The Wages of Whiteness

THE HAYMARKET SERIES

Editors: Mike Davis and Michael Sprinker

The Haymarket Series offers original studies in politics, history and culture, with a focus on North America. Representing views from across the American left on a wide range of subjects, the series will be of interest to socialists both in the USA and throughout the world. A century after the first May Day, the American left remains in the shadow of those martyrs whom this Haymarket Series honors and commemorates. These studies testify to the living legacy of political activism and commitment for which they gave their lives.

The Wages of Whiteness

Race and the Making of the American Working Class

———————◆———————

D A V I D   R .   R O E D I G E R

VERSO

London · New York

Cover illustration: From *The Union* (14 June 1836). The classic labor republican symbol of 'hammer and hand' in this instance called New Yorkers to a mass protest against 'tyrant masters', who were charged with reducing white workers to 'a level with the slaves of the South' as a result of the conviction of organized tailors in a celebrated conspiracy case.

First published by Verso 1991
© David R. Roediger 1991
All rights reserved

Verso
UK: 6 Meard Street, London W1V 3HR
USA: 29 West 35th Street, New York, NY 10001-2291

Verso is the imprint of New Left Books

British Library Cataloguing in Publication Data

Roediger, David R.
    The wages of whiteness : race and the making of the American working class.
    I. Title
    305.800973

    ISBN 0-86091-334-1
    ISBN 0-86091-550-6   pbk

US Library of Congress Cataloging-in-Publication Data

Roediger, David R.
    The wages of whiteness : race and the making of the American working class /
David R. Roediger.
    p. cm. — (The Haymarket series in North American politics and culture.)
    Includes index.
    ISBN 0-86091-334-1. — ISBN 0-86091-550-6 (pbk.)
    1. Discrimination in employment—United States—History. 2. Race
discrimination—United States—History. 3. Working class—United States—
History. 4. Slavery—United States—History. I. Title II. Series.
HD4903.5.U58R64   1991
305.8'00973—dc20

Typeset in Janson by NorthStar, San Francisco, California
Printed in Great Britain by Biddles Ltd

Contents

Acknowledgements

This book could not have been written without the help of the late George Rawick. The influence of his written work on mine will be clear at various points in the text, but even more important were the many meandering conversations we had, in which race and class usually figured prominently, but alongside sports, family, wildlife, the left and so much else. George never cared whose ideas were whose, but looking back and missing those talks, I know that the best were usually his.

In graduate school at Northwestern University, I studied largely with Sterling Stuckey and George Fredrickson, two of the most penetrating writers on race in the United States. Then, and more recently, they provided superb guidance and support for my own research. In conceptualizing and carrying through this project, I have also benefited greatly from the advice of Sundiata Cha-Jua, James Barrett, Steven Rosswurm, Alexander Saxton, Noel Ignatiev, Herbert Hill, Mike Davis, Philip Foner, Patrick Huber, Paul Garon, Al Young, Robert Wiebe, Steven Watts, Franklin Rosemont, Archie Green, Mary Cygan and Eli Zaretsky. Kerby Miller, Mark Lause and the late Henry Rosemont generously shared research materials. Susan Porter Benson provided not only encouragement and ideas but also an example of how to combine commitment, principle and scholarship. Mike Davis, Steve Hiatt and Mike Sprinker have been demanding and supportive editors. Research assistance from Brett Rogers and the expert typing of Patricia Eggleston halved the time it took to write this book.

Funding for research at the Newberry Library in Chicago has come from grants from the University of Missouri Research Council and from the Lloyd Lewis Fellowship, supported by the National Endowment for the Humanities. During my year in residence at the Newberry, I benefited from the friendship and criticism of Louise Wade, James Grossman, Francis Jennings, Cheryl Johnson-Odim and Richard Brown. The library staff at the Newberry was a model of helpfulness, as was the staff at the University of Missouri Library where Anne Edwards paid particularly prompt attention to my often unusual requests for dissertations and theses.

Opportunities to test some of my ideas in print and in presentations made this a bolder book. For those opportunities I thank the editors of *New Politics* and of *The Year Left*, and the history departments at Northwestern University and the University of Chicago, the Marxist Theory Seminar at the University of the Western Cape (South Africa), the Conference on Workers' Self-Organization, the Peter Tamony Lecture Series at the University of Missouri, the Fellows Colloquium at the Newberry Library, and the American Association for Irish Studies. Especially crucial were the remarks of John Jentz, Susan Hirsch and Toni Gilpin when I presented an early version of this research at a meeting of the Chicago Labor History Group.

My wife, Jean Allman, has greatly broadened my thoughts about race and class, drawing on her own work on the history of Ghana and of South Africa. She has been the best supporter and keenest critic of the project. My sons, Brendan and Donovan, have given me much, including the hope that the future does not belong to white supremacy. Responsibility for any errors of opinion or fact that remain in the text lies with four-year-old Donovan.

David R. Roediger

PART I

Introducing the White Worker

'The reality, the depth, and the persistence of the delusion of white supremacy in this country causes any real concept of education to be as remote, and as much to be feared, as change or freedom itself.'

James Baldwin
The Price of the Ticket (1985)

1

On Autobiography and Theory: An Introduction

When I was ten, it suddenly became possible to hit Little League pitching and, after my first (and only) five-hit game, the league's best player asked if I'd go to the carnival with him. This was a sign of acceptance, but as we walked to the fairgrounds the stakes increased. My new friend produced a long knife that he was not supposed to have and I was not supposed to know he had. 'This', he told me conspiratorially, 'is a nigger gigger.' Neither of us knew if this meant that the knife was for attacking Blacks or of a sort used by them. Neither of us knew any Blacks. None lived in the small German-American quarrying and farming town in which we were growing up. Local folklore held that laws barred Blacks from being in town after sundown. And yet the value of that knife, in terms of preteen male bonding, attached at least as much to its name as to its fake-pearl handle.

Even in an all-white town, race was never absent. I learned absolutely no lore of my German ancestry and no more than a few meaningless snatches of Irish songs, but missed little of racist folklore. Kids came to know the exigencies of chance by chanting 'Eeny, meany, miney, mo/Catch a nigger by the toe' to decide teams and first batters in sport. We learned that life – and fights – were not always fair: 'Two against one, nigger's fun.' We learned not to loaf: 'Last one in is a nigger baby.' We learned to save, for to buy ostentatiously or too quickly was to be 'nigger rich'. We learned not to buy clothes that were a bright 'nigger green'. Sexuality and blackness were of course thoroughly confused.

My mother's family came from Cairo, the half-Black city where the Ohio and Mississippi rivers meet, and we spent lots of each summer in a changing Cairo neighborhood. In the early sixties, the civil rights movement came to Cairo and so did a furious white backlash. Decisive from my child's point of view was the decision of the city fathers – one was a distant relative I called 'uncle' – to close Cairo's swimming pool rather than integrate it. Since there were few white kids to play with and it was unthinkable to play with Blacks, this defeat for civil rights seemed very much aimed at me. I also noticed that Black kids my age were challenging authority in a very appealing way: they crossed streets in front of angry white drivers with all deliberate speed, and sometimes rather less.

At the time none of this made me rethink racism. My family, all workers and many of them union supporters and minor officers in quarrying, telephone work, printing, teaching and pipefitting, held no doubts about white supremacy, and I knew no antiracists through junior high school. Racial attitudes did vary somewhat, however. My father's family held to the reticent racism of the insular German small town. On my mother's side, my aunts from Cairo were far more open in their somewhat contradictory denunciations of Blacks on welfare and of Blacks taking 'our' jobs. But they also had a small paternal streak, expressed especially toward a domestic who came for a half-day every two weeks and who pleased everyone (including, I later figured out, herself) by repeatedly referring to one of my cousins as 'pretty good-looking for a white girl.' At the first sign of civil rights activity, such paternalism vanished. Nor could German reticence be relied upon. In family arguments, my paternal (all-German) relatives floated the idea that the Irish heritage of my maternal relatives was a Black one, as the 'Black Irish' had resulted from intermixing with shipwrecked slaves.

As late as my freshman year in high school I repeated to my classmates the arguments I'd heard from white relatives in Cairo – Blacks paid no taxes and therefore ought not vote. No one dissented politically, but the mold of racism showed some slight cracks. We all hated Blacks in the abstract, but our greatest heroes were the Black stars of the great St. Louis Cardinals baseball teams of the sixties. The style, as well as the talent, of players like Lou Brock, Bob Gibson and Curt Flood was reverenced. More grudgingly, we admired Muhammad Ali as our generation's finest sportsman. We listened to Chuck Berry and Tina Turner, both based in the St. Louis area, though not yet to Miles Davis, born a few miles up the road. A few of us became firm fans of Motown music, especially Smokey Robinson. A small signal of rebellion in high school was to have the car radio blaring music from St. Louis's soul station – KATZ.

These tastes did not supplant racism. Most of them were decidedly

4

prepolitical. But they did open the possibility of antiracism, and my own experiences pushed me in that direction. The city of Cairo continued to decline, now with my 'uncle' as mayor. I had developed the habit of going to church at the small Catholic church for Blacks there, originally because that church's white priest raced through mass in half the time that it took at the white church. This Black parish gradually became a center of civil rights activity in Cairo, and I increasingly was made to wonder whether whites were ruining the town, as they had the swimming pool, in order to hold on to white supremacy. The common wisdom in my hometown held that it was impossible to take buses, or even to drive, through downtown East St. Louis, a nearby city deindustrializing and becoming almost wholly Black. But three days a week, in order to play public parks tennis in St. Louis, I rode the bus through East St. Louis with no incidents but pleasant ones. My best friends among tennis players were also Black, students of Dick Hudlin, Arthur Ashe's coach. Racism increasingly just made no sense to me.

In my junior year of high school, 1968–69, George Wallace swept votes in the school's mock presidential election after a student's nominating speech, which declared, to a full assembly of students, 'I have nothing against niggers. Every American should own one.' My senior year was much spent in counselors' and principals' offices because a few of us raised the issue of racism in the school newspaper, before it was censored, and later in an underground paper. When the student government voted to send money to the Black United Front in Cairo, all hell broke loose. As we were threatened with expulsion, some of the rebellious students who had spoken most vociferously for Wallace – oddly or maybe not – became our best supporters.

Until very recently, I would have skipped all this autobiographical material, sure that my ideas on race and the white working class grew out of conscious reflection based on historical research. But much of that reflection led back to what my early years might have taught me: the role of race in defining how white workers look not only at Blacks but at themselves; the pervasiveness of race; the complex mixture of hate, sadness and longing in the racist thought of white workers; the relationship between race and ethnicity. My own youthful experiences – and they were not very different, except in outcome, from those of many white working class kids at the time – could have given me the central themes of this book. But the further tasks – of explaining how, when and why 'whiteness' became so important to white workers – do require conscious reflection and historical research.

Marxism and the White Problem

My question at age eighteen was why friends wanted to be white and why I didn't. In the two decades since, the Marxist tradition has furnished most of the intellectual tools I use, but in the main, it has not led me to press for answers to the question of why the white working class settles for being white. In my view, no answer to the 'white problem' can ignore the explanatory power of historical materialism, but neither does Marxism, as presently theorized, consistently help us focus on the central issue of why so many workers define themselves as white.

Writers of color have often raised the issue sharply, perhaps because they have had to. There is a long tradition, dating back at least to Cyril Briggs's writings of sixty years ago, of Blacks pointing out that race in the US was not a 'Negro problem' but a problem among whites. This tradition has explored the cost of whiteness to white workers, with W.E.B. Du Bois writing, 'It was bad enough to have the consequences of [racist] thought fall upon colored people the world over; but in the end it was even worse when one considers what this attitude did to the [white] worker. His aim and ideal was distorted. ... He began to want, not comfort for all men but power over other men. ... He did not love humanity and he hated niggers.' Or as James Baldwin put it, 'As long as you think you're white, there's no hope for you.'[1] Nor does this tradition revolve solely around the political problems whiteness raises. The white problem – the question of why and how whites reach the conclusion that their whiteness is meaningful – is an intellectual and even an artistic problem for Black writers like Ralph Ellison, who observes, 'Southern whites cannot walk, talk, sing, conceive of laws or justice, think of sex, love, the family or freedom without responding to the presence of Negroes.' Most recently, empowered by what Toni Morrison calls the 'successful assault that feminist scholarship [made] on traditional literary discourses', novelists and critics like Morrison, Hazel Carby, Bell Hooks and Coco Fusco have tellingly interrogated the concept of whiteness. Fusco reminds her readers that 'racial identities are not only Black, Latino, Asian, Native American and so on; they are also white. To ignore white ethnicity is to redouble its hegemony by naturalizing it.'[2]

The main body of writing by white Marxists in the United States has both 'naturalized' whiteness and oversimplified race. These weaknesses, and the fact that they largely reproduce the weaknesses of both American liberalism and neoconservatism where race is concerned, have limited the influence of the very real Marxist contributions to the study of race. The central Marxist contributions are thoroughly presented in Barbara Fields's provocative 'Ideology and Race in American History'. Fields argues that race cannot be seen as a biological or physical fact (a 'thing') but must be seen as 'a notion that is profoundly and in its very essence ideological.' Race, for Fields, is then entirely socially and historically constructed as an ideology in a way that class is not. Because people really do own or not own land and workplaces, class has 'objective' dimensions. Moreover, race is constructed differently across time by people in the same social class and differently at the same time by people whose class positions differ. These latter points, not peculiar to Fields but expressed by her with considerable force and eloquence, underpin this book. They implicitly call for historical studies that focus on the racism of a class as well as of a society.[3]

But with certain exceptions, writers within the Marxist tradition have not often acted on such insights. The point that race is created wholly ideologically and historically, while class is not wholly so created, has often been boiled down to the notion that class (or 'the economic') is more real, more fundamental, more basic or more *important* than race, both in political terms and in terms of historical analysis. Thus, the pioneering Black sociologist, Oliver Cromwell Cox, writes, 'We shall assume that economic relations form the basis of modern race relations.' This view, which informed and deformed the practice of the socialist movement during its heyday in the US, leads in Cox's case to the political conclusion that Blacks and whites should look to class-based revolution as the solution to racism. Cox observes, 'There will be no more "crackers" or "niggers" after a socialist revolution because the social necessity for those types will have been removed.'[4]

That rosy view of a literal correspondence between racism and 'social necessity' and of the possibility of an unambiguous revolutionary solution to racism is largely gone. But the idea that class should be politically privileged has not, as is witnessed by the outpouring of recent left and left-liberal arguments that the Black freedom movement must now couch its appeals in terms of class rather than race.[5] Nor has the privileging of class over race by any means given way within Marxist and neo-Marxist historical analysis. Even Fields wavers. At times she nicely balances the ideological creation of racial attitudes with their manifest and ongoing importance and their (albeit ideological) *reality*. She writes, 'It follows that there can be no understanding the problems arising from slavery and its destruction which ignores their racial form; recognizing that race is an ideological notion and that not all white Americans held the same ideology does not mean dismissing racial questions as illusory or unreal.' But shortly thereafter we learn that, during Reconstruction, however much 'the Republicans may have perceived the situation through the veil of racial ideology, their frustration with the freedmen had nothing to do with color.' Instead, their frustrations were those that 'have … appeared again and again, in every part of the world, whenever an employer class in process of formation has tried to induce men and women unbroken to market discipline to work … for a wage.'[6] Race disappears into the 'reality' of class.

These are tricky but important matters. It is certainly true that racism must be set in class and economic contexts. Cox was right to quote delightedly Julius Boeke: 'Europeans did not sail to the Indies to collect butterflies.' Clearly, as Edmund Morgan and others have shown, labor control and land ownership provided the context for the emergence of strong white racial consciousness in early Virginia.[7] This book will argue that working class formation and the systematic development of a sense of whiteness went hand in hand for the US white working class. Nonetheless, the privileging of class over race is not always productive or meaningful. To set race within social formations is absolutely necessary, but to reduce race to class is damaging. If, to use tempting older Marxist images, racism is a large, low-hanging branch of a tree that is rooted in class relations, we must constantly remind ourselves that the branch is not the same as the roots, that people may more often bump into the branch than the roots, and that the best way to shake the roots may at times be by grabbing the branch.

Less botanical explanations of why the traditional Marxist habit of emphasizing class over race is not useful are in order before taking up consideration of better strategies. One major problem with the traditional Marxist approach is that what it takes as its central task – pointing out the economic dimension of racism – is already done by those in the political mainstream. In a quite meaningless way, the 'race problem' is consistently reduced to one of class. For example, when the outspoken racist and former Ku Klux Klan leader David Duke won a seat in the Louisiana legislature in early 1989, one expert commentator after another came on the morning news shows to announce that unemployment was high in Duke's nearly all-white district and therefore the election turned on economic grievances rather than racism. Viewers were thus treated to the exotic notion that, when white workers react to unemployment by electing a prominent white supremacist *who promises to gut welfare programs*, they are acting on class terms, rather than as working class *racists*. Such an argument is to be expected from the 'Today' show, but a viable left must find a way to differentiate itself strongly from such analysis. Similarly, it is worth noting that both neoliberalism and neoconservatism argue that race is not (or ought not to be) 'the issue' but that economic growth – neatly separable from race – will solve conflicts that only seem to revolve round race.[8]

A second problem with traditional Marxist analyses of race is that, while trying to show the class dimension of racism, they have tended to concentrate on the ruling class's role in perpetuating racial oppression, and to cast white workers as dupes, even if virtuous ones. Communist party leader Earl Browder's account of Jack Johnstone's experiences in the packinghouse union struggles of 1919 – struggles in which the working class was deeply split by race – provides one revealing, if extreme, example:

> … all obstacles to unity and solidarity came not from either group of workers themselves, but from the enemies of the working class – from the capitalist press, from the bosses, from the bourgeois politicians … and from the reactionary A.F. of L. officialdom.[9]

Cox echoes this view in theoretical language. Racism, he argues, is 'the socio-attitudinal concomitant of the racial exploitative practice of a ruling class in a capitalistic society.' Or again, in writing of the Jim Crow system in the South, he explains that 'every segregation barrier is a barrier put up between white and black people by their exploiters.' Cox later adds that it was the exploiters who maintained those barriers.[10] The workers, in this view, largely receive and occasionally resist racist ideas and practices but have no role in *creating* those practices.

The neo-Marxist perspectives that have in the past twenty years come to dominate the study of the working class, personified in the US by Herbert Gutman and in Britain by E.P. Thompson, should help us call into question any theory that holds that racism simply trickles down the class structure from the commanding heights at which it is created. The 'new labor history', whatever its weaknesses, has made the tremendous political and analytical contribution of showing that workers, even during periods of firm ruling class hegemony, are historical actors who make (constrained) choices and create their own cultural forms.

However, for reasons I have tried to explore elsewhere,[11] the new labor history has hesitated to explore working class 'whiteness' and white supremacy as creations, in part, of the white working class itself. Few historians would adopt an outlook that simply characterizes racism, as Communist party chair Gus Hall does, as monopoly capital's 'deliberate strategy for superprofits'.[12] Some have, wrongly I think, even suggested that capital and the state do not foster racism, or that capital does not profit from racism and acts to see racism ended.[13] But movements away from conspiratorial views of racism and toward a consideration of the agency of the working class in the social construction of race have not resulted in many class-specific studies of racism. The valuable general histories of racism, especially those by George Fredrickson and Thomas Gossett, rely mainly on evidence from political leaders, intellectuals and scientists.[14] Equally useful studies of race and popular culture generally do not explore the difficult question of the specific role of the working class in creating popular cultural treatments of race nor the specific meanings of racism in popular culture for workers.[15] Studies bringing race and labor together, including the pioneering work of Herbert Hill and Philip Foner, mainly stay on the terrain of trade union practices regarding race.[16] When the motivations of the white working class in accepting racism are considered, overly simple economic explanations hinging on advantages of 'white skin privilege' within the labor market too easily prevail.[17]

Nor are the efforts of historically minded economists and sociologists wholly satisfying in providing alternative interpretations. The 'segmentation' theories of Michael Reich, David Gordon, Richard Edwards and others make the useful point that racism benefits the capitalist class, but at times in language so careful to avoid any notion of conspiracy that it is clear they are not offering a theory of racism but an empirical observation about racism. Reich, for example, writes, 'Capitalists benefit from racial divisions whether or not they have individually or collectively practiced racial discrimination.' The other major socioeconomic model for discussing racism emphasizes split labor markets, which are seen as vexing to capital and as benefiting 'dominant workers' against 'cheap labor'. But this theory at best explains the results, not the origins, of white working class privilege. Edna Bonacich, the most prominent theorist of split labor markets, holds that the 'dominant workers' did not originally gain their position by racially exclusionist movements but rather by 'historical accident'. Typically, neither segmentation theory nor split labor market theories offer the possibility that racism comes from *both* above and below. Neither entertains the possibility that racism is not a matter of bread alone, but is in addition a way in which white workers have come to look at the world.[18]

There are signs, in the ongoing work of such scholars as Gwendolyn Mink, Robin D.G. Kelley, Eric Arnesen, Dan Letwin, Joseph Trotter, Dolores Janiewski, Roger Horowitz, Michael Honey, Daniel Rosenberg and, above all, Alexander Saxton, that a flowering of a new social and cultural history of race and labor may be beginning. Certainly the new areas opened by scholars in social history – the study of gender, of popular republicanism and of the roles of labor control and industrial discipline in class formation, for example – make possible far more sophisticated studies of working class racism. Indeed, this study begins with the insights of the new labor history and is within that broad tradition. In many ways it represents an attempt to apply to the question of race relations scholarship that takes the agency of working class people seriously. It sees working class whiteness as a gendered phenomenon, particularly expressing and repressing male longings and the perils and pride of republican citizenship among men. To the extent that it can range widely over space, time and subject matter – frankly depending on secondary accounts supplemented by primary research – it rests on the rich, if too often separated, bodies of historical writing on class and on race in the United States.

But some of the old problems found in the work of Oliver Cox still recur in recent labor historiography. Perhaps most serious is the continuing tendency to romanticize members of the white working class by not posing the problem of why they came to consider themselves white and with what results. As the Black historian Nell Irvin Painter has recently remarked:

> They [US labor historians] often prefer to wrap themselves in fashionable Europeanisms and to write as though their favorite, northern, European-American workers lived out their destinies divorced from slavery and racism, as though, say, Chartism meant more in the history of the American working class than slavery.[19]

Painter's observations bring us nicely back to the suppressed question of whiteness and the need for Marxists to fully reconceptualize the study of race and class. There can be no assumption that the whiteness of the white working class deserves exploration only when we begin to discuss the history of race relations in labor organizations. Rather, race has at all times been a critical factor in the history of US class formation.

The Essential Du Bois

The analysis offered in the preceding section suggests that, at least in the US, the most pressing task for historians of race and class is not to draw precise lines separating race and class but to draw lines connecting race and class. We can get this attention to how race and class interpenetrate from several sources – for example, in the best of Stuart Hall's and Alexander Saxton's works, and to an extent in recent studies of 'racial formation'[20] – but no body of thought rivals that of W.E.B. Du Bois for an understanding of the dynamics, indeed dialectics, of race and class in

11

the US. Du Bois wrote as a Marxist but also brought additional perspectives to the study of race and class. He was within the broad Black nationalist tradition that Sterling Stuckey has so well portrayed, and from that tradition gained a perspective intelligently critical of oversimplified class analysis.[21] He, like Toni Morrison, C.L.R. James, James Baldwin and other acute African-American students of the 'white problem', clearly saw whiteness not as natural but nevertheless as real and as problematic in intellectual, moral and political terms. Finally, Du Bois enjoyed the advantage of a critical appreciation of Max Weber's thought on race and status and an ability to borrow critically from Weber as well as from the Marxist tradition.[22]

Thus, Du Bois's *Black Reconstruction* continually creates jarring, provocative theoretical images, mixing race and class by design. Black reconstruction is, for Du Bois, the key to the story of 'our [the US] labor movement'. The book is organized around the activities of workers, but those workers function, for Du Bois tragically, within racial categories: the first chapter is entitled 'The Black Worker' and the second 'The White Worker'. White labor does not just receive and resist racist ideas but embraces, adopts and, at times, murderously acts upon those ideas. The problem is not just that the white working class is at critical junctures manipulated into racism, but that it comes to think of itself and its interests as white.[23]

Du Bois regards the decision of workers to define themselves by their whiteness as understandable in terms of short-term advantages. In some times and places, he argues, such advantages showed up in pay packets, where the wages of white, native-born skilled workers were high, both compared with those of Blacks and by world standards.[24] But vital for the white workers Du Bois studied most closely was, as he puts it in a brilliant, indispensable formulation, that even when they 'received a low wage [they were] compensated in part by a ... public and psychological wage.' Here Du Bois not only emphasizes status but the extent to which status was bound up with real social gains. He continues:

> They were given public deference ... because they were white. They were admitted freely, with all classes of white people, to public functions [and] public parks. ... The police were drawn from their ranks and the courts, dependent on their votes, treated them with leniency. ... Their votes selected public officials and while this had small effect upon the economic situation, it had great effect upon their personal treatment. ... White schoolhouses were the best in the community, and conspicuously placed, and cost anywhere from twice to ten times colored schools.[25]

As important as the specifics are here, still more important is the idea that the pleasures of whiteness could function as a 'wage' for white workers. That is, status and privileges conferred by race could be used to make up for alienating and exploitative class relationships, North and South. White workers could, and did, define and accept their class positions by fashioning identities as 'not slaves' and as 'not Blacks'.

[margin annotation: mutually exclusive dichotomies]

When they did so, Du Bois argued, the wages of whiteness often turned out to be spurious. America's 'Supreme Adventure ... for that human freedom which would release the human spirit from lower lust for mere meat, and set it free to dream and sing' gave way to a racism that caused 'capitalism [to be] adopted, forwarded and approved by white labor' and that 'ruined democracy'. Race feeling and the benefits conferred by whiteness made white Southern workers forget their 'practically identical interests' with the Black poor and accept stunted lives for themselves and for those more oppressed than themselves.[26]

Du Bois argued that white supremacy undermined not just working class unity but the very *vision* of many white workers. He connected racism among whites with a disdain for hard work itself, a seeking of satisfaction off the job and a desire to evade rather than confront exploitation. Du Bois held that this would have been a better and more class-conscious nation and world had the heritage of slavery and racism not led the working class to prize whiteness.[27] Although these are positions that some neo-Marxists and post-Marxists have criticized as essentialist, they nonetheless seem to me a model that takes us a long step toward seeing the whiteness of the white worker in the broad context of class formation rather than in the narrow confines of job competition.[28] Likewise, the tone here strives to emulate that of *Black Reconstruction*, and thus to be more tragic than angry.

Argument and Methods

In its broadest strokes, this book argues that whiteness was a way in which white workers responded to a fear of dependency on wage labor and to the necessities of capitalist work discipline. As the US working class matured, principally in the North, within a slaveholding republic, the heritage of the Revolution made independence a powerful masculine personal ideal. But slave labor and 'hireling' wage labor proliferated in the new nation. One way to make peace with the latter was to differentiate it sharply from the former. Though direct comparisons between bondage and wage labor were tried out ('white slavery'), the rallying cry

of 'free labor' understandably proved more durable and popular for antebellum white workers, especially in the North. At the same time, the
white working class, disciplined and made anxious by fear of dependency,
began during its formation to construct an image of the Black population
as 'other' – as embodying the preindustrial, erotic, careless style of life
the white worker hated and longed for. This logic had particular attractions for Irish-American immigrant workers, even as the 'whiteness' of
these very workers was under dispute.

In terms of periodization, this suggests that the first sixty-five years of
the nineteenth century were the formative period of working class
'whiteness', at least in the North, though obviously earlier habits of mind
and patterns of settler colonialist oppression of Native Americans form an
important part of the prehistory of working class whiteness. The Civil
War, and particularly the blows struck by Blacks on behalf of their own
freedom during the war, called pride in whiteness into question. However,
whiteness was by that time firmly established and well poised to remain a
central value, founded, in Du Bois's phrase, not just on 'economic exploitation' but on 'racial folklore'.[29]

In terms of method and evidence, this study is, after its debts to Du
Bois and to the labor historians, most influenced by recent work in the
historiography of slavery. It particularly seeks to use the sources that have
enriched the study of slavery – folklore, humor, song and language – with
the same subtlety as have Lawrence Levine and Sterling Stuckey.[30] The
analysis of whiteness as the product of specific classes' attempts to come
to terms with their class – never simply economic – problems by projecting their longings onto a despised race grows directly out of George
Rawick's closing chapters in *From Sundown to Sunup: The Making of the
Black Community*, in which Rawick probes the racism of the seventeenth-
and eighteenth-century Anglo-European bourgeoisie.[31] Rawick's largely
unacknowledged debt is to the Freudian tradition. I owe a similar debt,
especially to the work of Frantz Fanon and Joel Kovel, who forcefully
insist on the need for dialectical and materialist approaches within the
psychoanalytic framework. 'Just as the creation of white wealth pushed
Blackspp. down', Kovel writes, 'so must the presence of degraded black
bodies have exerted a continual stimulation to the continued pursuit of
abstracted money.'[32] In the work of both Rawick and Kovel, projection of
desires onto others is very far from being an idealist enterprise.

Because I have emphasized construction of identity through otherness
and have often used changes in language as complex evidence of race and
class perceptions, this study might appear to bear heavy influences from
poststructuralist literary theories. In fact, it does not do so except in mak-

ing use of the older ideas of Mikhail Bakhtin, ideas rediscovered by poststructuralism. With certain important exceptions, attempts to apply poststructuralism to history have foundered not only because they agonize so painfully about whether documents and language can reveal anything about the past, but also because they are prone to examining the interaction between 'the individual' and the text or settling for the idea that each *generation* finds different meanings in texts.[33] Bakhtin, on the other hand, holds that 'at any given moment ... language is stratified not only into linguistic dialects ... but also – and for us this is the essential point – into languages which are socio-ideological.' Meaning is thus always multifaceted and socially contested, but it is neither absent nor unconnected with social relations. Indeed, for Bakhtin and for such brilliant modern, but not poststructuralist, students of language as Raymond Williams and Archie Green, the ambiguity of language affords it meaning.[34]

The point that language is fluid and yet meaningful will have to be carried at this early point by a brief example. The socialist writer and maritime worker Stan Weir recalls that in the 1930s and 1940s at the port of San Francisco, the drums on the hoisting winches on the decks of ships were called *niggerheads* by deck seamen. Within two years of the outset of the Second World War, the longshore workforce in San Francisco went from having only a tiny African-American minority to a Black majority. Though the union representing the deck seamen continued to exclude Black American members, the seamen acknowledged the presence of Black longshoremen by changing their language. The drums became *gypsyheads*.[35] The change in signifiers itself signalled a new set of social realities and racial meanings. These meanings were different for the white seamen in a Jim Crow union, the white longshoremen in an integrated union, and the Black longshoremen. Gypsies might well have had still another view. If such a simple local example yields such complexity, we can approach discussion of a diverse working population defining and redefining terms such as *hireling, master, boss, white slave, coon, servant* and *free white labor* with considerable trepidation but also with excitement.

Notes

1.   Cyril Briggs, 'Further Notes on [the] Negro Question in Southern Textile Strikes', *The Communist* 8 (July 1929): 394; W.E.B. Du Bois, *The World and Africa: An Inquiry into the Part Which Africa Has Played in World History*, New York 1965, 18–21; James Baldwin as he spoke in the film about his life, *The Price of the Ticket*. See also Baldwin, 'Dark Days', in his *The Price of the Ticket*, New York 1985, 666.

2.   Ralph Ellison, *Shadow and Act*, New York 1972, 116; Coco Fusco as quoted by Bell Hooks, 'Representing Whiteness: Seeing Wings of Desire', *Zeta* 2 (March 1989): 39; Toni

Morrison, 'Unspeakable Things Unspoken: The Afro-American Presence in American Literature', *Michigan Quarterly Review* 28 (Winter 1989): esp. 2–3 and 38. See also Manning Marable, 'Beyond the Race–Class Dilemma', *Nation* 232 (11 April 1981): 432.

3. Barbara Fields, 'Ideology and Race in American History', in J. Morgan Kousser and James M. McPherson, eds, *Region, Race and Reconstruction*, New York 1982, 143. See also Alexander Saxton's introduction to *The Rise and Fall of the White Republic*, London 1990, a study of race, class and politics in the nineteenth-century US; Michael Omi and Howard Winant, *Racial Formation in the United States*, New York 1988, 62–69; Oliver Cromwell Cox, *Caste, Class and Race: A Study in Social Dynamics*, New York 1970 (1948), 319–20; Calvin C. Hernton, *Sex and Racism in America*, New York 1965, 175.

4. Herbert M. Hunter and Sameer Y. Abraham, eds, *Race, Class and the World System: The Sociology of Oliver C. Cox*, New York 1987, 31, and Cox, *Race Relations: Elements and Social Dynamics*, Detroit 1976, 6.

5. See, for example, the work of William Junius Wilson, esp. *The Declining Significance of Race*, Chicago 1978, and *The Truly Disadvantaged: The Inner City, the Underclass and Public Policy*, Chicago 1987; Adolph L. Reed, Jr., *The Jesse Jackson Phenomenon*, New Haven, Conn. 1986; Karen Winkler, 'Civil Rights Scholars Say Economic Equality Eludes Minorities', *Chronicle of Higher Education*, 29 November 1989, A-11.

6. Fields, 'Ideology and Race', 165.

7. Cox, *Race Relations*, 6; Edmund Morgan, *American Slavery, American Freedom: The Ordeal of Colonial America*, New York 1975.

8. For example, Winkler, 'Civil Rights Scholars', A-11, and Walter E. Williams, *The State Against Blacks*, New York 1982.

9. Earl Browder, 'Some Experiences in Organizing the Negro Workers', *The Communist*, January 1930, 40.

10. Cox, *Caste, Class and Race*, 470; Hunter and Abraham, *Race, Class and the World System*, 24–25.

11. See David R. Roediger, 'What Was So Great about Herbert Gutman?' *Labour/Le Travail* 23 (Spring 1989): 255–61, and 'Labor in White Skin: Race and Working Class History', in Mike Davis and Michael Sprinker, eds, *Reshaping the US Left: Popular Struggles in the 1980s*, London 1988, 287–308.

12. Gus Hall as quoted in E. San Juan, Jr., 'Problems in the Marxist Project of Theorizing Race', *Rethinking Marxism* 2 (Summer 1989): 59.

13. See, for example, Wilson's *Declining Significance of Race* and Edna Bonacich, 'Advanced Capitalism and Black–White Relations in the United States', *American Sociological Review* 41 (February 1978): 44.

14. George Fredrickson, *The Black Image in the White Mind: The Debate on Afro-American Character and Destiny: 1817–1914*, New York 1917; Thomas F. Gossett, *Race: The History of an Idea in America*, New York 1983.

15. Among the best such works are William L. Van Deburg, *Slavery and Race in American Popular Culture*, Madison, Wis. 1984, and Joseph Boskin, *Sambo: The Rise and Decline of an American Jester*, New York 1986.

16. Philip Foner, *Organized Labor and the Black Worker* New York 1976; Herbert Hill, *Race and Ethnicity in Organized Labor*, Madison, Wis. 1987. Alexander Saxton's *The Rise and Fall of the White Republic* is a pathbreaking exception here.

17. Roediger, 'Labor in White Skin', passim.

18. Omi and Winant, *Racial Formation*, 30–37; Michael Reich, *Racial Inequality: A Political-Economic Analysis*, Princeton, N.J. 1981, 268–313, quote from p. 269; Reich also (p. 268) allows that skilled workers may gain from racial discrimination but solves this problem for his theory by placing skilled workers among 'high income whites'. Bonacich, 'Advanced Capitalism and Black–White Relations', 35.

19. Nell Irvin Painter, 'French Theories in American Settings: Some Thoughts on Transferability', *Journal of Women's History* 1 (Spring 1989): 93.

20. Stuart Hall, 'Race, Articulation and Societies Structured in Dominance,' in UNESCO, *Sociological Theories: Race and Colonialism*, Paris 1980, 340–45; Omi and Winant, *Racial*

Formation, esp. 57–69; Saxton, 'Historical Explanations of Racial Inequality', *Marxist Perspectives* (Summer 1979): 146–68. See also Colette Guillaumin, 'Race and Nature: The System of Marks', *Feminist Issues* 8 (Fall 1988): 25–44.

21. Sterling Stuckey, *Slave Culture: Nationalist Theory and the Foundations of Black America*, New York, 1987.

22. See George Fredrickson, *The Arrogance of Race: Historical Perspectives on Slavery, Racism and Social Inequality*, Middletown, Conn. 1988, 4–5; Herbert Aptheker, ed., *The Correspondence of W.E.B. Du Bois*, Amherst, Mass. 1973–78, 1:106–7 and 3:44–45.

23. W.E.B. Du Bois, *Black Reconstruction in the United States, 1860–1880*, New York 1977 (1935), 727 and passim.

24. Ibid., 30 and 633–34.

25. Ibid., 700–701.

26. Ibid., 30 and 700. ✓

27. Du Bois, *Black Reconstruction*, 27–30, 347, 633–34 and 700–701. See also Du Bois, 'Dives, Mob and Scab, Limited', *Crisis* 19 (March 1920): 235–36.

28. Sean Wilentz, 'Against Exceptionalism: Class Consciousness and the American Labor Movement, '*International Labor and Working Class History* 26 (Fall 1984): esp. 2–3. See also Norman Geras, 'Ex-Marxism Without Substance: Being a Reply to Laclau and Mouffe', *New Left Review* 169 (May-June 1988): 43–46; and Cornel West, 'Rethinking Marxism', *Monthly Review* 38 (February 1987) for some good sense on essentialism.

29. W.E.B. Du Bois, *Dusk of Dawn: Autobiography of a Race Concept*, New York 1940, 205.

30. Stuckey, *Slave Culture*; Lawrence W. Levine, *Black Culture and Black Consciousness: Afro-American Folk Thought from Slavery to Freedom*, New York 1977.

31. George Rawick, *From Sundown to Sunup: The Making of the Black Community*, Westport, Conn. 1972, esp. 125–47. For the specific debt this book owes to Rawick, see my 'Notes on Working Class Racism', *New Politics* [Second Series] 7 (Summer 1989): 61–66. Rawick's (and my) debt, to Hegel, is also obvious.

32. Kovel, *White Racism: A Psychohistory*, New York 1970, 197. See also Frantz Fanon, *Black Skins, White Masks*, New York 1967.

33. The exceptions include work by the group centered on the journal *Subaltern Studies* in India and Joan Wallach Scott, *Gender and the Politics of History*, New York 1988.

34. Michael Holquist and Caryl Emerson, eds, *The Dialogic Imagination: Four Essays by M.M. Bakhtin*, Austin, Tex. 1981, esp. 271–72. See also Raymond Williams, *Keywords: A Vocabulary of Culture and Society*, New York 1976, and Archie Green's forthcoming studies of *fink* and of *wobbly*.

35. Stan Weir, letter to the author, 30 May 1989.

2

The Prehistory of the White Worker: Settler Colonialism, Race and Republicanism before 1800

When US elections are won or lost these days, the voting patterns of the 'white worker' receive considerable attention. In popular usage, the very term *worker* often presumes whiteness (and maleness), as in conservative Democrats' calls for abandoning 'special interests' and returning the party to policies appealing to the 'average worker' – a line of argument that blissfully ignores the fact that the 'average worker' is increasingly Black, Latino, Asian and/or female. Most fascinating are sociologist David Halle's recent observations on the self-identification of white workers. Halle writes that the New Jersey chemical workers he has studied prefer to call themselves 'working men' (and 'lower middle class' or 'middle class' when describing their consumption patterns). The phrase *working men* speaks at once, Halle observes, of a class identity and of a gender identity. But its actual usage also suggests a *racial* identity, an identification of whiteness and work so strong that it need not even be spoken. That is, the white chemical workers do not describe as 'working men' Blacks who do similar jobs and who are more likely to be AFL-CIO members than are the white chemical workers' neighbors. That category is instead seen as 'naturally' white, and Black workers become 'intruders' who are strongly suspected of being 'loafers' as well.[1]

Perhaps the 'naturalness' of the category of 'white worker' has likewise blinded historians. The best work bringing together race, slavery and pre–Civil War labor has tended to focus narrowly on whether and why white working people supported or opposed antislavery initiatives. The kind of

[handwritten margin note: transparency that veils racism]

19

work analogous to David Brion Davis's brilliant studies of the extent to which the existence of slavery and of an abolitionist critique of slavery made wage labor a more defensible practice for the Anglo-American bourgeoisie still remains to be done with respect to slavery's influence on the consciousness of the US working class. Nor do we have a study of nineteenth-century workers analogous to Edmund Morgan's probing account of the ways in which slavery shaped white perceptions of race, freedom and work in colonial Virginia. And yet we know that from 'white slave' to 'free labor', antebellum white workers could not begin to describe themselves without reference to the fact of slavery and, increasingly, to the ideology of race. If, as Davis shows, the discourse of slavery and abolition shaped that of labor reform in mid-nineteenth-century Britain, which held no slaves, we should not be surprised that a similar process occurred in the US, which held four million.[2]

This book not only views the white worker as a historical phenomenon whose rise needs explanation but also as one of rather recent origin. The argument is that the words *white* and *worker* (or more often analogous terms like *free white labor*, *white slave* and a host of more euphemistic usages connecting race and class) became meaningfully paired only in the *nineteenth* century. They became paired during a time in which the United States, whose citizens were taught by their revolutionary victory and republican ideology to expect both political and economic independence, became a nation in which, by 1860, roughly half the nonslave labor force was dependent on wage labor and subject to new forms of capitalist labor discipline.[3] In this slaveholding republic, where independence was prized but where, especially among Northern artisans, it was also threatened, the bondage of Blacks served as a touchstone by which dependence and degradation were measured. Racial formation and class formation were thus bound to penetrate each other at every turn. However, this process took place only *after* the Revolution and early industrial capitalist economic changes had combined to defuse the complicating issues of American political 'slavery' to Britain and of various forms of nonwage dependency among whites. The white worker arrived in the early nineteenth century, an arrival coinciding with a considerable rise in popular racism in the urban North.[4]

This is not to say that the seventeenth and eighteenth centuries were a period of nonracial utopia in America. Nor is it to say that artisans and laborers in these early years were necessarily less likely than other Americans to view society in racial terms. Instead, it is to argue that, whatever racist attitudes were present, there were by and large no compelling ways to connect whiteness with a defense of one's independence as a worker. The varieties of economic dependency, white and Black, along with the perception of Native Americans as overly independent, made equations of color and servility problematic. The range of dependent relationships did not permit stark comparisons between wage labor and slavery. Moreover, only with the intense politicization of the Revolutionary generation did the ideal of independence itself take on its full and many-sided force among the 'lower orders' in white America. This chapter therefore discusses the 'prehistory' of the white worker. It explores the importance of settler colonialism and anti-Black attitudes in creating a popular sense of whiteness in colonial America. But it also shows why *white* could not in the colonial period modify *worker* in the same way that it would in the nineteenth century, and how the Revolution helped to change the social meaning of whiteness by creating new possibilities – which would be realized during the accelerated formation of the working class in the nineteenth century – to conflate terms like *freeman* or *independent mechanic* with *white*.

White Settlers and Red Indians

The term *white* arose as a designation for European explorers, traders and settlers who came into contact with Africans and the indigenous people of the Americas. As such, it appeared even before permanent British settlement in North America. Its early usages in America served as much to distinguish European settlers from Native Americans as to distinguish Africans from Europeans.[5] Thus, the prehistory of the white worker begins with the settlers' images of Native Americans. Moreover, the images developed by colonists to rationalize dispossession of Native Americans from the land had a strong connection to work and to discipline. Settler ideology held that improvident, sexually abandoned 'lazy Indians' were failing to 'husband' or 'subdue' the resources God had provided and thus should forfeit those resources. Work and whiteness joined in the argument for dispossession. Settlers, whether or not they worked harder or more steadily than Native Americans, came to consider themselves 'hardworking whites' in counterpoint to their imagination of Indian styles of life.[6]

By the early nineteenth century, the small and dwindling numbers of Native Americans, especially in the Northeast where the laboring and artisanal white population was concentrated, made direct experience with Indians less than common. However, anti-Indian racism and frontier myths had considerable staying power. As Herman Melville sardonically put it, 'Indian rapine having mostly ceased through regions where it once prevailed ... Indian-hating has not in like degree ceased with it.' 'Civilization' continued to define itself as a negation of 'savagery' – indeed, to invent savagery in order to define itself. 'White' attitudes toward manliness, land use, sexuality, and individualism and violence were influenced by real contacts with, and fanciful ideas about, Native Americans. Working people certainly did not escape these attitudes, even if they did not internalize them in exactly the same way as other social groups. Moreover, the question of expansion into lands occupied by Native Americans remained an important political issue and one of particular interest to working people through the Revolution and early Republican and Jacksonian years. Land was, as we shall see, a central issue in the early labor movement, an issue that many organizers closely connected to the possibilities of economic independence in the United States. Not surprisingly, anti-Indian thought played a huge role in the development of 'American Racial Anglo-Saxonism', the particular brand of 'whiteness' that Reginald Horsman has convincingly argued was intellectually ascendant in the US by 1850.[7]

But despite the manifest importance of anti-Indian racism in fashioning the self-perceptions of white Americans, Indians were not ultimately the counterpoint against which Euro-American workers could define themselves as white. After the failure of early attempts to 'reduce the savages to civility' by enslaving them, it became clear that the drama of white–Indian contact outside the fur trade would turn on land and conquest, not on labor. By the time that significant numbers of Americans came to grips with wage labor, those Native Americans who did remain were in any case often confusingly categorized, legally at least, as 'colored' or even 'mulatto', sometimes because they had mixed with more numerous Black populations and sometimes even when they had not. In folk usage, the interesting term *red nigger* appeared in the 1820s as a description of Native Americans through racial language originally applied to the more familiar Black population.[8]

Even on a mythic level, without widespread direct white–Indian contact Native Americans served poorly as foils against which whites could measure themselves as workers. Comparisons with Black slaves or even Northern 'free' Blacks were tempting precisely because whites had defined these groups as servile. Thus, by considering a range of comparisons with Blacks in weighing his status as a white worker, the white laboring man could articulate a self-image that, depending on his wont, emphasized either his pride in independence or his fears of growing dependency. But the mythical/historical Native American male was seen as *independent*, so much so that he was used, oddly enough, as a symbol of the American Revolution, not just at the Boston Tea Party but by many political cartoonists of the day. Any systematic social construction of the white worker's position that used the Native American as the 'other' would therefore have had to take people of color as a model rather than as a negative reference point. This image would not catch on in any way more widespread than the 'going native' of a few whites in the fur trade.[9]

In the context of the Western land question, workers who did reflect on Indians shared the general propensity of colonial settler populations to minimize the numbers of natives in contested areas and the amount of land to which they could lay claim. The idea that the Indian was disappearing made him less available as a yardstick against which white labor could measure its own position. One nineteenth-century minstrel book, for example, included an elaborate sketch titled 'Races', full of puns turning on the distinction between race as a social category and horse races. The short, single pun on Native Americans simply observed, 'The Indian's race is nearly run.' For a variety of reasons, the white worker could meaningfully speak of being a 'wages slave' but not of being a 'wage Indian'. He could complain of having to 'work like a nigger' but not of having to 'work like an Indian'.[10]

White over Black

If the 'white worker' developed as a self-conscious social category mainly by comparing himself to Blacks, we might ask whether this process did not begin in the seventeenth century rather than the nineteenth. Indeed, Winthrop Jordan's full and eloquent *White over Black* traces the roots of American racism before Jamestown, showing that the animus toward things and people who were dark was already a powerful force in the British worldview. Whether the package of 'American attitudes' toward race gave rise to a full-blown and coherent ideology of racism able to shape white supremacist actions before 1800 remains a matter of sharp debate among historians. So too do the related questions of whether racism made for a relatively speedy and unconsidered embrace of slavery by Americans, or whether slavery gradually evolved, driven mainly by social tensions and labor demands among whites and was less the result than the cause of racist attitudes.[11] These issues are difficult enough when considering evidence drawn from the records left by the political leaders, theologians and intellectuals – the sources most favored by leading historians of racial thought. Far less studied, and probably far more complex, is the question of how far nonelite white colonists had coherently divided the world into racial terms and had internalized white supremacy. Attempting to view seventeenth- and eighteenth-century white American attitudes toward Blacks 'from the bottom up' provides almost perfect illustration of Barbara Fields's comment that racial attitudes are 'promiscuous critters', sometimes coexisting quite cheerfully with their seeming opposites.[12] Nonetheless, the overall picture is clear enough to justify regarding early anti-Black attitudes as important parts of the prehistory, but not history, of the white worker.

In certain places and at certain times between 1607 and 1800, the 'lower sorts' of whites appear to have been pleasantly lacking in racial consciousness. Perhaps they had never fully imbibed the white supremacist attitudes of the larger society described by Jordan. Or perhaps, as Alden Vaughn has suggested, they came as racists but showed 'signs of eroding prejudice [on becoming] more familiar with Black men and women.'[13] In any case, racial lines were often drawn quite waveringly at the bottom of society. Before 1680, Virginia's 'giddy multitude' was biracial and shared not only a desire for land but also social occasions, solidarity in rebellion and sometimes the same household. North and South, white indentured servants fled at times with Black (and even Indian) servants or slaves, an act that brought extra scrutiny to the white escapee because his or her companion was more likely to be stopped and questioned than he or she was.[14] G.S. Rowe's fine study of Black defendants and criminal courts in late eighteenth-century Philadelphia argues that 'the lower classes of both races often accepted each other on terms of equality much more readily than did their social betters.' Rowe shows poor whites harboring Black fugitive servants, dancing with Blacks and at times engaging in a life of biracial petty crime. Steven Rosswurm's study of Revolutionary Philadelphia shows the city fathers to be anxious to abolish fairs as places in which not only white servants but white journeymen artisans mixed freely with African-Americans.[15] Major urban slave revolts, such as that in New York City in 1741 and Gabriel's Rebellion in Richmond in 1800 included white participants. In early Virginia revolts, such limited support was said to come from the 'very poor' whites.[16]

Blacks dominated late eighteenth-century community festivals such as the huge Negro Election Day celebrations held in a score of New England cities and the Pinkster festivities in New York and New Jersey. These events greatly worried authorities, not the least because of sizeable participation by 'the lower class of ... our own complexion', as James Newhall of Lynn, Massachusetts put it. Indeed, mixed lower class entertainments throughout the year were common in New York, and Black

24

influence on white popular entertainment was marked.[17]

Some artisans, most eloquently Benjamin Franklin, defended not only the slave's right to freedom but also the intellectual abilities of Blacks.[18] In the Revolutionary era and the very early Republic, artisans generally appear to have favored abolition of slavery in the North and even to have exhibited some unease, in Maryland, about *formally* disfranchising free Blacks.[19] And the proportions of Black artisans among urban craft workers were greater than they would ever be again. In Philadelphia, 14 percent of identifiable Black male occupations in Gary Nash's sample for 1795 were artisanal, and in Shane White's New York City research a surprising 37.8 percent of male free Black heads of households held artisanal jobs in 1800, a proportion that was to decline by a fourth within the next decade.[20]

The many gradations of unfreedom among whites made it difficult to draw fast lines between any idealized free white worker and a pitied or scorned servile Black worker. Indentured servitude, impressment, apprenticeship, convict labor, farm tenancy, wage labor and combinations of wage labor and free farming made for a continuum of oppression among whites. Of course (notwithstanding scattered references to white 'enslavement' in colonial court cases) that continuum did not extend to the extreme of chattel slavery as was inflicted on people of color.[21] But neither were sweeping and unambiguous distinctions between stations in life and kinds of work appropriate for whites and those to be confined to Blacks yet possible. One could occasionally find attempts to make such sharp distinctions, as in the comment a Carolina merchant is said to have made to the Earl of Edgmont in 1740: '... where there are Negroes, a white Man despises to work [in the fields], saying, *what will you have me a Slave and work like a Negroe?*'[22] But in general, wide varieties of whites (not just indentures) were called *servants* and the same term was used, with adjectives like *perpetual* and *negro* to describe slaves. This usage, which would become absolutely intolerable to employed whites within three decades after the Revolution, reflected the fact that in labor-short seventeenth- and eighteenth-century America the work of slaves and that of white servants were virtually interchangeable in most areas.[23]

None of this is to argue that working people in the seventeenth and eighteenth centuries were not aware of race or that they were unwilling to use white supremacy when it could work to their advantage. Racial attitudes did behave promiscuously and coexist with their opposites. Thus the egalitarian Franklin could also hope to make America a land of 'White People' and consider whiteness (in which he regarded even the 'swarthy' Germans as insufficient) as the 'Complexion of my Country'.[24] Similarly the race-mixing whites of Virginia's 'giddy multitude' of the 1670s were, after a series of economic, political and demographic changes, recruited to the cause of white unity. Artisans were frequently slaveholders – indeed they were the largest slaveholding group in New York City through 1790.[25]

But in most places, and the point is crucial for present purposes, such attempts to connect a consciousness of whiteness with a consciousness of status as a worker failed. There was certainly a long tradition, centered in New York City and Charleston, of protesting against the use of slave labor because it 'soe much impoverisht' white workers, as a late seventeenth-century complaint put it. But though this hatred of having to compete with slave labor was expressed sporadically in many cities and towns, it fought an uphill battle. In a few cases, white workers succeeded in gaining public policies supporting their demand for limits on competition from slaves, but enforcement was uncertain. It is unclear how much of this agitation was racially based. Some appeals seem to conflate 'slave' and 'Black', implying calls for color bars against free Blacks as well. But there were also organized complaints about the employment of 'outsiders', and 'soldiers'. Not surprisingly, workers tried to enhance their position in the labor market. They did so by making appeals as 'your Majestys white Subjects' or by whatever other logic had a chance of working. On the whole, as Jordan puts it, 'What is impressive about the evidence of economic competition [with Blacks] is its occasional character.' Faced with the rights of powerful slaveholders to use their property as they wished, having no compelling evidence that they were better off competing against white indentured servants than against slaves, and perhaps hopeful of one day acquiring a slave themselves, most artisans continued to work in relatively open labor markets.[26] Even after the Revolution, the abolition of slavery in the North cannot be regarded in any simple way as a victory for white workers seeking to limit labor competition.[27]

A brief discussion of New York City's carters, a group of atypical colonial workers who did manage to become white workers, illuminates the difference between episodic agitation for labor market advantages based on racial appeals and a self-image that brought together race, work and citizenship. The carters, who transported commodities in one-horse carts, monopolized their trades because they were, after 1695, licensed by the city government as 'freemen'. The municipal government secured a licensing fee and compliance with regulations from the cartmen. The cartmen received protection against competition from transient, usually farm-based, laborers and got the right to vote in city elections and protection from being seized by press gangs for impressment as sailors. Based on Dutch and declining British traditions of freemanship, this licensing arrangement offered to British officials the opportunity to cultivate loyal political support by conferring 'freeman' status. The system extended, after Leisler's Rebellion of 1689–91, to twenty-eight trades and became a significant way to defuse class divisions and Anglo-Dutch tensions. Among the carters particularly, freemanship became the centerpiece of a prideful ideology. It combined civil rights, a trade and white supremacy, in that Blacks were never allowed freeman status. Moreover, and in contrast with other New York City occupations, the cartmen were able to use color bar legislation – passed even before the freemanship period, probably to cement ties between the young English regime and Dutch carters – and their own political power to keep *slaves* from being hired out as carters. Carters were not only insulated from competition from the city's large Black population, and from merchants owning slaves, but they could and did hire Blacks as helpers, paying a small fraction of white helpers' wages and sometimes paying only in alcohol. In such a situation, whiteness, civic entitlement and job issues had become one and were summed up by one word: *freeman*.[28] The American Revolution would help create an America in which many more working 'freemen' would be tempted to define themselves against slaves.

Political Slavery, White Servitude and Republican Liberty

During the period of intense politicization surrounding the American Revolution metaphoric usages of *slavery* to describe the political plight of whites abounded. The allusions to the 'political slavery' of whites were rife, and some observers compared white indentured servants to slaves, though the servants generally did not openly make such comparisons themselves. But the plethora of metaphors did not yet signal the rise of the 'white worker' as a form of self-identification in the United States. Instead, the constant references to unfreedom among whites spoke of a situation in which whiteness and independence were not firmly connected. Nor was Blackness yet fully linked with servitude. But the success of the Revolution in spreading independence as a reality and as an ideal among whites and its failures in addressing Black oppression helped to change all that.

In the rhetoric of Anglo-American freedom-lovers, as Marcus Cunliffe points out, 'the opposite of "liberty" was "slavery".'[29] Americans consistently interpreted the designs of the British and other enemies as plots to enslave free people. 'There are but two sorts of men in the world, freemen and slaves', John Adams wrote just before the Revolution. He

the Revolution, in not making women part of equality, gendered whiteness. working class identity.

I'm not so sure. Cf p. 26 Conflation of Black : slave, cf. p. 28 - Adams' quote added that the 'very definition of a freeman is one who is bound by no law to which he has not consented' and that capitulation to Parliament could make Americans 'not only ... slaves. But the most abject sort of slaves to the worst sort of masters!'[30] Because revolutionaries, and particularly artisan revolutionaries, so thoroughly conflated the opportunity to accumulate and secure productive property with the 'pursuit of happiness', the power to tax particularly implied the power to 'enslave'. Adams foresaw a nation 'oppressed to death with debts and taxes.' Stephen Hopkins, writing in 1764, reproduced republican logic on this score clearly, if schematically: 'They who are taxed at pleasure by others cannot possibly have any property. ... They who have no property, can have no freedom, but are indeed reduced to the most abject slavery.'[31]

Such rhetoric is so extravagant when constraints on white American liberties are compared with constraints on Black slaves that one is tempted to conclude that the revolutionary critique of political 'slavery' merely echoed old Anglo-American radical rhetoric and had little to do with actual chattel slavery.[32] This would be a mistake. Although the metaphoric use of *slavery* for any threat to liberty had deep roots in virtually slaveless England, Scotland, Venice and Florence, its special force in the American colonies derived in large part from proximity to chattel slavery. American revolutionaries consistently exhibited a terror of being treated, as one of them put it, 'like *Guinea slaves*'. When Arthur Lee, slaveholder and revolutionary, protested the Declaratory Act, he almost incoherently registered fears that must have seemed exceptionally vivid to those who knew and ran a slave system:

> I see already men torn from their weeping and distressed families, without hope, without redress, never to return, by an unrelenting, lawless crew, unbridled by our own civil and legislative authority, and wantonly cruel in the exercise of despotic power. I see every endearing tie of father, husband, son and brother, torn asunder, unrespited, unpitied, unreprieved.

John Adams, pseudonymously writing a humorous newspaper series designed to solidify yeoman and artisan revolutionary commitment, promised 'we won't be their [Britain's] negroes. Providence never designed us for negroes. I know, for if it had it would have given us black hides and thick lips ... which it han't done, and therefore never intended us for slaves.'[33]

For working people of the revolutionary generation metaphors regarding enslavement, and the consciousness of the difference between mastery and servitude, must have been particularly vivid. John Locke had argued that chattel slavery could apply only to Africans because such a condition was 'so vile and miserable an estate' that it could find no application among Englishmen. American radicals were not so certain. The greatest artisan radical, Benjamin Franklin, wrote in 1770:

> A slave ... is a human creature stolen, taken by Force, or bought of another or of himself with Money. ... He may be sold again or let for Hire, by his Master. [He] must wear such Cloaths as his Master thinks fit ... and be content with such Food ... as his Master thinks fit to order for him: [He] must never absent himself from his Master's Service without Leave [and is] subject to severe Punishments for small Offenses.

Franklin's definition, a rare direct connection by an (albeit prosperous) white artisan of economic dependency and slavery, covered not only Black slavery but also indentured servitude and even the apprenticeship Franklin himself had served. He argued that there were 'many thousands of "slaves"' in Britain, citing Scottish miners and English sailors in particular.[34] Such white servitude, as John Van Der Zee has written, 'gave to words like "liberty," "freedom" and "tyranny" a physical reality that people were willing to suffer and die for' in the American Revolution.[35]

But the 'physical reality' of servitude was made still more meaningful because indenture was so dramatically poised *between* independence and chattel slavery. On the one hand, the artisanate was a remarkably independent group. As David Brody observes, 'the artisan labor force was substantially a labor force of masters.' Generally unfettered by guild restrictions, an artisan became a master simply by setting up for himself. 'The term master', Brody continues, '... meant any self-employed artisan', a position within reach of most skilled craftsmen in the late colonial period and the early Republic. Brody adds that many of the 'settled unskilled' in cities were likewise self-employed.[36]

However, in its origins the artisan population was particularly unfree, dependent and subjected to treatment often compared with that meted out to Black slaves. According to Bernard Bailyn's sample of registered white migration to the colonies on the 'eve of the Revolution', 'four-fifths of the [arriving] artisans in the most highly skilled crafts' came under indenture, with the proportion being only just slightly less in 'less highly skilled trades'. These are, as Bailyn recognizes, 'remarkable' figures, and the best explanation for them is that skilled craft workers, rather than exhausting scarce resources for passage, came with small savings into servitude, enduring indenture in order to establish themselves independently more rapidly after four or five years of suffering.[37]

By most accounts the indenture's unfreedom and hardship, though of short duration, were in some respects worse than any institutionalized form of labor exploitation in Britain. *Indentured servitude* was a term which, like *kidnapping*, gained currency because it described the particularly harsh realities of labor recruitment to the colonies. Sharon Salinger's work on servitude in Pennsylvania moreover suggests that the institution only became more 'American' and more debasing as the Revolution approached.[38] Transported in abysmal conditions alongside convicts, often sick and always filthy on arrival, indentured servants were sold at auction, sometimes after being stripped naked. If not sold retail on the coast, they were wholesaled to 'soul drivers' who marched the white servants, sometimes in coffles, through the countryside, selling them individually or in small lots. Not surprisingly, British contemporaries likened this 'infamous traffic' to chattel slavery. A letter in a Yorkshire newspaper, for example, found the indentures to be 'sold for slaves at public sale' and 'subject nearly to the same laws as the Negroes [with] the same coarse food and clothing.' Unfree whites often worked alongside slaves in cities like Philadelphia and New York City and sometimes ran away with slaves.[39] The indentured servant was legally 'chattel of the master', though with greater protection – through custom, terms of indenture and recourse to magistrates – than slaves had and, of course, with an end to bondage in sight.[40]

Indentured servitude, along with apprenticeship, imprisonment for debt, tenant farming, hiring out of convicts and impressment of sailors,[41] gave ordinary whites of the revolutionary generation galling experience of a variety of social oppressions and increased their receptivity of critiques of white political enslavement. When, celebrating the eleventh anniversary of the British evacuation of New York City, the artisan-based Tammany Society issued a ringing republican call for 'a speedy abolition of every species of slavery throughout America', its language reflected a tendency to subsume a range of evils under the heading of 'slavery'.[42]

The proximity of unfree whites and Black chattel slaves on a continuum of oppression helped create sympathies that ensured that the 'contagion of liberty' during and after the upheaval of the Revolution would result in attacks on racial slavery as well as on indentured servitude. Tom Paine, who had in 1774 sold his corsetmaking shop in London to avoid imprisonment for debt, made an attack on 'African Slavery in America' practically his first order of business in Philadelphia in 1775. Writing under the names 'Justice and Humanity' in the *Pennsylvania Magazine*, Paine accepted the gist of Samuel Johnson's criticism that revolutionary ideas came from the 'drivers of negroes'. He demanded an answer as to how Americans could 'complain so loudly of attempts to enslave them, while they hold so many hundreds of thousands in slavery; and annually enslave many thousands more.'[43] Paine's solution, unlike Johnson's, was to attack many 'species of slavery'. The momentum of the Revolution, the ability of Blacks to strike for their own freedom during the upheaval and, in part, the activities of politicized artisans like Paine contributed decisively to the gradual abolition of slavery in New England and the middle colonies, to the nonextension of slavery into most of the Northwest Territory and, in 1807, to an end of US participation in the slave trade. However, Paine and others also toyed with the idea that chattel slavery was the result of actions by the anti-Republican British and therefore not the responsibility of Americans – an idea that found sharp expression in the Declaration of Independence. Even among radical artisans, the revolutionary heritage did not lead to unambiguously antislavery conclusions.[44]

Toward Racism: White Freedom and Black Slavery

But indentured servitude was not chattel slavery, and in the long run the differences contributed to a republican disdain for *slaves* as well for slavery. This issue is best approached via a thesis in David Brion Davis's *The Problem of Slavery in the Age of Revolution*. 'Prior to the [American] Revolution', Davis writes, 'few colonists were capable of the imaginative leap of placing themselves' in the position of the slave. Colonists were, Davis argues, '"fully encased" in their identity as free white men.' Only the 'uncertainty, self-doubt and unpredictable identity' brought by the Revolution made such an imaginative leap possible.[45] This may have been the case in Southern colonies like Virginia, where a huge slave population, a decrease in the numbers of indentures and in the horrors of white servitude, and the growth of a unique politics of deference and populism had made for a very early and complete 'creation of the white race'.[46] But if Davis had concentrated more on the position of unfree, formerly unfree and precariously free whites, and on long-standing fears of political slavery, he might have reached a rather more complicated conclusion: a large body of whites could imagine themselves as slaves – and on socioeconomic, as well as political, grounds.

Complexities arose precisely because their identification with slaves, though important, was imaginary. Conditions were close enough to permit, perhaps necessitate, such an imagination, but the differences remained and mattered both for how ordinary whites saw slaves and how they saw themselves. Indentures were part of a late colonial population that was sometimes careful to claim rights as 'freeborn *British White*

31

subjects'. They would soon again be free.[47] Slaves were born Black, not British, and were often born in chains. Those chains would last a lifetime and would be passed on to their children. Sharp fears of rebellion and retribution by slaves and exslaves existed, while servants were, a century after Bacon's Rebellion, seen as unruly but not given to insurrection. Far more laborers were chattel slaves than indentured servants and, since indentures so quickly became free, Americans could envision the assimilation of the white unfree into citizenship, but could not envision such an assimilation of chattel slaves. Nor was it easy to see how slaveholders would be compensated for their loss of productive property. The economic and political interests defending Black slavery were far more powerful than those defending indentured servitude.[48]

In short, white servitude was a problem that could be and was conquered both at the social and at the individual level in a way that Black slavery was not. The metaphoric 'political slavery' of which Americans of all classes complained was swept away by an uneven, but by world standards remarkably successful, process of democratization among whites. The long decline of urban indentured servitude, which had begun during the two decades of economic uncertainty before the Revolution, continued during the war because freedom was offered in exchange for military service, and because of the drying up of British immigration, the general decline in shipping, and republican attacks on the 'traffick in white people'.[49] Such servitude renewed after the war, but it brought unfreedom mainly to German and Irish ethnic minorities and to northern Blacks whose 'emancipation' often came only after long periods of servitude. In some areas at least, demand for white bound labor had slowed during years of slow economic growth after the Revolution. By the early nineteenth century, indentured servitude was 'quantitatively insignificant' within the US labor system.[50]

Perhaps more important, significant numbers of indentured servants of the revolutionary generation had served their indentures, and, if lucky, received their 'freedom dues'. Among indentured artisans, many had undoubtedly gone on to the full independence of becoming masters. Mobility was surely not always so easy as was implied in Warren Smith's study of indentures in South Carolina, which held that 'the white servant in Charles Town when "out of his time" might simply hang out his own shingle.' But before, during and after the Revolution, American society was sufficiently open to the self-employed, if still poor, artisan to justify Abbott Smith's well-phrased contention that America offered 'a far better chance of attaining decent independence than did Europe.' Bonds, for the whites in the young United States, were things to be broken, slipped or outlasted by free men. Especially after 1763, paternalist labor relations, such as hiring out by the month or year, declined in urban areas, both as a result of the desires of employers and those of workers. Fragile urban economies, before and after the Revolution, did not promise much opportunity for gaining wealth to the 'lower orders'. But amidst poverty and anxiety, independence could be won.[51]

Critically, white urban workers connected their freedom and their work. At the Independence Day celebration in 1788 of the ratification of the federal Constitution, parading Philadelphia craftsmen swelled with pride and linked their trades and political liberty. 'By Unity We Support Society' punned the chairmakers' banner, while that of the hatters announced 'With the Industry of the Beaver We Support Society'.[52] Old terms received new meanings and acquired wider currency to express such pride and self-confidence. *Mechanic* had carried negative connotations before the revolutionary movement began, describing 'low workmen' and 'mean' or even 'servile' workers. But, as Howard Rock put it, 'For the mechanic, the Revolution catalyzed previous economic and political gains into a new and prideful sense of being active participants in the creation of a new republic.'[53]

The very word *mechanic* took on a luster. Journeymen, employing artisans, and even former artisans who had become considerable manufacturers, embraced the term as mechanics' revolutionary organizations proliferated during the conflict with Britain, and mechanics' banks, institutes, societies, charitable organizations, reading rooms, newspapers, fire fighting brigades and insurance companies later arose. 'Mechanic consciousness' united masters and journeymen in the belief that those who produced, and especially those who produced useful commodities, deserved respect, full citizenship, value for their work and a measure of social power. Mechanics now claimed respect as 'men professing an ingenious art' and as intelligent citizens.[54]

The largely reasonable expectation was that journeymen mechanics would in time become masters and then would be *independent* in every sense of the word. The Revolution had already made them *freemen*, usually not in the restricted sense of the licensed New York City carters, but as full citizens who could protect their economic interests. *Freeman*, in eighteenth-century usage, implied either political freedom or economic independence. For republican artisans it implied both. Far into the nineteenth century, and even as the lines dividing masters and journeymen hardened, workers would see themselves and make their claims as 'industrious mechanics', as 'independent mechanics' and as 'freemen'.[55] But *freeman* had its opposite: *slave*.

And the number of chattel slaves kept increasing – in the South and even, through the 1790s, in some Northern areas such as New York City. The Constitution, as it codified an impressive range of freedom for whites, accepted that Black slavery would continue by providing for return of escaped slaves, by aggrandizing the representation of slaveholding districts through the partial counting of slaves for purposes of legislative apportionment and taxation and by allowing for twenty years of noninterference with the slave trade. Remarkably, the framers did all this without using the words *slave* or *slavery*. The presence of whites 'bound to service for a Term of Years' was acknowledged in the course of providing that such Americans should be counted as full citizens for purposes of taxation and representation.[56]

Even artisan-patriots with substantial antislavery credentials supported the Constitution as a compromise necessary to secure the world's greatest experiment in freedom. This was the position taken by Paine and Franklin, though the latter caustically noted the difference between Northern and Southern property protected by the Constitution. 'Sheep', he observed, using the animals to symbolize Northern property, 'will never make an insurrection.' For many, even on the Paineite-Jeffersonian left wing of the Revolution, chattel slavery had become by 1789 a necessary evil. Hopes lay in its gradual eradication over a period of decades. Indeed, even in the North it took decades for gradual emancipation schemes to eliminate Black slavery completely.[57] It proved easy to suspect that those injecting the issue of slavery into politics were less advocates of Black freedom than enemies of the compromise that undergirded America's great experiment in liberty among whites. In 1790, the writer of a letter to the *Maryland Gazette* eloquently expressed one kind of republican logic in arguing for abolition and signing himself 'Freeman'. He was answered by another kind of republican logic, which saw slavery, albeit regrettably, as part of the ongoing 'fabric of government' in the South. That letter was signed 'A True Friend to the Union'.[58]

Revolutionary success in defeating the 'servile' and 'slavish' Tories provided, according to Reginald Horsman, 'an overt sign that Providence had marked [Americans] for great deeds.' At the same time the Revolution strengthened the case for pride in 'special American accomplishments and a distinguished historical heritage', often a specifically Anglo-Saxon heritage.[59] But by no means did such pride necessitate the growth of racism or even national chauvinism. The Revolution taught optimism and an awareness that people could change with astonishing speed, and therefore a belief that, especially given the American example, 'other peoples ... could build free institutions.' Some theorists even held that skin color was merely a short-term result of exposure to a given environment and that Blacks would literally whiten over time, without mixing of the races. Such extreme environmentalism was common but looked to quite long-range improvements, while whites saw changes in their own lives occurring at a rapid pace. Moreover, the plantation was seen as a powerful environment, one whose destructive, even degenerative, servility-inducing effects might be harder to change than skin color itself. It was increasingly difficult to find signs that such a transformation was occurring among people of color, either among the 'savage nations' scattering before American expansion or the growing numbers of enslaved Blacks.[60] Republicanism had long emphasized that the strength, virtue and resolve of a people guarded them from enslavement, and that weakness and servility made those most dependent a threat to the Republic, apt to be pawns of powerful and designing men.[61] From such a stance it was not difficult to move toward considering the proposition that Black oppression was the result of 'slavishness' rather than slavery.

White revolutionary pride could thus open the way for republican racism. By 1805, Black Philadelphians were driven from Independence Day celebrations; they could return in subsequent years 'only at their peril'. Similar attacks on Blacks on Independence Day also occurred in New York City.[62] It was less easy, for a time, for ordinary whites, now 'freemen', to imagine themselves, even inexactly, as slaves. They were by the nineteenth century, to use Davis's language, '"fully encased" in their identity as free white men.' To inquire too deeply into why the 'contagion of liberty' had resulted in increased slaveholding in the South, and indentures and unfreedom for Blacks elsewhere, was painful if not treasonous. Perhaps, an appealing argument ran, events had shown Blacks to be unfit for freedom, proven so because they did not thrive in republican America. Duncan MacLeod's suggestion that 'southern whites preserved their commitment to republicanism by formally reading blacks out of the polity, thereby separating black slavery from white freedom', begins an understanding of this process, but the connection between republicanism and racism was made nationwide, not just in the South.[63] Moreover, the gulf between black slavery and white freedom was a reality in early American politics and society. Such a separation was not invented by proslavery Southerners. Instead, its existence and growth opened the way for proslavery thought, racism and the coming of the white worker.

James Flint was a British traveller whose 1822 book on the United States so resolutely made the case that the revolutionary society it described was an unprecedented success that it has a charmingly modern ring and a special usefulness. Democratic and antislavery, Flint listened carefully to, and sympathized with, ordinary Americans, mostly in the North. Flint's brief apologia for US slaveholding – he opposed extension of slavery – distills what he heard:

> The Americans, no longer the vassals of England, were at liberty to pursue an independent course of policy [regarding slavery, which had previously been supported by the Crown]. The subject of negro slavery engaged their attention at an early period; but, unhappily for the new government, their territory was overspread with an unfortunate race who, by education, habits and resentment of former injuries, were the enemies rather than the members of the social compact.[64]

This remarkable passage suggests how easily historical and environmental explanations for Black oppression could be conflated with 'racial' ones. It shows how Blacks, free and slave, could be stigmatized precisely because slavery thrived in republican America, indeed that they could be stigmatized as the *antithesis* of republican citizens. In the changed circumstance of the nineteenth century, they would further be seen as the opposites of 'free white labor'.

Notes

1. David Halle, *America's Working Men: Work, Home and Politics among Blue-Collar Property Owners*, Chicago 1984, 202–30.
2. David Brion Davis, *The Problem of Slavery in the Age of Revolution, 1770–1823*, Ithaca, N.Y. 1975, and *Slavery and Human Progress*, Oxford 1984; Edmund Morgan, *American Slavery, American Freedom: The Ordeal of Colonial Virginia*, New York 1975.
3. Eric Foner, *Free Soil, Free Labor, Free Men: The Ideology of the Republican Party before the Civil War*, New York 1970, 32; David Montgomery, *Beyond Equality: Labor and the Radical Republicans, 1862–1872*, New York 1967, 7 and 26–30.
4. Gary Nash, *Forging Freedom: The Formation of Philadelphia's Black Community, 1720–1840*, Cambridge, Mass. 1988, 172–279; Leon F. Litwack, *North of Slavery: The Negro in the Free States, 1790–1860*, Chicago 1961, esp. 153–86; Paul A. Gilje, *The Road to Mobocracy: Popular Disorder in New York City, 1763–1834*, Chapel Hill, N.C. 1987.
5. *Oxford English Dictionary*, 2d edn (*OED2*), Oxford 1989, 12:72; *A Dictionary of American English, On Historical Principles* (*DAE*), Sir William A. Craigie and James R. Hulbert, eds, Chicago 1938, 4:2475–78.
6. On how the 'lazy Indian' was used by settlers in counterpoint to the provident and steady colonists – who were hardly such – see Morgan, *American Slavery*, esp. 59–68; Carolyn Merchant, *Ecological Revolutions: Nature, Gender and Science in New England*, Chapel Hill, N.C. 1989; William Cronon, *Changes in the Land: Indians, Colonists and the Ecology of New England*, New York 1983; David Smits, 'We Are Not to Grow Wild: Seventeenth-Century New England's Repudiation of Anglo-Indian Intermarriage', *American Indian Culture and Research Journal* 11 (1987): 1–32; David R. Roediger and Philip S. Foner, *Our Own Time: A History of American Labor and the Working Day*, London 1989, 4; James Axtell, *The European and the Indian: Essays in the Ethnohistory of Colonial North America*, New York 1981, 39–86.
7. Herman Melville, *The Confidence-Man: His Masquerade*, New York 1971 (1857), 125;

see also Roy H. Pearce, *The Savages of America: A Study of the Indian and the Idea of Civilization*, Baltimore 1953, 244; Richard Drinnon, *Facing West: The Metaphysics of Indian-Hating and Empire Building*, Minneapolis, Minn. 1980; Richard Slotkin, *Regeneration Through Violence: The Mythology of the American Frontier, 1600–1860*, Middletown, Conn. 1973; Rogin, *Fathers and Children: Andrew Jackson and the Subjugation of the American Indian*, New York 1975; Reginald Horsman, *Race and Manifest Destiny: The Origins of American Racial Anglo-Saxonism*, Cambridge, Mass. 1981.

8. Quoted in Michael Zuckerman, 'Identity in British America: Unease in Eden', in Nicholas Canny and Anthony Pagden, eds, *Colonial Identity in the Atlantic World, 1500–1800*, Princeton, N.J. 1987, 149 and passim; Robert F. Berkhoefer, Jr., 'The North American Frontier as Process and Context', in Howard Lamar and Leonard Thompson, eds, *The Frontier in History: North America and South Africa Compared*, New Haven, Conn. 1981, 53–55; Stephen Cornell, 'American Indians, American Dreams, and the Meaning of Success', *American Indian Culture and Research Journal* 11 (1987): 66–67 and 70 n12 for references to some exceptions. On *red niggers*, see Walter Blair and Franklin J. Meine, *Mike Fink: King of the Mississippi Keelboatmen*, New York 1933, 10–11, and Robert Montgomery Bird, *Nick of the Woods*, New York 1939 (1837), 22; on labor in the fur trade, see John Morris's forthcoming doctoral dissertation (University of Missouri).

9. Francis Jennings, *The Invasion of America: Indians, Colonialism and the Cant of Conquest*, Chapel Hill, N.C. 1975, 15–31; Bruce Collins, *White Society in the Antebellum South*, London 1985, 41; Jack D. Forbes, *Black Africans and Native Americans: Color, Race and Caste in the Evolution of Red-Black People*, Oxford 1988, 190–220 and 249–64; Zuckerman, 'Identity in British America', 154–55; James Axtell, 'Colonial America without the Indians', in Frederick E. Hoxie, ed., *Indians in American History*, Arlington Heights, Ill. 1988, 64; Axtell, *European and Indian*, 49–50, discusses the settler view that independence was confined to Indian males and rested on exploitation of women.

10. Frank Dumont, *Burnt Cork; or, The Amateur Minstrel*, New York 1881, 45; Horsman, *Race and Manifest Destiny*, 76–77, 155–56 and 198; Thomas Hart Benton in *Congressional Globe*, 29th Cong., 1st sess., 1846, 917–18; Mark Lause, 'Land, Labor and Race: A Reconsideration of Agrarian Social Reform', forthcoming.

11. Winthrop Jordan, *White over Black: American Attitudes toward the Negro, 1550–1812*, Chapel Hill, N.C. 1968. Compare George Fredrickson, *The Black Image in the White Mind: The Debate on Afro-American Character and Destiny, 1817–1914*, New York 1972, xi and 1–2; Alden Vaughn, 'The Origins Debate: Slavery and Racism in Seventeenth-Century Virginia', *Virginia Magazine of History and Biography* 97 (July 1989): 347–49 and passim; Morgan, *American Slavery, American Freedom*.

12. Barbara Fields, 'Ideology and Race in American History', in J. Morgan Kousser and James M. McPherson, eds, *Region, Race and Reconstruction*, New York 1982, 155.

13. Vaughn, 'Origins Debate', 347–49.

14. T.H. Breen, 'A Changing Labor Force and Race Relations in Virginia', *Journal of Social History* (Fall 1973): 3–25; Lawrence W. Towner, 'A Good Master Well Served: A Social History of Servitude in Massachusetts' (Ph.D. dissertation, Northwestern University, 1954), 319–21.

15. G.S. Rowe, 'Black Offenders, Criminal Courts, and Philadelphia Society in the Late Eighteenth Century', *Journal of Social History* 22 (Summer 1989): 695; Steven Rosswurm, *Arms, Country and Class: The Philadelphia Militia and 'Lower Sort' during the American Revolution, 1775–1783*, New Brunswick, N.J. 1987, 37.

16. Thomas J. Davis, *A Rumor of Revolt: 'The Great Negro Plot' in Colonial New York*, New York 1985, ix; James Hugo Johnston, 'The Participation of White Men in Virginia Negro Slave Insurrections', *Journal of Negro History* 16 (April 1931): 159–62.

17. Melvin Wade, 'Shining in Borrowed Plumage: Affirmation of Community in the Black Coronation Festivals of New England, ca. 1750–1850', *Western Folklore* 40 (July 1981): 171–82; Joseph P. Reidy, 'Negro Election Day and Black Community Life in New England, 1750–1860', *Marxist Perspectives* 1 (Fall 1978): 102–17; Shane White, 'Pinkster: Afro-Dutch Syncretization in New York City and the Hudson Valley', *Journal of American Folklore* 102

(January–March 1989): 71ff; William J. Mahar, '"Backside Albany" and Early Blackface Minstrelsy', *American Music* 6 (Spring 1988): esp. 13–14.

18. Jordan, *White over Black*, 282; Nash, *Forging Freedom*, 30–31.

19. Edgar J. McManus, *A History of Negro Slavery in New York*, Syracuse, N.Y. 1966, 183–84; Charles F. Steffen, *The Mechanics of Baltimore: Workers and Politics in the Age of Revolution, 1763–1812*, Urbana, Ill. 1984, 131; Gary Nash, *The Urban Crucible: Social Change, Political Consciousness and the Origins of the American Revolution*, Cambridge, Mass. 1979, 320–21.

20. Nash, *Forging Freedom*, 149; Shane White, '"We Dwell in Safety and Pursue Our Honest Callings": Free Blacks in New York City, 1783–1810', *Journal of American History* 75 (September 1988): 453–54 and 469.

21. Towner, 'Good Master', 280.

22. As quoted in Jordan, *White over Black*, 129–30.

23. Christopher L. Tomlins, 'The Ties That Bind: Master and Servant in Massachusetts, 1800–1850', *Labor History* 30 (Spring 1989): 199–209; Edmund Morgan, *The Puritan Family: Religion and Domestic Relations in Seventeenth-Century New England*, New York 1966, 109; Towner, 'Good Master', 150; Jordan, *White over Black*, 86–88 and 129–30; Albert Matthews, 'The Terms Hired Man and Help', *Publications of the Colonial Society of Massachusetts* 5 (1898): 230 and passim. See also Chapter 3 below.

24. Jordan, *White over Black*, 143.

25. Morgan, *American Slavery, American Freedom*, 235–362; Nash, *Urban Crucible*, 109; White, 'Dwell in Safety', 455.

26. Quotes from Litwack, *North of Slavery*, 5; Jordan, *White over Black*, 129. See also Nash, *Urban Crucible*, 107–10; Richard B. Morris, *Government and Labor in Early America*, New York 1946, 182–88; Graham R. Hodges, *New York City Cartmen, 1667–1850*, New York 1986, 4–5.

27. Litwack, *North of Slavery*, 6, and McManus, *Slavery in New York*, 183–84, give more weight to labor competition in Northern abolition initiatives than would I in the absence of much evidence that abolition was immediately followed by white labor efforts to bar freed-people from employment.

28. Hodges, *New York City Cartmen*, 4–5, 25–31, 35 and 189n.

29. Marcus Cunliffe, *Chattel Slavery and Wage Slavery*, Athens, Ohio 1979, 8.

30. Quoted in John Van Der Zee, *Bound Over: Indentured Servitude and American Conscience*, New York 1985, 304.

31. Bernard Bailyn, *Ideological Origins of the American Revolution*, Cambridge, Mass. 1967, 55–100 and 232–46; quotes from Van Der Zee, *Bound Over*, 169 and 304.

32. This is in essence the position of Bailyn, cited in n. 31, and of Duncan Macleod, *Slavery, Race and the American Revolution*, London 1974.

33. F. Nwabueze Okoye, 'Chattel Slavery as the Nightmare of the American Revolutionaries', *William and Mary Quarterly* 37 (January 1980): 14–15 and passim; Adams as quoted in Alexander Saxton, *The Rise and Fall of the White Republic: Class Politics and Mass Culture in Nineteenth-Century America*, London 1990.

34. Benjamin Franklin, 'Conversation on Slavery', *Public Advertiser*, 30 January 1770, as reprinted in Verner W. Crane, ed., *Benjamin Franklin's Letters to the Press*, Williamsburg, Va. 1950, 190–92; on Locke, property and slavery, see James Farr, '"So Vile and Miserable an Estate": The Problem of Slavery in Locke's Political Thought', *Political Theory* 14 (1986): 263–89; Seymour Drescher, '"So Vile and Miserable an Estate"', *Political Theory* 16 (1988): 502–3; and Farr, ''Slaves Bought with Money': A Reply to Drescher', *Political Theory* 17 (1989): 471–74.

35. Van Der Zee, *Bound Over*, 32.

36. David Brody, 'Time and Work during Early American Industrialism', *Labor History* 30 (Winter 1989): 13.

37. Bernard Bailyn with Barbara DeWolfe, *Voyagers to the West: A Passage in the Peopling of America on the Eve of the Revolution*, New York 1988, 172–74.

38. For a judicious account of the novelty of indentured servitude and its continuities with British patterns of service, see David Galenson, *White Servitude in Colonial America: An*

Economic Analysis, Cambridge, Mass. 1981, 5–15; and Sharon Salinger, *To Serve Well and Faith-* ✓ *fully: Labor and Indentured Servants in Pennsylvania*, New York 1987; on kidnapping and indenture see *OED2* and Anna L. Keaton, 'Americanisms in Early American Newspapers', Chicago 1936 (a private edition of part of Keaton's 1933 University of Chicago Ph.D. dissertation), 22.

39. Bailyn, *Voyagers*, 324 and 296–353, passim; E.M. Riley, ed., *The Journal of John Harrower: An Indentured Servant in the Colony of Virginia, 1773–1776*, Williamsburg, Va. 1963, 39.

40. Abbott Smith, *Colonists in Bondage*, Chapel Hill, N.C. 1947, 233 and 226–301 passim.

41. On impressment, see Marcus Rediker, *Between the Devil and the Deep Blue Sea: Merchant Seamen, Pirates and the Maritime World, 1700–1750*, Cambridge, Mass. 1987, 32–34 and 249–53, and Jesse Lemisch, 'Jack Tar in the Street: Merchant Seamen in the Politics of Revolutionary America', *William and Mary Quarterly* 25 (1968): 381–400. On convict labor, A. Roger Ekrich, *Bound for America: The Transportation of British Convicts to the Colonies, 1718–1775*, Oxford 1987. See also Staughton Lynd, *Anti-Federalism in Duchess County, New York*, Chicago 1962.

42. Philip S. Foner, ed., *The Democratic-Republican Societies: 1790–1800: A Documentary Sourcebook of Constitutions, Declarations, Addresses, Resolutions and Toasts*, Westport, Conn. 1976, 204.

43. Philip S. Foner, *Labor and the American Revolution*, Westport 1976, 160. See Bailyn, *Ideological Origins*, 230–319, for the 'contagion of liberty'.

44. Davis, *Problem of Slavery*, 255–342; Robin Blackburn, *The Overthrow of Colonial Slavery, 1776–1848*, London 1988, 109–28 and 265–92; Peter H. Wood, '"The Dream Deferred": Black Freedom Struggles on the Eve of White Independence', in Gary Y. Okiro, ed., *In Resistance: Studies in African, Caribbean and Afro-American History*, Amherst, Mass. 1986, 172–81.

45. Davis, *Problem of Slavery*, 279.

46. Morgan, *American Slavery, American Freedom*; and for the 'creation of the white race', see the Theodore William Allen pamphlet 'Class Struggle and the Origin of Racial Slavery', Somerville, Mass. 1976, 1.

47. Blackburn, *Colonial Slavery*, 92.

48. Davis, *Problem of Slavery*, 321–26; W.E.B. Du Bois, *The Suppression of the African Slave Trade in the United States of America, 1638–1870*, New York 1896; Donald Robinson, *Slavery in the Structure of American Politics*, New York 1970.

49. Nash, *Urban Crucible*, 320; Smith, *Colonists in Bondage*, 284; P. Foner, *Labor and the American Revolution*, 181–82 and 200. Vermont's revolutionary constitution outlawed indentured servitude, appenticeship and slavery of adults. See Blackburn, *Colonial Slavery*, 117.

50. Galenson, *White Servitude*, 179; Sharon Salinger, 'Colonial Labor in Transition: The Decline of Indentured Servitude in Late Eighteenth Century Philadelphia', *Labor History* 22 (Spring 1981): 183–91. Arthur Zilversmit, *The First Emancipation: The Abolition of Slavery in the North*, Chicago 1967. See also Lynd, *Antifederalism*, 78–81, on the revolutionary period and the mixed successes of white tenants in gaining freedom from neofeudal oppression.

51. Warren B. Smith, *White Servitude in Colonial South Carolina*, Columbia, S.C. 1961, 88; Smith, *Colonists in Bondage*, 301; Nash, *Urban Crucible*, 258–59 and 340–72; Billy G. Smith, 'The Vicissitudes of Fortune: The Career of Laboring Men in Philadelphia, 1750–1800', in Stephen Innes, ed., *Work and Labor in Early America*, Chapel Hill, N.C. 1988, 239–41, stresses limits on mobility but the figures he cites show that a young journeyman had a good chance to become a master, especially in the 1780s and 1790s.

52. Edward Countryman, *The American Revolution*, New York 1985, 215.

53. Howard B. Rock, 'The Independent Mechanic: The Tradesmen of New York City in Labor and Politics During the Jeffersonian Era' (Ph.D. dissertation, New York University, 1974), 1–4; *OED2*, 6:284.

54. Rock, 'Independent Mechanic', 87 and passim; Paul Faler, *Mechanics and Manufacturers in the Early Industrial Revolution*, Albany, N.Y. 1981, 28–51; Bruce Sinclair, *Philadelphia's Philosopher Mechanics: A History of the Franklin Institute, 1824–1865*, Baltimore 1974, 1–17; Steffen, *Mechanics of Baltimore*, 53–142; Alfred F. Young, 'The Mechanics and the Jeffer-

sonians: New York, 1785–1801', *Labor History* 5 (1964); Nash, *Urban Crucible*, 359, 369, 372, 376; Gary J. Kornblith, '"Cementing the Mechanic Interest": Origins of the Providence Association of Mechanics and Manufacturers', *Journal of the Early Republic* 8 (Winter 1988): 355–88.

55. *OED2*, 4:526; *DAE2*, 1063; Rock, 'Independent Mechanic', 359; Rosswurm, *Arms, Country and Class*, 55; John R. Commons et al., *A Documentary History of American Industrial Society*, Cleveland 1910, 3:279.

56. Shane White, '"Dwell in Safety"', 448; Staughton Lynd, *Class Struggle, Slavery and the United States Constitution*, New York 1967; Davis, *Problem of Slavery*, 322–23; Blackburn, *Colonial Slavery*, 122–26; on white freedom and the Constitution, see Alfred Young, 'The Framers of the Constitution and the "Genius" of the People', and the various responses in *Radical History Review* 42 (Fall 1988), 8–47; on emancipation and discrimination, see McManus, *Slavery in New York*, 183–84; Litwack, *North of Slavery*, 15–19; Zilversmit, *First Emancipation*, 127–28.

57. Franklin, quoted in Robinson, *Slavery and American Politics*, 148; Eric Foner, *Tom Paine and Revolutionary America*, New York 1976 , 205; Zilversmit, *First Emancipation*; Blackburn, *Colonial Slavery*, 276–77.

58. Davis, *Problem of Slavery in the Age of Revolution*, 342; Macleod, *Slavery, Race and the American Revolution*, 92.

59. E. Foner, *Tom Paine*, 140; Horsman, *Race and Manifest Destiny*, 84–85. This is not to say that postrevolutionary society witnessed unambiguous triumphs for the 'lower orders'. See Rosswurm, *Arms, Country and Class*.

60. Horsman, *Race and Manifest Destiny*, 85–86; Ronald Takaki, *Iron Cages: Race and Culture in Nineteenth-Century America*, New York 1979, 32.

61. Gordon Wood, *The Creation of the American Republic, 1776–1787*, Chapel Hill, N.C. 1969; Countryman, *American Revolution*, 61–63; Fredrickson, *Black Image*, 2; Jordan, *White over Black*, 512–69; Nash, *Forging Freedom*, 3; Rowland Berthoff, 'Free Blacks, Women and Corporations as Unequal Persons', *Journal of American History* 76 (December 1989): 760.

62. Nash, *Forging Freedom*, 177; Gilje, *Road to Mobocracy*, 159.

63. Duncan Macleod, 'Toward Caste', in Ira Berlin and Ronald Hoffman, eds, *Slavery and Freedom in the Age of the American Revolution*, Charlottesville, Va. 1983, 231. See also Takaki, *Iron Cages*, Chaps. 1 and 2 and for a similar but abstruse argument, see Benjamin B. Ringer, *'We the People' and Others: Duality and America's Treatment of Racial Minorities*, New York 1983, 3–14 and passim.

64. James Flint, *Letters from America, 1818–1820*, London 1822, 33, 288–90; Nash, *Forging Freedom*, 178–79.

PART II
Race and the Languages of Class from the Revolution to the Civil War

'Names are the turning point of who shall be master.'

Walt Whitman
An American Primer (1904)

3

'Neither a Servant Nor a Master Am I': Keywords in the Languages of White Labor Republicanism

This chapter takes its title from a line in Walt Whitman's *Chants Democratic*, a line that also is featured in the epigraph to the first section of Sean Wilentz's recent study of the rise of the working class in New York City.[1] The idea that a recently revolutionary and strongly republican working population tried in the nineteenth century to build a Whitmanesque economy and society without masters and servants undergirds not only Wilentz's work but most of the best of the new labor history on the making of the American working class. The power of republicanism in informing labor's rhetoric and practice is now amply demonstrated. As Herbert Gutman and Ira Berlin have put it, when 'preindustrial workers became a wage-earning class, republicanism neither disappeared nor remained a set of stale patriotic pieties. Instead, workers in Jacksonian America remade it into a distinctive and radical – but nonsocialist – argument against the pervasive inequalities associated with nineteenth-century capitalism.'[2] The insights, and considerable drama, of recent histories of early labor derive largely from a focus on this remaking of republicanism by labor. The new labor history illuminates the question of how workers creatively pursued the vision of a republic of small producers in which, again in Whitman's words, 'I will be even with you, and you shall be even with me', even as the United States became a land whose citizens increasingly worked 'in shops they did not own and control, at a pace ... often

43

determined by others.'[3]

But labor republicans in the United States did not only attempt to abolish mastery and servanthood among white Americans. Many of them also acquiesced in the even sharper social divisions between Black Americans and slavemasters. Thus Whitman: 'Slaves are [probably] there because they must be – when the time arrives for them not to be ... they will leave.'[4] Moreover, republicanism itself carried a strong suspicion of the powerless, not just of the powerful, and a fear that the top and bottom in society would unite against the 'producing classes' in the middle. As virtually all working whites were included in the 'producing classes', that suspicion could fall heavily on slaves and free Blacks. *All* labor republicans existed in a society that offered the opportunity for white workers to measure their situations not only against the dream of a republic of small producers but also against the nightmare of chattel slavery. If early languages of class have already been located by historians within the context of republican thought and accelerating working class formation, they need also to be located within a *slaveholding* republic in which the constant, even increasing, presence of slavery was, as the Black abolitionist H. Ford Douglass remarked, 'completely interwoven into the passions of the ... people.'[5]

The Hireling and the Slave

In 1814, Francis Scott Key wrote, in a verse of 'The Star-Spangled Banner' not sung before baseball games, 'No refuge could save the hireling and the slave/From the terror of flight or the gloom of the grave.' The significant pairing of 'hireling and slave' would echo even into the 1850s as the status of white workers was debated. For Key's original audience the pair of words carried meanings within the context of the War of 1812. Britain prosecuted that war using hated mercenary or 'hireling' soldiers. Also in the British ranks were about three hundred former slaves, promised freedom and protection by British commanders in exchange for their military service. Some of these exslaves helped to burn the White House in 1814.[6] But Key's words also carried much broader meanings, embodying what a young, republican nation hated and perhaps feared that it might become. We have already examined the multifaceted connotations of *slave*. Those of *hireling* deserve similar attention.

In castigating 'hirelings', Key used a word that captures much of what republicans despised. A nation that depended on hirelings simply could not be a republic. Anglo-American usages of *hireling* current by the early nineteenth century connected a hireling soldier with a propensity to flee under fire. More broadly, hirelings in various fields, but particularly in politics, behaved as the very opposite of self-sacrificing republican citizens. They made 'reward or material remuneration the motive of [their] actions'; They were prostitutes – indeed Webster's 1829 dictionary of American English gives 'prostitute' as a synonym for *hireling* and further defines *hirelings* as 'perjurers by virtue of their avarice'. As an adjective, *hireling* typically meant both 'venal' and 'mercenary'. In usage it was often preceded by *press* and *politicians*, adumbrating various aspects of the critique of British corruption that had been a staple of American republican rhetoric since before the Revolution.[7] As Steve Watts's *Republic Reborn* demonstrates, Americans by 1814 had substantial doubts, and substantial reasons to doubt, with regard to their nation's ability to preserve a republican vision against 'hireling' corruption.[8]

But *hireling* conjured up yet another threat to republican liberty, one perhaps less easily conquered in the long run than the mercenary soldier or even than the acid of corrupt self-interest. *Hireling* meant, of course, 'one who is hired or serves for wages'. That usage, as the *Oxford English Dictionary* observes, was 'opprobrious', with 'serving for hire or wages' being all too nearly synonymous with 'to be had for hire'.[9] The term was especially opprobrious for American republicans. In particular, the artisanal followers of Tom Paine and Thomas Jefferson held that a free government required 'independent' small producers who owned productive property and therefore were neither cowed nor mercenary, as lifelong 'hirelings' would inevitably be. For Paine, 'freedom [was] destroyed by dependence' and *servant* was an opprobrious term. Hirelings and slaves were sometimes connected in popular logic, as in the observation that those who labor for others become 'mere Negroes [growing] lazy, and careless' and in the frequent references to sailors, the outstanding occupational group of waged adult males, as children and as slaves.[10]

Thus, the gradual transition to wage labor from 1800 to 1860 (and beyond) was an extremely serious matter for labor republicans. There were, of course, elements within republican thought that discouraged panic and encouraged long-term faith in republican solutions. From Tom Paine to Abraham Lincoln ran a line of thought that held that wage labor was not degrading *per se* – for Paine, man was free in large part because he held 'property in his own labor'. Wage labor could then be a rite of passage on the road to the economic independence of free farming or of self-employed craft labor.[11] Moreover, many labor republicans shared with their British counterparts the view that political plots – the corruption

45

and machination of the powerful and the acquiescence of the servile – gave rise to social inequality. In a republic of freemen, these political evils could be identified and checked, in the long run if not the short.[12]

Finally – and this is the point is least understood by historians – forms of wage labor emerging in the late eighteenth and early nineteenth centuries were themselves sometimes seen as less productive of dependency and as more 'republican' than traditional arrangements. Not only did the number of white indentured servants decline greatly between 1763 and 1830, but practices such as living in with the employing family, agreeing to long-term work for a single family and taking meals at the employer's table also declined in some areas with astonishing speed. Apprenticeship even came regularly to involve cash payments.[13] We know far too little about whether these changes were initiated mainly by employers or workers, but it is clear that the worker who struck wage bargains by the day and boarded out was considered less 'dependent' (if more anxious) than one who worked by the month or the year and boarded in. Paine could thus argue for extending the vote to some propertyless males but not to 'servants in families'.[14] Sean Wilentz has nicely shown how, without stepping outside the bounds of republican categories, labor radicals in New York City rehabilitated the wage relationship in the 1830s. They argued – admittedly with the rather significant exceptions that journeymen should get the full value for their labor in wages and should themselves decide what that value was – that a wage relationship was compatible, at least temporarily, with a just society.[15]

As Asa Briggs emphasizes, populist leaders in early nineteenth-century Britain who had labor followings lamented the loss of the 'chain of connection' or the 'bond of attachment' between the rich and the poor. Bonds and chains, seen as ties of dependency rather than of sharing, were far less valued in US labor republican thought.[16]

But, as reference to bonds and chains should sharply remind us, it was impossible to think about dependency on wages merely in comparison with the position of labor in an ideal republic; the comparison with the truly enslaved also loomed. Such a comparison cut hard, and it cut in two ways. On the one hand, the spectre of chattel slavery – present historically in no other nation during the years of significant working class formation – made for a remarkable awareness of the dangers of dependency and a strong suspicion of paternalism. On the other hand, hard thought about 'the hireling and the slave' could make the position of hireling comparatively attractive. The white hireling had the possibility of social mobility as the Black slave did not. The white hireling was usually a political freeman, as the slave, and with very few exceptions the free Black, were not. The comparison could lead to sweeping critiques of wage labor as 'white slavery' but it also could reassure wage workers that they belonged to the ranks of 'free white labor'. In their early attempts to develop a language of labor, working Americans therefore expressed soaring desires to be rid of the age-old inequalities of Europe and of any hint of slavery. They also expressed the rather more pedestrian goal of simply not being mistaken for slaves, or 'negers' or 'negurs'. And they saw not nearly so great a separation between these goals as we do.

From Servants to Hired People

As early as 1807, the British investor Charles W. Janson published the indignant replies he had received when he visited an acquaintance in New England and asked the maid who answered the door, 'Is your master home?' Not only did the maid make it clear that she had 'no master' but she insisted, 'I am Mr. ___'s *help*. I'd have you to know, *man*, that I am no *sarvant*; none but *negers* are *sarvants*.' The *Massachusetts Spy* in 1815 reported that exactly such exchanges occurred frequently, when visitors attempted to address *servants* or to ask about *masters*. Two decades later, a more celebrated observer of American life, Frances Trollope, lamented the difficulty of 'getting servants' in Ohio, but then corrected herself to write 'getting help'. She explained that in the United States, 'It is more than petty treason to the republic to call a free citizen a *servant*.' One of her own 'help' anxiously expressed to Trollope the hope that she would not think whites in service to be 'just as bad as if we are negurs.'[17]

Trollope and Janson were among many foreigners and American citizens to note such avoidance of the term *servant* and the reasons for such avoidance. As the American lawyer John Bristed put it in 1818, 'There is no such relation as *master and servant* in the United States: indeed the name is not permitted.' In explaining the disappearance of these terms, especially among farm and domestic laborers, Bristed commented on the tendency of US citizens toward 'confounding the term *servant* with that of *slave*.' There was good reason for such confounding, dating from the early imprecisions of colonial usages of *slave* and *servant* right through Noah Webster's inconsistent distinctions between the two terms in his dictionary of 1828 and the tendency in the South to apply *servant* overwhelmingly to slaves in the antebellum years. Yet another complicating factor was that free Blacks often worked as domestic servants, with the result that the degradations suffered by slaves, by Blacks generally and by

47

domestics all came to be associated under the heading *servant*.[18]

The *Oxford English Dictionary* counts 'hired man, woman, girl [and] people' all as Americanisms of probable early nineteenth-century origins. It stresses connections with slavery, finding the words to have been coined to be 'applied to free men or women engaged as servants (the latter word being formerly used to include slaves).' The *OED* adds that the terms particularly applied to workers 'on a farm' and in or 'around a house'.[19] Albert Matthews's close study of American usages of *hired man* and *help* shows the words to be more complex and even more interesting than the *OED* allows. Matthews establishes some colonial examples of the terms and, in the former case, some British antecedents. But he emphasizes an increase in their popularity in the early nineteenth century and attributes that increase both to a desire to be set apart from Blacks and to postrevolutionary ideals. On the latter point, Matthews agrees with the domestic service reformer Lucy Salmon who, writing in 1897, explained the decline of the term *servant* in postrevolutionary America by pointing out that it was an 'incongruous term in the face of the declared equality of all men, and an obnoxious term in view of the service performed at the South by negro slaves.'[20] This juxtaposition of the search for a language of freedom and for a language that would simply set apart and racially stigmatize the wholly unfree makes the popularity of terms like *hired man* and *help* extremely suggestive.

In one sense the developing language of labor was certainly egalitarian; it was largely the creation of those who worked. Daniel Rodgers, in an interesting short passage on antebellum labor and language, argues that euphemistic terms like *help* were inventions of the employers and 'reflected the vain hope that labels would rectify the anomaly of dependence in a society in which self-employment was the moral norm.' He adds that capitalists 'had good reason for the evasion' because they wanted to avoid associating the 'worker who labored at the will ... of another [with] the oldest, bluntest and most troubling word of all: "slave".'[21] Whether words like *help* functioned in the way Rodgers argues is a fascinating question. Whether they came into being through upper-class initiatives is quite another. On the latter score, the evidence from the early nineteenth century, when *help* and *hired man* became popular evasions, does not support Rodgers's point. Virtually all primary accounts show the new usages being enthusiastically initiated by those whose work was being described. James Fenimore Cooper, who hated the new terms as 'subterfuges', regarded them as creations of the workers themselves: of *help*, he snickered, 'A man does not usually hire his cook to *help* him cook his dinner, but to cook it herself.' The British traveller Charles Mackay similarly counted the new words for *servant* as marks of self-assertion, however quaint, among whites who did domestic work, and even suggested that the now-familiar 'help wanted' ads took that wording to avoid ruffling the racial and republican sensibilities of those who worked as servants.[22] The *Dictionary of American English* aptly summarizes a range of usages substituting *helps* and *hands* for *servants* by saying that the substitutions reflect what the employed 'chose to call themselves'. White female household workers in particular 'resisted' the designation *servant*, in favor of 'helps, helpers or hands'.[23]

In popularizing such new words, farm and household workers were not simply becoming racists, but neither were they simply being militant republicans. Rather, they were becoming *white workers* who identified their freedom and their dignity in work as being suited to those who were 'not slaves' or 'not negurs'. White workers were not slaves, and there were excellent reasons, quite without manipulation by employers, for their not wanting to be considered 'like a slave'. Not all these reasons had to do immediately with race. The first recorded instance of an American objecting to being called a servant, in 1784, reflected the sentiments of a white freeman who apparently hated being compared to indentured *whites*. US republicans, moreover, were used to railing against those who sought to enslave others, and several primary accounts of the rise of substitutes for *servant* set the changes squarely in the context of a quest for 'republican liberty' and a desire to be rid of models that had been inherited from 'slavish Europe'.[24]

But in a society in which Blackness and servility were so thoroughly intertwined – North and South – assertions of white freedom could not be raceless. To criticize Europe as 'slavish' or full of 'dastardly slaves' inevitably called to mind chattel slavery and in several cases high republicanism and high race feeling cohabit on the same page.[25] James Flint, a British visitor in the second decade of the nineteenth century, noted that among the poor in the free states that bordered slaveholding states 'certain kinds of labour are despised as being the work of slaves.' He counted shoeblacking and, at times, 'family manufactures' as tabooed and told of paupers in an Ohio poorhouse who 'refused to carry water for their own use' for fear of being considered 'like slaves'.[26] We can see in such actions both the frayed strands of republican self-assertion and a sense of whiteness that could at times be self-defeating.

The existence of slavery (and increasingly of open Northern campaigns to degrade free Blacks) gave working Americans both a wretched touchstone against which to measure their fears of unfreedom and a friendly reminder that they were by comparison not so badly off. It encouraged an early language of labor that was at once suffused with concern for 'republican liberty' and at the same time willing to settle for what Rodgers calls 'evasions'. Amidst much assertion of independence, the term *hired* subtly became one to be embraced. As *hired* was increasingly placed in front of *man*, *woman* and *girl*, it was also placed before the old term *hand*, especially when referring to farm laborers. In the latter usage – apparently first commented upon when James Flint observed in 1818 that where he visited in the North, 'Laborers are not *servants*, all are hired *hands*' – labor is clearly a commodity, separable from its owner and for sale.[27] Some of the sting had been taken from the connection between *hireling* and *slave*.

No Masters: The Mechanic Gets a Boss

Among urban craftsmen, the group that by the Age of Jackson had initiated a significant national labor movement and had launched labor parties and an identifiable artisan wing of the Democratic party, the language of labor displayed more continuity and, seemingly, more self-confidence than did that of farm and domestic workers. The favorite terms to emerge after the Revolution continued to be popular, with *mechanics'* societies proliferating and labor appeals being consistently addressed to *freemen*.[28] Other terms, like *artisan*, *member of the working classes*, *tradesman* and *workingman* also achieved significant popularity. No surviving evidence suggests that these terms – with the partial exception of *freeman* – bespoke any conscious desire to set white workers apart from slaves. *Mechanic* and *freeman* blurred lines – or reflected the fact that lines were indeed blurry – between employed and employing artisans. Such words bespoke the tendency, so often remarked upon by historians of antebellum craftsmen, to see the interests of all of the 'producing classes', including working masters and small manufacturers, as united against the parasitic designs of bankers, undeserving paupers, monopolists, aristocrats and corporations.[29]

But the independence of wage-earning journeymen mechanics increasingly came under a double attack. With wage labor becoming more and more common, the prospect of rising through wage labor to run one's own shop became increasingly problematic. Moreover, journeymen complained that masters required harder, more subdivided work, with fewer informal breaks during the day. Since living standards for most urban artisans did not improve, and may in fact have declined, between 1820 and the 1850s, the extent to which artisans continued confidently to call themselves *freemen* and *mechanics* reflected the strength of the republican vision associated with those terms.[30] On the other hand, since this very group was producing leaders who by the middle 1830s were calling workers *white slaves*, subterranean tensions and subtle worries about bondage also deserve attention.

Nationally, groups representing the interests of journeymen artisans proliferated in the late 1820s and the 1830s. These organizations sometimes took care to call themselves 'journeymen mechanics' groups but usually they simply and assertively followed earlier local traditions and made themselves the embodiment of *mechanic* interests generally. One of the first great US labor pamphlets was written by William Heighton under the pseudonym 'An Unlettered Mechanic'. Heighton's Philadelphia witnessed, in 1827, the early rise of a city central, the Mechanics' Union and, the following year, of a first experiment in trade union journalism, the *Mechanics' Free Press*.[31] Perhaps because skill with machines was becoming more vital in many trades, the meaning of *mechanic* as one 'skilled in making machines' took on special importance.[32]

In the early thirties, craftsmen in New York City's main shipbuilding district erected a bell to regulate the hours that masters required of journeymen. They called it the Mechanics' Bell, and its earliest historian, himself a labor leader, observed that 'As the "Liberty Bell" rang out the proclamation of liberty from monarchical control, so the "Mechanics' Bell" proclaimed the liberty of leisure for the sons of toil.' 'Mechanics' libraries' and 'mechanics' institutes' sprang up, often with explicit reform purposes. Advocates of Christian labor reforms, including temperance, would later also use the term to name their groups. *Mechanic* gave a name to New York's state labor organization, to important New England and New York labor papers of the 1840s, to secret societies and to the Nashville anticonvict labor forces of 1850.[33] In sum, *mechanic* had the capacity to unite craftsmen as proud republican workers, to evoke images of social harmony among producers and to legitimate the challenges that employed artisans mounted to the powers of capital. Significantly enough, antilabor organizations of employing master craftsmen and of merchant capitalists avoided calling employed artisans *mechanics*, preferring *journeymen*.[34]

But even *mechanic* was not an unproblematic term. It was too narrow for broad political and class mobilization, such as attempts to form labor parties, and therefore was at times supplanted by *workingmen's* in the titles of labor groups. Organizations sometimes referred to 'Mechanics and Other Workingmen' in their rather unwieldy titles.[35] More important, *mechanic*, for all its egalitarian connotations, still could not avoid raising the issue of dependency in a slaveholding republic that was unable to put aside fully long-standing suspicions of manual labor. Webster's 1829 dictionary illustrates tensions within the ways the word was used. One noun definition of *mechanic* is neutral and descriptive: 'a person whose occupation is to construct machines or goods. ... ' A second definition is even somewhat exalted: 'one skilled in a mechanical ... art'. But negative connotations appear among the definitions of *mechanic* as an adjective. 'Skilled in the art of making machines', one such entry flatly begins, before adding, 'bred to manual labor'. Another reads, 'pertaining to artisans or mechanics, vulgar'.[36] A brief item, filling space at the bottom of a column in the radical Jacksonian, urban artisan–oriented *Democratic Exposition and United States Journal for the Country* suggests that some artisans themselves embraced these prejudices: '*The Mechanic* who is ashamed of his frock is himself a shame to his profession.'[37]

Moreover, in the South a large number of slaves and free Blacks were still mechanics, and there was little denying that Black workers could do craft labor. *Mechanic* was a term pridefully used by, and respectfully applied to, white artisans in the South.[38] Southern labor organizations and trade associations used the term. But at the same time there was a clear recognition that 'negro mechanics' and 'negro mechanical labor' existed. No small part of the activities of white mechanics and their allies was directed against Black artisans and at times, in alliance with slave-owning artisans versus free Black mechanics. In arguing for preferential treatment for themselves, white Southern mechanics generally eschewed baiting 'niggers'. Nor did white mechanics often cast Black artisans as inferior workers in their appeals. Instead, such appeals were grounded in the white mechanics' contributions to the communities as taxpayers and as citizens, and as 'white men', the 'legal, moral and civil proprietors of this country and state.' Moreover, it was argued in a way that somewhat undercut the dignity of existing white mechanics that a better class of artisans could be attracted if the trades were 'honourably associated' by virtue of Blacks being expelled.[39]

Even with these complications, *mechanic* was a term that survived healthily, especially when interspersed with references to the rights of 'American Freemen'.[40] But journeymen mechanics had *masters*, according to time-honored usage, and it was here that republican values, worries about wage labor, and anxieties about being compared to slaves conspired to change the language of labor. So long as the master was called by that term because of his craft skills, no violation of republican principles occurred. As Marx observed, the master typically owned the tools used in production and the product and therefore was a capitalist. 'But it is not as a capitalist that he is a *master*', Marx went on. 'He is an artisan in the first instance and is supposed to be a master of his craft. Within the process of production he appears as an artisan, like his journeymen, and it is he who initiates his apprentices into the mysteries of his craft.'[41]

But real changes in small workshops in the US in the early nineteenth century, changes often caused by pressures from merchant capitalists, made many masters act like masters of men rather than of crafts.[42] As the masters sought greater production and lower costs in a postrevolutionary and slaveholding society, their motivations were closely scrutinized by journeymen whose reactions mixed republicanism and whiteness. It was particularly difficult to be mastered by someone who was not a master of his craft. Thus the Philadelphia General Trades Union in 1836 complained that the 'veriest *botch*' among craftsmen too often assumed '*kingly supremacy* to himself the very moment he becomes a "MASTER MECHANIC".' Earlier and smaller labor organizations had made similar points. During 1806, in the Philadelphia journeymen shoemakers' conspiracy case, a labor appeal referred to 'these masters, as they are called, and who would be masters and tyrants if they could.'[43] Well before the term *wages slavery* came into common use, journeymen criticized *masters* as so-called 'after the slavish style of Europe'. A very early carpenters' organization scored the 'haughtiness and overbearance' of masters as more appropriate to those who 'give laws to slaves ... depriving free men of their just rights.'[44]

A New York City cordwainers' conspiracy case in 1809 saw the defense call for labor rights as a counterweight to the 'rapacity of the masters' who enforced 'despotic servitude'. Workers, according to the pioneer labor pamphleteer William Heighton, suffered 'under a grievous and slave-like system of labor'.[45] From Heighton's image it was but a short leap to the conclusion that *master mechanics*, as foremen and master craftsmen came to be called perhaps for the first time in the 1820s, were one with slavemasters and that workers were 'white slaves'.[46] But a different, sidelong leap was also possible. Just as farm and domestic workers addressed the 'servant problem' by finding new words, artisans could find reassurance with regard to the 'master problem' by attempting to abolish the term *master*. Characteristically, workers jumped in both directions at once. Use of the term *white slavery* and avoidance of *master* grew together. The labor movement itself adopted *both* the embrace of blunt, indeed overdrawn, comparisons with slavery, and euphemistic usages of a newly popular word: *boss*.

As early as the late eighteenth century, the British traveller Richard Parkinson had commented on an American aversion to using the word *master*. Parkinson, who arrived in 1798 and spent considerable time in rural Maryland but also stayed in Virginia and in Philadelphia and Baltimore, succinctly showed how republicanism and race intermingled. He found the typical white servant unwilling 'to acknowledge that he works for a master' and therefore insistent on calling the employer *mister* or *sir*. These usages, according to Parkinson, resulted from the 'boast of American liberty and equality', from the servant's 'think[ing] himself more on an *equality* with the master than with the negro' and from the servant's desire to 'be not a slave'. By 1818, these same sentiments were resulting in the increased popularity of *boss* as a substitute for *master*. In that year, James Flint, author of the most perceptive of the British travel accounts, wrote, '*Master* is not a word in the vocabulary of hired people. *Bos*, a Dutch one of similar import, is substituted. The former is used by negroes and is by free people considered as synonymous with slavekeeper.' Another Briton, Isaac Holmes, wrote in 1823 of *boss* in words almost precisely echoing Flint's, except that they stressed the status of the United States as a 'republican country' rather than a slaveholding one in accounting for the use of the Dutch term.[47] Thus, the *OED* records *boss* as a word adopted particularly in the United States in the early nineteenth century to avoid the use of *master*. The use of *boss* in this sense was not common enough to find its way into Webster's 1829 dictionary. By 1872, M. Schele DeVere's *Americanisms* could count *boss* the most familiar Dutch-derived word in American English.[48]

By the 1830s, *boss* was specifically and popularly embraced by employed artisans amidst the rapidly developing Jacksonian labor movement. The pioneering labor historian John R. Commons thus identifies the *boss* in labor documents of the period as the 'contractor – successor of the master workman'.[49] Paul Johnson's study of labor, religion and society in Rochester notes that when one editor there used *boss* in 1829 it was felt necessary to follow it with an asterisk and to provide the definition: 'A foreman or master workman. ... Of modern coinage, we believe.' Five years later, Johnson adds, *boss* could stand by itself without explanation.[50] The Cincinnati *People's Paper* meanwhile explained that *boss* meant 'master mechanic'.[51] James Fenimore Cooper's *American Democrat*, published in 1837, bristled at the newly popular term, holding that 'the laboring classes of whites' moved by a desire not to be connected with 'negro-slaves' had dispensed with the term *master*. 'So far has this prejudice gone', Cooper lamented, that 'they have resorted to the use of the word *boss*, which has precisely the same meaning in Dutch!'[52]

Race and the Freeman's Freedom

Cooper regarded those who used euphemisms for *master* or *servant* as lacking in 'manly' qualities. But to see such choices as merely silly, feckless or cowardly is to miss the drama, and tragedy, of workers caught in a situation in which it was difficult not to compare themselves to slaves, almost unbearable to make such a comparison, and impossible to sustain the metaphor. Nor were the new usages without meaning and impact. If republicanism meant different things to different groups, it still carried a resonance; and white supremacy was widely shared, if also variously interpreted. In such a society it was desirable, even imperative, not to be taken for a slave or anything like one. Conventions of *Black* reformers declared, 'To be dependent, is to be degraded.' A *hired hand* could claim and perhaps insist upon small privileges that a *servant* could not. He could see himself in a different way. White native-born Americans not only changed the language of domestic service but also, by the 1830s, in fact largely abandoned domestic service as a job. Avoidance of connections to dependency and to blackness paid, in Du Bois's language, 'public and psychological' wages.[53] But there were costs as well, not only in terms of race relations but also the wedding of labor to a debased republicanism.

If there was a 'manly' Jacksonian-era alternative to the kinds of workers' self-identification that Cooper deplored, it was *freeman*. The evolution of this long-used term illustrates the impossibility of avoiding race in constructing a class identity. The evolution of *freeman* also richly suggests the payoffs of whiteness and the tendency of those payoffs to prove spurious – spurious, that is, if we regard an attack on lifelong wage labor to have been a legitimate goal of labor republicanism.

The term *freeman* remained much-prized in the Age of Jackson. Indeed, in an urban society in which work and home became more radically separated and masculinity underwent extensive redefinition, its masculine ending may have had special appeal. Labor appeals often featured calls to 'men' – a term that was sometimes used without 'working', 'trades', or 'journey' in front of it to refer to wage earners collectively. *Workingman* and *Workingmen's* consistently graced the titles of labor groups and the mastheads of the labor press. One important labor newspaper was simply titled *The Man*.[54] The title *freeman* was worth fighting over. Abolitionist papers took it for their names, as did antiabolitionist Catholic ones. When Walt Whitman launched a democratic experiment in journalism, designed to win a readership of neither *masters* nor *servants*, he called it the *Brooklyn Freeman*.[55]

55

The word reverberated throughout labor's appeals, with Seth Luther's famous *Address to the Workingmen of New England* setting a standard for highlighting its importance by promising to show 'all TYRANTS, that we are not only determined to have the name of freemen, but that we will LIVE FREEMEN and DIE FREEMEN.' The earliest protests by female textile workers couched their appeals for better treatment in terms of their status as the 'daughters of freemen'.[56]

Freeman continued to carry the double meaning of economic and political independence. Webster's 1829 dictionary gave as its first definition of *freeman* 'one who enjoys liberty ... one not a slave or a vassal', and as its second 'one who enjoys or is entitled to a franchise'.[57] Before the Revolution, these various freedoms were only imperfectly linked to whiteness amidst patterns of deference, varied forms of economic vassalage among whites, colonial status and limits on suffrage. By the Age of Jackson, the correspondence between who was white and who was a freeman has become a far closer one. Although imprisonment for debt among whites remained a fearsome problem in some areas, the range of economic unfreedom felt by native-born whites had come to be increasingly concentrated on the single category of wage labor. While this dependency was sometimes defined metaphorically as 'wages slavery', it could also be seen in republican terms as merely temporary, as more free than older, paternalistic labor relations and certainly as vastly more free, in republican terms, than chattel slavery. Moreover, given their wide political freedoms – wide in comparison not only with those of slaves and of free Blacks but also with those of the common people of the whole of Europe – white male workers in the United States could and did count themselves as *freemen* even as they protested seeming plots to enslave them economically.[58]

Blackness meanwhile almost perfectly predicted lack of the attributes of a freeman. In 1820, 86.8 percent of African-Americans were slaves – in 1860, 89 percent. Free Blacks in the South lacked political rights, as they did in the North to a nearly equivalent extent. As white manhood suffrage became the norm, perhaps one free Black male in fourteen could legally vote in the North by 1860, with tradition barring the participation even of many of these who were technically so qualified. With jury duty, militia service and other civil responsibilities and rights barred to Black Northerners, the typical 'free' Black had, as the historian Jean Baker has tellingly observed, a single accepted public role: that of the victim of rioters.[59]

The very powerlessness of free Blacks made them not only easy but, in republican terms, appropriate and logical victims of the popular masses of white freemen. Because they were dependent, free Blacks were seen as

pawns of the rich and powerful. At exactly the moment that voting re-
quirements reflected the tendency to drop the traditional republican concern about voting by *whites* who were not economically independent,
concern focused on the possibility that 'servile' Blacks would vote. The
1821 'Reform Convention' in New York provided the vote to virtually
'every white male citizen' under the new state constitution. The convention also instituted a steep $250 property requirement and harsher resi-
dency laws for Black male voters. The logic of the Republican-dominated
convention – Blacks had largely voted Federalist – was, as one historian
has recently summarized it, that 'many Negroes had been born in slavery
[and] they were filled with a spirit of dependence and consequently would
vote according to the wishes of their employers ... which would foster an
aristocracy.' In 1825, about one New York City African-American in two
hundred was qualified to vote. In 1846, when the issue of expanding Black
voting rights in New York was briefly raised, a printer and activist in the
artisan wing of the Democratic party stood on his republicanism and his
race. 'We want no masters', he began, briefly echoing Whitman before
continuing, 'and least of all no negro masters.'[60]

In Connecticut in 1818, a similar pairing of expanded white suffrage
and narrowed Black rights occurred, in this case the elimination of Black
voting rights altogether. In North Carolina and Tennessee, anomalous
Southern states where free Blacks with property had voted, universal
white manhood suffrage and Black disfranchisement likewise came
together. The broad white suffrage of states in the Old Northwest was
from the start joined, with very minor exceptions in Wisconsin, to bars on
Black voting. Referenda repeatedly proved such regulations hugely
popular among whites.[61]

That Blacks were largely noncitizens will surprise few, but it is important to emphasize the extent to which they were seen as *anticitizens*, as
'enemies rather than the members of the social compact.' As such they
were driven from Independence Day parades as 'defilers' of the body
politic and driven from their homes by Sons of Liberty and Minute
Men.[62] The more powerless they became, the greater their supposed
potential to be used by the rich to make freemen unfree. Thus, it was
necessary to watch for the smallest signs of power among Blacks, and,
since Blacks were defenseless, it was easy to act on perceived threats. We
shall see this dynamic very much at work later in discussions of antebellum race riots, but worth considering here are the vehement and usually
successful popular objections to any hint that Blacks could be freemen,
objections that at times also bolstered white workers' labor market positions.

In New York City, for example, the licensing of cartmen – a group that had perhaps singularly come to define itself as a body of white freemen even during colonial days – continued to be racially based. Though Irish carters were at times licensed, over hot objections, a fully qualified Black candidate found the chief magistrate unwilling to grant a license because 'the populace would likely pelt him [the magistrate] ... when it became known.'[63] In the brutal Columbia, Pennsylvania race riot of 1834 defenders of the white rioters modelled their appeal directly on the Declaration of Independence, charging a plot by employers and abolitionists to open new trades to Blacks, and 'to break down the distinctive barrier between the colors that the poor whites may gradually sink into the degraded condition of the Negroes – that, like them, they may be slaves and tools.' Though the animus was ostensibly directed toward the weak Blacks and their designing manipulators, the fear that any change in the status of Blacks could show white freedom to be illusory runs through the document, and 'colored freeholders' were singled out for removal from the borough.[64]

Much popular energy was in fact expended to make the literal legal title of *freeman* absolutely congruent with *white* adult maleness. In Rhode Island in 1822 provision was made to let only 'freemen' vote and to allow only whites to become freemen. But Rhode Island atypically barred many poorer whites from voting, and a strongly artisan-based movement to expand the franchise matured in the mid-1830s. Seth Luther followed his 1832 *Address to the Workingmen* with an equally strong indictment of Rhode Island's 'aristocratic' voting system. The reform forces eventually followed the leadership of the abolitionist attorney Thomas Dorr, but they did not follow his racial liberalism. The Dorr forces' People's Convention of 1841 not only adopted white manhood suffrage but overwhelmingly rejected any attempt to make freemen and voters of Blacks, despite pleas from Providence's overwhelmingly working-class Black community and from the abolitionist William Lloyd Garrison. If some delegates made a considered decision that liberalization of the suffrage for whites would be jeopardized by taking up racial issues, others cited a simpler logic. One speaker explained that if Blacks could vote they could also win election and 'a nigger might occupy the chair where your honor sits.' The rebellion of the Dorrites ended in defeat, in part because the Black community rallied against the Dorr forces which had spurned them and supported the conservative opposition to Dorr, strengthening loyal militia units. In 1842, a new state constitution broadened the franchise to whites but also to Blacks, who were rewarded for their opposition to Dorr.[65]

58

In Pennsylvania, suffrage for white males extended to all who were on the tax roles, as an overwhelming proportion of white males were. However, the 1790 state constitution also left open the possibility of Blacks voting and, despite intimidation and subterfuge, a few Blacks did cast ballots. In Philadelphia whites could brag to Alexis de Tocqueville in 1831 that Blacks were effectively driven from the polls by 'public opinion', but in other areas small numbers of Black votes were counted and, in 1837, these ballots apparently turned the tide against Democratic candidates in a county election. Any such exercise of Black power, symbolic or otherwise, loomed as a tremendous threat in a state known for its race riots. The 1837–38 constitutional convention featured protracted hearings on the necessity of denying the franchise to Blacks – hearings that almost precisely coincided with the initial hearings on child labor and labor conditions generally in Pennsylvania. The franchise hearings and concurrent court cases featured arguments holding that Pennsylvania was traditionally 'a political community of white men exclusively', that Black suffrage and racial amalgamation were synonymous, and that Black voters would surely be manipulated by 'evil forces'. Another rationale suggested how thoroughly whiteness could undermine a sense of self-reliant republicanism: if voting meant having to 'jostle with negroes', the white electorate would withdraw altogether. The courts, then the consitutional convention, and finally and resoundingly a referendum disfranchised Blacks. Technically the latter remained 'freemen', but the new constitution limited voting to 'white freemen'.[66]

The case of Pennsylvania illustrates the problem of applying the much-debated term *herrenvolk democracy* to goals of the militant popular racism of the North. *Herrenvolk democracy*, used by the sociologist Pierre L. van der Berghe to denote the ideology of 'regimes like those of the United States or South Africa that are democratic for the master race but tyrannical for the subordinate groups', does partially describe the coupling of gains by poorer whites in political rights and the loss of rights by free Blacks during the early nineteenth century. But subordinate groups, notably 'hirelings', still existed among whites and, in situations such as that in Pennsylvania in 1837 and 1838 racism was not effectively linked to any significant social or political levelling among whites. The labor hearings of the same years produced no action, for example. Rather than levelling, there was a simple pushing down on the vulnerable bottom strata of society, even when there was little to be gained, except psychologically, from such a push. Since republicanism encouraged fear of plots between those above and those below against the independent producers, we should perhaps speak of a *herrenvolk* republicanism, which read African-Americans out of the ranks of the producers and then proved more able to concentrate its fire downward on to the dependent and Black than upward against the rich and powerful. Only sometimes was that choice of targets effective, in the narrow sense that white supremacy was popular and could be tied, as in New York or North Carolina, to political gains for poorer whites. *Herrenvolk* republicanism had the advantage of reassuring whites in a society in which downward social mobility was a constant fear – one might lose everything but not whiteness. Like republicanism generally, for all its talk about a white people's government, *herrenvolk* republicanism placed mainly negative demands on the state. And *herrenvolk* republicanism could become an unconsidered habit, a turning into the easiest of possible roads. Sometimes this was literally so, as in the numerous antebellum riots that began with more controversial targets and then settled into attacks on the Black community.[67]

Plebeian goals could degenerate, for understandable though tragic reasons, from a republican hatred of slavery to a republican disdain for slaves and for free Blacks, and then to a mere racial pettiness that robbed republicanism of any remaining grandeur. Identifying oneself by negation was a risky business. It was a long way down from Tom Paine to Huck Finn's Pap, who railed:

'Oh, yes, this is a wonderful government, wonderful. Why, looky here. There was a free nigger from Ohio – a mulatter, most as white as a white man. He had the whitest shirt on you ever see, too, and the shiniest hat; … and there ain't a man in that town that's got as fine a clothes as what he had; … And what do you think? They said he was a 'fessor in a college, and could talk all kinds of languages, and knowed everything. And that ain't the wust. They said he could *vote* when he was at home. Well, that let me out. Thinks I, what is this country acoming to? It was 'lection day, and I was just about to go and vote myself if I warn't too drunk to get there; but when they told me there was a state where they'd let that nigger vote, I drawed out. I says I'll never vote again.'[68]

Notes

1. Walt Whitman, *Leaves of Grass*, Boston 1860, 144; Sean Wilentz, *Chants Democratic: New York City and the Rise of the American Working Class, 1788–1850*, New York 1984, 21.

2. Herbert Gutman with Ira Berlin, 'Class Composition and the Development of the American Working Class, 1840–1890', in Herbert Gutman, *Power and Culture: Essays on the American Working Class*, New York 1987, 381.

3. Whitman, *Leaves of Grass*, 144. For a good recent synthesis reflecting the impact of an approach that stresses labor's republicanism, see Bruce Laurie, *Artisans into Workers: Labor in Nineteenth-Century America*, New York 1989.

4. Lorenzo D. Turner, 'Walt Whitman and the Negro', *Chicago Jewish Forum* 15 (Fall 1956): 8; Rowland Berthoff, 'Free Blacks, Women and Corporations as Unequal Persons',

Journal of American History 76 (Dec. 1989): 760.

5.   Quoted in Eric Foner, *Reconstruction: America's Unfinished Revolution, 1863–1877*, New York 1988, 26.

6.   Robin Blackburn, *The Overthrow of Colonial Slavery, 1776–1848*, London 1988, 288–89.

7.   *OED2*, 5:299–300; Noah Webster, *An American Dictionary of the English Language*, New York 1829, 412.

8.   Blackburn, *Colonial Slavery*, 289.

9.   *OED2*, 5:300.

10.   Quoted in Eric Foner, *Tom Paine and Revolutionary America*, New York 1976, 134, and in David Brody, 'Time and Work during Early American Industrialism', *Labor History* 30 (Winter 1989): 13–15. See also Edward Countryman, *The American Revolution*, New York 1985, 61–62, and Marcus Rediker, *Between the Devil and the Deep Blue Sea: Merchant Seamen, Pirates and the Maritime World, 1700–1750*, Cambridge, Mass. 1987, 111. On Paine and *servant*, see Elizabeth Blackmar, *Manhattan for Rent, 1785–1850*, Ithaca, N.Y., 1989, 116.

11.   E. Foner, *Tom Paine*, 40 and 143–44. On Lincoln, see Eric Foner, *Free Soil, Free Labor, Free Men: The Ideology of the Republican Party before the Civil War*, New York 1970, 23, 29–30. On the extent of the transformation to wage labor by the time of the Civil War, see David Montgomery, *Beyond Equality: Labor and the Radical Republicans, 1862–1872*, New York 1967, 25–31.

12.   John Ashworth, *'Agrarians and Aristocrats': Party Political Ideology in the United States, 1837–1846*, London 1983, 25 and 40–41; Wilentz, *Chants Democratic*, 243.

13.   William Rorabaugh, *The Craft Apprentice: From Franklin to the Machine Age in America*, New York 1986, 3–130; Gary Nash, *The Urban Crucible: Social Change, Political Consciousness and the Origins of the American Revolution*, Cambridge, Mass. 1979, 258–60; Paul E. Johnson, *A Shopkeeper's Millennium: Society and Revivals in Rochester, New York, 1815–1837*, New York 1978, 32–48.

14.   E. Foner, *Tom Paine*, 40 and 143–44; Nash, *Urban Crucible*, 258–60 and 320–31; Rorabaugh, *Craft Apprentice*, 68–69.

15.   Wilentz, *Chants Democratic*, 242–43.

16.   Asa Briggs,'The Language of "Class" in Early Nineteenth-Century England', in *The Collected Essays of Asa Briggs*, Urbana, Ill. 1985, 1:4–6. See also Craig Calhoun, *The Question of Class Struggle: Social Foundations of Popular Radicalism during the Industrial Revolution*, Chicago 1982, 74–77.

17.   Charles W. Janson, *The Stranger in America*, New York 1946 (1807), 88; Richard H. Thornton, ed., *An American Glossary, Being an Attempt to Illustrate Certain Americanisms on Historical Principles* (hereafter *AG*), Philadelphia 1912, 1:428; Frances Trollope, *Domestic Manners of the Americans*, New York 1839, 45.

18.   John Bristed, *America and Her Resources*, London 1818, 460. Compare Adam Fergusson, *Practical Notes Made during a Tour in Canada, and a Portion of the United States*, London 1833, 233–34. See Webster, *American Dictionary*, 743; *OED2*, 5:508; and Christopher Tomlins,'The Ties That Bind: Master and Servant in Massachusetts, 1800–1850', *Labor History* 30 (Spring 1989), passim, for the complexities of usage but also an argument that *servant* did have more or less precise, limited legal meanings in colonial Massachusetts. See Edmund Morgan, *American Slavery, American Freedom: The Ordeal of Colonial Virgina*, New York 1975, 327–32; Winthrop Jordan, *White over Black: American Attitudes toward the Negro, 1550–1812*, Chapel Hill, N.C. 1968, 80–81; Albert Matthews, 'The Terms Hired Man and Help', *Publications of the Colonial Society of Massachusetts* 5 (1898), esp. 229–38; [Thomas Hamilton], *Men and Manners in America*, Edinburgh 1834, 1:104; and *AG*, 1:428. See also Blackmar, *Manhattan*, 116–22.

19.   *OED2*, 5:299, and *DAE*, 2:1250.

20.   Albert Matthews, 'Hired Man', 229–54, esp. 232, and for the Salmon quote, 230 n1.

21.   Daniel T. Rodgers, *The Work Ethic in Industrial America, 1850–1920*, Chicago 1979, 30–31. See Matthews, 'Hired Man', 243–54, on *help*.

22.   James Fenimore Cooper, *The American Democrat; or, Hints on the Social and Civic*

Relations of the United States of America, Cooperstown, N.Y. 1838, 122; Charles Mackay, *Life and Liberty in America*, London 1859, 2:45–46; Trollope, *Domestic Manners*, 44–45; Janson, *Stranger*, 88. A partial exception is Francis J. Grund, *The Americans in Their Moral, Social and Political Relations*, Boston 1837, which sees the employer and employed both acting to find substitutes for *servant* out of a shared republicanism. The labor leader Seth Luther satirizes *help* in Appendix H of his *Address to the Workingmen of New England*, Boston 1832.

23. *DAE*, 1:288 and 2:1236. See also Christine Stansell, *City of Women: Sex and Class in New York, 1789–1860*, New York 1986, 272 n7.

24. Matthews, 'Hired Man', 229; Janson, *Stranger*, 88; Trollope, *Domestic Manners*, 44–45; Grund, *Americans*, 236.

25. Webster, *American Dictionary*, 262; Bristed, *America*, 460; Trollope, *Domestic Manners*, 44–45.

26. James Flint, *Letters from America, 1818–1820*, London 1822, 218.

27. Ibid., 98. On *hired hand*, see also *DAE*, 2:1212 and 1250, and David E. Schob, *Hired Hands and Plowboys: Farm Labor in the Midwest, 1815–60*, Urbana, Ill. 1975.

28. See Chapter 2 and pages 52–56 in the balance of this chapter on *mechanic* and *freemen*.

29. E. Foner, *Free Soil, Free Labor, Free Men*, 15; Paul Faler, *Mechanics and Manufacturers in the Early Industrial Revolution*, Albany, N.Y. 1981, 30–31; Laurie, *Artisans into Workers*, 70–71.

30. David R. Roediger and Philip S. Foner, *Our Own Time: A History of American Labor and the Working Day*, London 1989, 1–42; Laurie, *Artisans into Workers*, 59; Robert William Fogel, *Without Consent or Contract: The Rise and Fall of American Slavery*, New York 1989, 354–62.

31. 'Unlettered Mechanic' [Heighton], *An Address Delivered before the Mechanics and Working Classes Generally*, Philadelphia 1827?; *Mechanics' Free Press*, 21 June 1828; Louis H. Arky, 'The Mechanics Union of Trade Associations and the Formation of the Philadelphia Workingmen's Movement', *Pennsylvania Magazine and History and Biography* 76 (April 1952): 145–51.

32. Webster, *American Dictionary*, 523.

33. George McNeill, ed., *The Labor Movement: The Problem of Today*, Boston 1887, 345–48; Wilentz, *Chants Democratic*, 197, 347–48; Norman O. Ware, *The Industrial Worker, 1840–1860*, Gloucester, Mass. 1959, xiv, 200–201; Philip S. Foner, *History of the Labor Movement in the United States*, New York 1947, 1:115 and 203; W.T.M. Riches, *Industrialisation, Paternalism and Class Conflict: White Workers in Antebellum Southern Industry, 1830–1860*, Coleraine, Northern Ireland 1987, 11.

34. *Columbian Centinel*, 23 April 1825; Roediger and P. Foner, *Our Own Time*, 24.

35. Pessen, *Uncommon Jacksonians*, 3.

36. Webster, *American Dictionary*, 523; Faler, *Mechanics and Manufacturers*, 30–31.

37. *Democratic Exposition and United States Journal for the Country*, 6 September 1845, 135; Howard B. Rock, 'The Independent Mechanic: The Tradesmen of New York City in Labor and Politics during the Jeffersonian Era' (Ph.D. dissertation, New York University, 1974), 1–5, deepens this point.

38. On the prevalence of *mechanic* in Southern speech and in the titles of artisan organizations, see Riches, *Industrialization and Class Conflict*, 11; P. Foner, *Labor Movement*, 1:263; Herbert Aptheker, *The Unfolding Drama: Studies in US History*, New York 1978, 34; Roger W. Shugg, *Origins of Class Struggle in Louisiana: A Social History of White Farmers and Laborers during Slavery and After, 1840–1875*, Baton Rouge, La. 1972, 115 and note 39 below.

39. Quote from John R. Commons et al., *A Documentary History of American Industrial Society*, Cleveland 1910, 2:360 and 2:356–75 passim, and Philip S. Foner and Ronald L. Lewis, eds, *The Black Worker: A Documentary History from Colonial Times to the Present*, Philadelphia 1978, 1:87–88 and 1:71–88 passim; see also Laurie, *Artisans into Workers*, 108–9; Robert S. Starobin, *Industrial Slavery in the Old South*, London 1970, 18–19 and 209–14; Charles H. Wesley, *Negro Labor in the United States*, New York 1927, 69–74; Ira Berlin and Herbert G. Gutman, 'Natives and Immigrants, Free Men and Slaves: Urban Workingmen in the Antebellum South', *American Historical Review* 88 (1983): 1175–1200.

40. Perhaps the most vivid such a combined appeal to 'Brother Mechanics' and 'American Freemen' is the Boston 'Ten-Hour Circular' of 1835, reprinted in Commons et al., *Documentary History*, 6:94–99.

41. Karl Marx, *Capital* Volume 1, trans. Ben Fowkes, London 1976, 1029. The passage is not in Marx's *Capital* as first published but is from a projected, and dropped, Part Seven, of Volume 1 of that work. Fowkes's is the first published English translation.

42. John R. Commons et al., *History of Labour in the United States*, New York 1918–35, 1:103ff, remains useful on this point. See also Alan Dawley, *Class and Community: The Industrial Revolution in Lynn*, Cambridge, Mass. 1972, 20–32.

43. The 1836 quote is from *The Pennsylvanian*, 31 March 1836, emphasis in the original as cited in Richard A. McLeod,'The Philadelphia Artisan, 1828–1850' (Ph.D. dissertation, University of Missouri–Columbia, 1971), 192; 1806 quote from Anthony Bimba, *The History of the American Working Class*, New York 1927, 79.

44. Mark Lause's forthcoming book on early labor organizations records the first two uses while the third is from Rock, 'Independent Mechanic', 94.

45. Philip S. Foner, 'An Early Trades Union and Its Fate', *Labor History* 14 (Summer 1973): 423–24; Commons et al., *History of Labour*, 1:158–60; Commons et al., *Documentary History*, 5:80.

46. On *master mechanic*, see *DAE*, 3:1494, for a first use in 1838, but there were earlier uses in the 1830s. For one in Boston in 1832, see Commons et al., *Documentary History*, 6:82, and in 1829; P. Foner and Lewis, *Black Worker*, 1:155, and McLeod, 'Philadelphia Artisan', 192.

47. Richard Parkinson, *The Experienced Farmer's Tour in America*, London 1805, 18–19; Flint, *Letters from America*, London 1822, 33 and 288–90; Isaac Holmes, *An Account of the United States of America*, London 1823, 342. An unpublished account of his pre-1818 apprenticeship in New Jersey by the American sculptor John Frazee uses *boss* for master, but the account was written much later in Frazee's life. See John B. Jentz, 'Artisans, Evangelicals, and the City: A Social History of Abolition and Labor Reform in Jacksonian New York' (Ph.D. dissertation, City University of New York, 1977), 124.

48. *OED2*, 1:1009; *DAE*, 1:288; Webster, *American Dictionary*, 99; M. Schele DeVere, *Americanisms: The English of the New World*, New York 1872, 91–92; *AG*, 1:91–92.

49. Commons et al., *History of Labour*, 1:7.

50. Johnson, *Shopkeeper's Millennium*, 39 and 42. See also Commons et al., *Documentary History*, 4:287.

51. Commons et al., *Documentary History*, 8:222.

52. Cooper, *American Democrat*, 114. See also [Thomas Hamilton], *Men and Manners*, 1:229, for the view that the 'better orders' were not responsible for spread of *boss*.

53. Quoted in Leon F. Litwack, *North of Slavery: The Negro in the Free States, 1790–1860*, Chicago, 1961, 174; W.E.B. Du Bois, *Black Reconstruction in America, 1860–1880*, New York 1935, 700; Stansell, *City of Women*, 155–58.

54. On gender and labor, see Stansell, *City of Women*, esp. 11–12 and 76–129, and the essays by Nancy Chodorow, Heidi Hartman and Mary Ryan in Zillah Eisenstein, ed., *Capitalist Patriarchy and the Case for Socialist Feminism*, New York 1979; for an early (1817) use of *men* to refer to workers collectively, see G.A. Kleene, *History of the Ten-Hour Day in the United States*, n.p. n.d., 5. On *The Man*, see Wilentz, *Chants Democratic*, 224 n11.

55. For example, the Pennsylvania *Freeman* (abolitionist), and New York *Freeman* (Catholic). On Whitman's *Brooklyn Freeman*, see Malcolm Cowley's introduction to *The Complete Poetry and Prose of Walt Whitman*, Garden City, N.Y. 1948, 7.

56. Luther, *Address to the Workingmen of New England*, Boston 1832, 31; *The Man*, 22 February 1834.

57. Webster, *American Dictionary*, 359.

58. For formal reforms in suffrage, see Chilton Williamson, *American Suffrage: From Property to Democracy, 1760–1860*, Princeton, N.J. 1960.

59. Ira Berlin, *Slaves without Masters: The Free Negro in the Antebellum South*, New York 1974, 137; Jean H. Baker, *Affairs of Party: The Political Culture of Northern Democrats in the*

Mid-Nineteenth Century, Ithaca, N.Y. 1983, 244–45.

60.   Philip S. Foner, *A History of Black Americans: From the Emergence of the Cotton Kingdom to the Eve of the Compromise of 1850*, Westport, Conn. 1983, 206–7 and 339; quote from Berthoff, 'Free Blacks, Women and Corporations', 771.

61.   P. Foner, *Black Americans*, 207–9; Berlin, *Slaves without Masters*, 190–92; Baker, *Affairs of Party*, 243.

62.   Flint, *Letters from America*, 122; Baker, *Affairs of Party*, 246.

63.   Rock, 'Independent Mechanic', 134–35.

64.   P. Foner and Lewis, *Black Worker*, 1:175–77.

65.   Marvin E. Gettleman, *The Dorr Rebellion: A Study in American Radicalism, 1833–1849*, New York 1973, 17–19, 37, 46–48, 53, 129–130.

66.   Litwack, *North of Slavery*, 84–86; P. Foner, *Black Americans*, 297–308; Williamson, *American Suffrage*, 267; Berthoff, 'Free Blacks, Women and Corporations', 772; J. Lynn Barnard, *Factory Legislation in Pennsylvania: Its History and Administration*, Philadelphia 1907, 7–17.

67.   On *herrenvolk democracy* in the US context, and for van der Berghe's definition, see George M. Fredrickson, *The Black Image in the White Mind: The Debate on Afro-American Character and Destiny, 1817–1914*, New York 1971, 61, 84, 90–94 and 322.

68.   Mark Twain, *The Adventures of Huckleberry Finn*, New York 1973 (1884), 36. The novel is set between 1836 and 1846.

4

White Slaves, Wage Slaves and Free White Labor

In 1836, supporters of New York City's journeymen tailors papered the city with handbills featuring a coffin. The tailors had just lost a conspiracy case and with it their right to organize. The handbill encouraged protest and demanded redress in strong republican language familiar since the Revolution. It appealed to 'Freemen' and to the power of 'Mechanics and workingmen'. But confidence that the cause of independence would prevail was at an ebb. The coffin signified that the 'Liberty of the workingmen [would] be interred!' at the sentencing of the tailors. 'Tyrant *masters*' had the upper hand, and the handbill's authors made a direct comparison that had been unthinkable even a decade before: 'Freemen of the North are now on a level with the slaves of the South.'[1]

The 'coffin handbill' shows both the new ease and the continuing hesitancy with which white workers in Jacksonian America began to describe themselves as slaves. Its unqualified North–South comparison is most striking, but the document also suggests some of the ways in which white workers remained beyond comparison with slaves. The whites, if slaves, were also simultaneously 'freemen'. If 'tyrant *masters*' had prevailed, according to one line of the handbill, another line settled for invoking the fear of 'would-be masters'. Nor was it clear that the 'slavery' of the tailors was 'wage slavery'. They were cast as slaves not because they were 'hirelings' but because the state had deprived them of the freedoms necessary for defending their rights. The emphasis on the 'slavery' of the tailors in fact proved rather short-lived. After hearing of a more favorable court decision in another conspiracy case upstate, 'the journeymen's fury abated'.[2]

Other instances of comparison between wage labor and chattel slavery between 1830 and 1860 were likewise both insistent and embarrassed. They could not have been otherwise. Labor republicanism inherited the idea that designing men perpetually sought to undermine liberty and to 'enslave' the people. Chattel slavery stood as the ultimate expression of the denial of liberty. But republicanism also suggested that long acceptance of slavery betokened weakness, degradation and an unfitness for freedom. The Black population symbolized that degradation. Racism, slavery and republicanism thus combined to require comparisons of hirelings and slaves, but the combination also required white workers to distance themselves from Blacks even as the comparisons were being made.

Chattel slavery provided white workers with a touchstone against which to weigh their fears and a yardstick to measure their reassurance. An understanding of both the stunning process by which some white workers came to call themselves slaves and the tendency for metaphors concerning white slavery to collapse thus takes us to the heart of the process by which the white worker was made. It also furnishes us with an excellent vantage point from which to view the vexed relations between the labor movement and movements to abolish slavery.

The Winding Road to *White Slavery*

Use of terms like *white slavery* and *slavery of wages* in the 1830s and 1840s presents an intriguing variation on the theme of American exceptionalism. US labor historians are usually pressed to explain why American workers have historically lacked the class consciousness said to have existed elsewhere in the industrializing world. But if the antebellum US labor movement was exceptional in its rhetoric, it was exceptionally militant as it critiqued evolving capitalist social relations as a kind of slavery. France, with a revolutionary tradition that forcefully used metaphors regarding slavery to press republican attacks on political oppression, apparently saw but slight use of phrases such as *wage slavery* before the Revolution of 1848. The German states, though they produced a great popularizer of the concept of wage slavery, likewise did not witness frequent use of the term. Only Britain, where the metaphoric term *wage slavery* apparently originated in the second decade of the nineteenth century, rivalled the US in producing a discourse that regarded white hirelings as slaves. But since the spread of the metaphor in Britain was as much associated with the Tory radical politician Richard Oastler as with its use by working class Chartists, one might regard the antebellum US labor movement as exceptional in being the world leader in militant criticisms of wage work as slavery.[3]

Of course, concern over 'slavery' was very much in the air in Jacksonian America, whose citizens worried variously that Catholics, Mormons, Masons, monopolists, fashion, alcohol and the national bank were about to enslave the republic. Nonetheless, the use of the white slave metaphor for wage workers ought not be dismissed as merely another example of the 'paranoid' style of antebellum politics.[4] It might instead be profitable to view the paranoid style itself as a republican tradition much enlivened by the horrific example of chattel slavery and fears engendered by the growing failure of the American republic to produce a society of independent farmers and mechanics among whites.

By the Age of Jackson, several changes had created the setting in which white workers would begin to make and press, as well as deny and repress, comparisons between themselves and slaves. The rise, after 1829, of a highly visible movement to abolish slavery evoked reexamination of the line between slavery and freedom. Since free Blacks and slave rebels played so central a role in the Black freedom movement, the tendency to equate blackness and servility was likewise called into question. If abolitionism did not recruit more than a minority of white workers, it did make clear that equations between race and fitness for liberty were not eternal truths but objects of political debate.[5]

Meanwhile, the experiences of the white artisans themselves encouraged the consideration of white slavery as a possible social category. In a nation agonizing over the fate of the Republic as the last of its revolutionary generation passed from the scene, urban craftsmen fought monumental struggles, concentrated between 1825 and 1835, for a ten-hour working day. Linking these struggles to time for self-education and full citizenship, the growing labor movement advocated the ten-hour system as the key to workers' independence and to the nation's. Seeking the immediate freedom of being less bossed by increasingly profit-driven masters – and ultimately to be free from having a boss – artisans who undertook concerted actions contrasted the fetters they felt and the liberty they longed for at every possible turn. The workers who gained the ten-hour day in the great 1835 Philadelphia general strike, for example, massed in Independence Square, marched to fife and drum and carried ten-hour banners alongside others proclaiming 'LIBERTY, EQUALITY AND THE RIGHTS OF MAN'.[6]

The responses of employers tended to sharpen the artisans' sense that a great contest between freedom and its opposite was unfolding and encouraged them to raise the issue in terms of white slavery. In some cases, employers made the initial comparison of free US labor with British 'slaves' and with Black slaves. They insisted that the ten-hour system could not function in the United States because the nation had to compete with Britain. The response of the *Working Man's Advocate* to this argument in 1832 reflected labor's view of the British system as utterly degrading. 'Are we to slave thirteen or fourteen hours a day', the *Advocate* asked, 'because the Manchester spinner or the Birmingham blacksmith so slaves?'[7] As ten-hour struggles continued, US workers learned more about British resistance to long hours and answered employers' objections that British competition must be met in new ways that challenged the idea that only British workplaces encouraged servility. The *New England Artisan* wondered in 1834, 'If the poor and oppressed but gallant working men of Great Britain have the daring hardihood to declare that they will work but eight hours ... , how should the comparatively free ... American working citizen feel?' In the midst of the shorter hours campaigns of the 1830s, some immigrant US workers also came to maintain that work in America was harder than it had been in Britain.[8] When it was later argued that the ten-hour system could not prevail in Northern states because workplaces on that schedule could not match the production of Southern slave labor, the extent of the republican freedom of the white worker was still more sharply called into question.[9]

Opposed to these substantial reasons for white workers to at least entertain comparisons of themselves and slaves was the continuing desire *not* to be considered anything like an African-American. Not only was the verb *slave* used, as we have seen, to indicate the performance of work in ways unbecoming to whites, but new and negative phrases such as *white nigger* (that is, 'drudge') and *work like a nigger* (that is, 'to do hard drudging work') came into American English in the 1830s, at roughly the same time that the term *white slavery* became prominent. Richard Henry Dana's searing indictment of the oppression of antebellum sailors in *Two Years before the Mast* took care to quote an irate captain screaming at his crew: 'You've got a driver over you! Yes, a *slave-driver*, – a *nigger driver*! I'll see who'll tell me he isn't a NIGGER slave!'[10]

Such usages, which should give considerable pause to those who believe race and class are easily disentangled, remind us that comparing oneself to a slave or to any Black American could not be lightly undertaken in the antebellum United States. Moreover, it should be obvious that for all but a handful of committed abolitionists/labor reformers, use of a term like *white slavery* was not an act of solidarity with the slave but rather a call to arms to end the inappropriate oppression of whites. Critiques of white slavery took form, after all, alongside race riots, racially exclusive trade unions, continuing use of terms like *boss* and *help* to deny comparison with slaves, the rise of minstrel shows, and popular campaigns to attack further the meager civil rights of free Blacks.

In such a situation, it is not surprising that labor activists rather cautiously backed into making comparisons between white workers and slaves. Many of the earliest comparisons emphasized not that whites were enslaved but rather that they were threatened with slavery. In Dover, New Hampshire in 1828, leaders of four hundred striking women textile workers both connected and disconnected themselves to chattel slavery by asking who among them could 'ever bear the shocking fate of slaves to share?'[11] In 1833, male and female members of the Manayunk (Pennsylvania) Working People's Committee refused a wage cut because it would, as they put it, 'rivet our chains still closer' and, over time, 'terminate, if not resisted, in slavery'.[12] In 1834 Lowell's female strikers permitted themselves considerable ambiguity. In a single paragraph they cast themselves as virtually in 'bondage', as threatened with *future* slavery by the 'oppressing hand of avarice' and as the 'daughters of freemen' still. Two years later protesting Lowell women sang:

> Oh! I cannot be a slave;
> I will not be a slave.
> For I'm so fond of liberty
> That I cannot be a slave.[13]

For male artisans, who led the first labor movement, the rise of a small sector of full-fledged factory production both symbolized threats to independence and offered the possibility to experiment with application of the slavery metaphor to white (often child and female) factory workers without necessarily applying it to *themselves*. The factory system tended to confine and discipline workers to an unprecedented extent, at least by the 1840s. Moreover, it was identified with the degrading, antirepublican labor said to be required in Europe, a comparison that gave force to labor leaders' branding of it as a 'gaol' or a 'Bastille'.[14]

That US textile factories employing large workforces of single women (and smaller ones employing whole families) justified their management practices as paternalistic ones only sharpened suspicions of them. Blacklists and the whipping of workers in some small mills likewise provoked outrage. In the 1834 textile strike in Dover, one complaint of the women workers was that management called them 'their *slaves*'. Perhaps the managers meant to refer to their own paternal responsibilities in adopting this usage, or perhaps to their dictatorial powers. In any case, they hit just the wrong note. Quitting and other forms of informal protest far outdis-

69

tanced strikes among early mill workers, but for male artisans contemplating the new industrial system the issue of permanent 'factory slavery' was a fearsome one.[15]

Many early references to white slavery thus focused on so identifying British manufacturing workers and on adding that women and children in the United States were, or were about to be, so enslaved. 'The Factory Girl', an abominable piece of British verse that was in the US perhaps the most widely reprinted of the early treatments of white slavery, combined the ideas that the British workers, and women workers in textiles, were in bondage. It portrayed the sad end of a female British worker:

> That night a chariot passed her
> While on the ground she lay;
> The daughters of her master
> An evening visit pay—
> Their tender hearts were sighing,
> As negroes' wrongs were told;
> While the white slave was dying,
> Who gained their fathers' gold.[16]

This highly sentimental pressing of the comparison with chattel slavery ran through much antebellum writing on white female and child workers by male activists. Seth Luther's stirring 1832 *Address to the Workingmen of New England*, for example, does not refer to American male journeymen as slaves, but it does find factory women in bondage and does quote sentimental verse describing child laborers as 'little sinless slaves'.[17]

Once made, comparisons to slaves could of course be extended, and artisans sometimes did come to be included in them. By 1835, for example, Luther was helping to write the 'Ten-Hour Circular', which bitterly castigated 'slavery among [white] mechanics'.[18] Stephen Simpson, intellectual leader and first Congressional candidate of the Philadelphia Working Men's party, began his 1831 *Working Man's Manual* by arguing that factory slavery had taken root in Britain where a 'serf class' worked in manufacturing but that it could never grow in the US, which had disconnected the age-old links among 'slavery, labor [and] degradation' and had made work the province of a 'community of FREEMEN'. Simpson then proceeded to take virtually all other possible positions. He noted the presence of huge numbers of slaves in the South, where he admitted that 'labour shares in ... disgrace, because it is a part of the slave.'[19] Within a few lines the US was characterized as a society sustained by a 'mixture of slavery and labor'. White women and children suffered special exploitation because 'custom ... classed them with slaves and servants.' And, for that matter, Simpson argued, all Northern workers faced a situation in which 'capital [was] the Master' and in which employers calculated wages in a manner like that of the 'lords of the South [who oppress] sable herds of brutalized humanity.'[20]

Some workers, usually in factories, did describe themselves and their peers as already and fully enslaved. As early as 1831, Vermont operatives protested that they were 'slaves in every sense of the word', while Lynn shoemakers of the 1840s saw themselves as having 'masters – aye, masters' and as being 'slaves in the strictest sense of the word.'[21] Lowell textile women echoed the Vermont millhands, describing themselves as slaves to long hours, as slaves to the 'powers that be' and as 'slaves in every sense of the word'.[22]

However, radical artisans remained more comfortable discussing the 'slavery' of others than that of themselves. George Henry Evans, the printer, labor leader and land reformer who probably did more than anyone else to popularize the terms *white slavery* and *slavery of wages*, could be direct and sweeping in describing even male artisans as, if land-less, then unequivocally enslaved. 'Stealing the man away from his land, or his land away from the man', he argued, 'alike produces slavery'.[23] Even Evans's individual writings did not tend to discuss the 'slavery' of artisans but instead to concentrate on that of tenant farmers, the unskilled, women workers and child laborers.[24] Though eloquent and expressive of the real fears of white workers, comparisons with slaves did not automatically lead to sustained self-examination among those groups of 'hirelings' who were most active in organized labor in the antebellum years.

White Slavery and Wage Slavery

Norman Ware's classic study of antebellum labor, *The Industrial Worker*, pointed out that some highly skilled and relatively well-paid artisans did see their own wage labor as a kind of slavery, citing pianoforte makers in New York City as an example. Ware added a musing footnote that should sensitize us to how language changes over time as well as to the considerable extent to which references to slavery had shaped the language of antebellum white labor:

> The term 'wage slave' had a much better standing in [the 1840s] than it does today. It was not then regarded as the empty shibboleth of the soap-box orator. This would suggest that it has suffered only the normal degradation of language not that it is a grossly misleading characterization.[25]

But in seeking to rescue the term *wage slavery* from the soapboxers, Ware failed to heed his own reminder that words have their own histories, for a closer look at the labor and radical Democratic press of the 1840s shows that *white slavery* was the most common phrasing of metaphors regarding white workers' oppression with *slavery of wages* second and *wage slavery* a very distant third. Indeed, the term *white slavery* was at times used even in articles speculating about the fate of free *Blacks* if abolition prevailed! Probably because *wage slavery* survived the Civil War in much wider currency and continued to be a phrase used by Marxist writers (and soapboxers) into the twentieth century, it was read back into antebellum history as the most common way for white workers to press comparisons with slavery. *White slavery* meanwhile came to be much more narrowly associated with female prostitution, and its use in accounts of the earlier period declined.[26]

Historians have more frequently discussed antebellum usage of *wage slavery* than of *white slavery*, and have so confuted the phrases that Marcus Cunliffe, in his recent studies of wage slavery and chattel slavery, comments that it hardly matters whether *wage* or *white* prefaced slavery since the two adjectives were used interchangeably.[27] Cunliffe's generally helpful work is wrong on this point: it makes considerable difference whether workers experimented with metaphors regarding *wage slavery* or *white slavery*. If some labor writers did at times freely substitute *white slavery* and *slavery of wages* for each other, that pattern needs to be explained, for the terms carry quite different implications.

Slavery of wages came to be used alongside *white slavery* by land reformers and utopian socialists in the last half of the 1840s, often in dialogue with abolitionists. Its wording raised the old issue of whether hireling labor and republican independence could coexist.[28] But its very precision and directness raised problems. Many of those being described as slaves were not wage-earners. Thus, tenant farmers and those imprisoned for debt were frequently discussed, but the problem of the latter was precisely that they could not enter the wage labor market.[29] Most early labor activists remained tied to one of the major political parties, usually the Democrats, and sought unity among the 'producing classes', including small employers.[30] To refer to such employers as 'masters, aye masters', made sense in terms of fleshing out the metaphor of slavery of wages, but it did not make political sense. Moreover, many masters were simply self-employed workers or men who sporadically employed others while depending mainly on their own labor. Many failed and again became wage-earners.[31] Some evidence suggests that small employers paid better than manufacturers with larger workshops, and clearly merchant capitalists often pressured masters to maintain tough labor policies. Journeymen *aspired* to run a small shop of their own. 'Men must be masters', Whitman wrote, 'under themselves.'[32]

Metaphors regarding the slavery of wages thus confronted the problem that, if the worker could be called a *slave*, the wage-paying master could not, except in the heat of labor conflict, really be regarded as a *slavemaster*. One stopgap solution was to hold that the master himself was a 'slave'. Boston's 'Ten-Hour Circular' thus argued:

> We would not be too severe on our employers [for] they are slaves to the Capitalists, as we are to them. ... But we cannot bear to be the servant of servants and slaves to oppression, let the source be where it may.[33]

Evans, in keeping with his emphasis on land and rent, similarly maintained that small manufacturers in Lynn were mastered by landlords who owned their shops, while the New York *Mechanic* complained of the 'capitalists ... bossing all the mechanical trades.'[34]

The advantages of the phrase *white slavery* over *wage slavery* or *slavery of wages* lay in the former term's vagueness and in its whiteness, in its invocation of *herrenvolk* republicanism. *White slavery* was particularly favored by radical Democratic politicians for a time because it could unite various elements of their coalition – wage workers, debtors, small employers and even slaveholders – without necessarily raising the issue of whether the spread of wage labor was always and everywhere anti-republican. Abolitionists, free Blacks, bankers, factory owners and prison labor could, in sundry combinations, be cast as villains in a loose plot to enslave white workers. Moreover, *white slavery* did not necessarily require a structural solution – arrest of the spread of hireling labor. Although some who employed the term did go on to argue that all long-term wage dependency was bondage, *white slavery* itself admitted solutions short of an attack on the wage system. White workers could be *treated* better – reforms could occur, as they did in the 'coffin handbill' case – and the comparison with slavery could be exorcised.[35]

White slavery also served well because it did not call into question chattel slavery itself, an issue that sharply divided the labor movement, the Jacksonians and the nation. Regarding *wage slavery*, Eric Foner has written:

> ... the idea of wage slavery contained condemnation of slavery itself. The central values of the early labor movement – liberty, democracy, personal independence, the right of the worker to the fruits of his or her labor – were obviously incompatible with the institution of slavery.[36]

73

Foner is largely right that such values ran through the term *wage slavery* and implicitly called all slavery into question. But the far more common term *white slavery* immediately undercut any such implications by leaving open the possibility that it was the 'slavery' *of whites* that deserved censure. Much of the labor discourse on *white slavery* took just that stance and at times strongly supported the slavery of Blacks.

White Slavery as Proslavery

Larry E. Tise, in his provocative *Proslavery: A History of the Defense of Slavery in America*, argues that much of the defense of slavery as a good social system, at least for the slaves, actually took shape in the North before it did in the South. He credits, if that is the right word, conservative Northern Federalists and ex-Federalists with providing the intellectual ammunition that John C. Calhoun, George Fitzhugh and other Southerners would later fire. But some proslavery Yankees discussed in Tise's book are far better characterized as *herrenvolk* republicans, even labor radicals, than as conservatives. Thomas Man, whom Tise identifies as a 'Rhode Island clergyman', was also perhaps the most militant, if perhaps eccentric, labor poet in Jacksonian America. He did, as Tise observes, regard abolitionists as godless fanatics prophesied by Scripture and did, in the oddly titled essay 'Order and White Man Contrasted', urge Northerners to 'enlist themselves under the banner of slavery.' But Man's point was to enlist under Southern slavery's banner in order to defeat *white* slavery in the North. He regarded the factory worker as a 'slave at morn, a slave at eve', the victim of a system twice as 'contemptible and oppressive' as Southern slavery.[37]

Similarly, Theophilus Fisk is identified by Tise as a lapsed Universalist clergyman from Massachusetts whose fierce 1836 antiabolitionist speech to South Carolinians pronounced slavery a 'blessing to the slave'. But Fisk was very far from being a conservative where politics among whites was concerned. A Connecticut Jacksonian Democratic editor and publisher of *Priestcraft Unmasked*, Fisk is counted a major radical leader of the early labor movement even by the stringent criteria of the historian Edward Pessen. When US workers mounted mass strikes for the ten-hour working day in 1835, Fisk issued a pioneering call for the eight-hour day. That same year he became probably the first US labor writer to use the term *white slavery*.[38] The tour of the South during which Fisk excoriated abolitionism was intended as a set of prolabor speeches to win popular support after he had addressed the National Trades' Union's convention.

But then Fisk did not see the two issues as separate. He found that America's slaves had 'pale faces' and, as abolitionism grew in Boston, called for an end to indulging sympathies for Blacks in the South and for 'immediate emancipation of the white slaves of the North.'[39]

Such examples could be greatly multiplied. One of the slave South's most eloquent defenders during the 1830s congressional debates over whether to accept petitions from abolitionists was Ely Moore, the nation's first labor Congressman, first president of the National Trades' Union and editor of the *National Trades' Union* newspaper. Moore denounced abolition not only as a 'blind, reckless, feverish fanaticism' but also as a plot to rob whites of their independence.[40] These charges found substantial echoes, though also some opposition, in the early labor press. The ex-Chartist Philadelphia typesetter, bookseller and labor reformer John Campbell followed his 1848 book, *A Theory of Equality*, three years later with *Negromania*, a cranky and vicious early attempt to popularize racist pseudo-science. Both the books were pleas for white unity inside the Democratic party. *America's Own and Fireman's Journal*, a labor paper of the 1850s, approvingly republished Las Casas's 'A Plea for Slavery'.[41]

In the New York City labor movement, despite George Henry Evans's tempering influence, the tendency to indict white slavery and to support Black slavery was especially strong. The historian Bernard Mandel, in arguing that only an 'insignificant element' of the early labor movement took an actively proslavery stance, dismisses Mike Walsh, the charismatic, labor-supported US congressman from New York City, as a 'drunk' who idiosyncratically 'endorse[d] every policy put forward by the politicians of Dixie.' Whatever one's view of Walsh – and I am inclined to credit both Sean Wilentz's characterization of him as a major contributor to 'the preservation of labor radicalism in hard times' and W.E.B. Du Bois's as 'that living embodiment of *Subterranean* filth and fury' – he cannot be so easily set aside.[42] Walsh's wild popularity from the early forties to the early fifties stemmed from the resonance of his freewheeling attacks on what he called 'white wages slavery' with the accent on both of the adjectives. 'You are slaves', he thundered to his followers, 'and none are better aware of the fact than the heathenish dogs who call you freemen', while outspokenly supporting Southern slavery and even its extension into Kansas and Nebraska.[43] Walsh's bitterest factional opponent within New York City's artisan Democracy, the lockmaker Levi Slamm, echoed this combination of proslavery and attacks on 'black-hearted tyrants' who held 'white slaves'. Slamm, editor of *The Plebeian*, organized the 'coffin handbill' protest whose dramatic characterization of white workers as slaves begins this chapter.[44] John Commerford, the New York chairmakers' leader who Pessen argues may have been the most popular Jacksonian labor leader, joined a number of trade unionists and radical Democrats who excoriated white slavery and gave political support to the South's premier proslavery politician, John C. Calhoun.[45]

The proslavery affinities of those who denounced white slavery have attracted some passing notice from historians, who have offered various explanations. The fear of job competition with emancipated Blacks has received emphasis – perhaps even overemphasis, in that only a minority of proslavery indictments of white slavery raised the issue of job competition and that it was then usually raised in combination with broader fears of amalgamation.[46] Labor's animosity to 'middle class' and moralistic abolitionist leaders has also been mentioned. So have the necessity to guard the Republic from potentially fatal divisions over slavery and the need to preserve the Democracy as the party of reform, even at the cost of conciliating slaveholders. John Ashworth's work offers the most forceful recent restatement of the old, much debated view of the Jacksonian Democrats as (among whites) a party of political egalitarianism and social levelling. Surely the Democrats' positions on such issues as free trade, banking, imprisonment for debt, prison labor and, to an extent, land reform, gave some substance to their populism. Ashworth adds an inventive twist that makes the radical labor/proslavery position seem less anomalous, arguing that because Jacksonians could imagine no citizenship but full, equal citizenship they were less able to imagine emancipation of Blacks than more elitist parties.[47] Other historians have even held that Yankee labor radicals were engaged in a sophisticated attempt to exploit splits within the ruling class by allying for a time with proslavery Southerners. This last position probably credits the labor radicals with more acumen than they in fact had, but it may describe what a particularly cerebral radical like Orestes Brownson thought he was doing for a time.[48]

However great the value of existing explanations for the considerable coming together of radical labor and proslavery, these explanations deserve to be supplemented by a simpler one: the very structure of the argument against white slavery typically carried proslavery implications. As Eric Foner has recently observed, radical labor's comparisons of 'white' and Black slavery often found the latter less oppressive than the former. Radicals argued, on shreds of evidence, that Southern masters worked their Black slaves far fewer hours per day – perhaps only half the number required by Northern employers.[49] They computed rates of exploitation that putatively showed that a much greater proportion of the value produced by a Black slave was returned to him or her than was returned to the white slave in the North.[50] Even writers who argued that white and

thus, this comp. begins not in S. defense but in N. wrs labor rads?

76

Black slavery were roughly equal nonetheless showed a sharp tendency to cite only comparisons favorable to this latter. For example, a comparison of the two labor systems in the *Mechanics' Free Press* in 1830 – probably the first such direct and significant one made by organized labor – set out to show that the two differed only 'in name'. But it then compared the life of a free laborer, full of the threat of starvation, over-exertion, deprived children and uncomforted sickness, with that of the slave with a 'master interested in prolonging his life.' Even Evans, who strove for balance, found that the 'slave to the Land-Lord and capitalist class is in a worse, aye a *worse* condition than the slave who has a master of his own' and reprinted arguments that emancipation without land reform would worsen Black slaves' positions tenfold.[51]

Artisan radical and early historian John Finch cited the 'well-known fact that the blacks of the South enjoy more leisure time and liberty and fare quite as well as the operatives in the northern or eastern manufacturing districts.' He added that the same comparison more or less applied to whites in 'other mechanical pursuits'.[52] Orestes Brownson, who at times found white workers closer to freedom than Blacks, could at other junctures argue that slave labor is 'except so far as feelings are concerned ... decidedly the least oppressive. ... The laborer at wages has all the disadvantages of freedom and none of its blessings, while the slave, if denied the blessings, is freed from the disadvantages.'[53]

The most common comparison, repeated by Walsh and several others, was that the 'poor negro' was a 'farm horse' with one master who would protect him when he could 'toil no more', while the 'poor white man' was a 'horse in a livery stable' hired to many masters and therefore overworked by all and without protection when infirmed.[54] Chattel slavery was, in this view, better than white slavery, a point fraught with proslavery paternalist implications and not lost on the Southern editors who reprinted articles carrying such opinions.[55]

but this comparison works only if it is unthinkable that whites be chattel slaves

whiteness : liberty already conjoined.

George Henry Evans: White Slavery and Antislavery

Attacking white slavery did not, however, necessarily mean accepting Black slavery. The very title of the New York Society for the Abolition of All Slavery, an organization active in the 1840s, signalled that some militants favored attacks on both chattel slavery and the wage system.[56] Some artisans, heirs to the radical democratic and antislavery traditions of Tom Paine, Benjamin Franklin and Robert Owen, did attempt to apply the principles of liberty and equality to both races. Craft workers and native-born women textile workers were important supporters of the abolitionist movement in the 1830s and 1840s. On a few occasions labor organizations took abolitionist positions and labor papers more often did so.[57] It was even possible, in theory at least, to hold that white slavery was more oppressive than Black slavery, but that both deserved to be abolished. In practice, however, the 'Down with all slavery!' position proved exceedingly hard to maintain, and its supporters were inconsistent in advocating emancipation. Its perils are best illustrated by a consideration of the career of George Henry Evans, its most committed leader.

Evans was originally a follower of Frances Wright and Robert Dale Owen, whose *Free Enquirer* he had helped to print. The *Free Enquirer* took a moderately antislavery position, carrying passionate attacks on the slave trade while rather wildly claiming that British traders 'forced [slaves] on the settlers' of America, by simply dropping off Africans, without recompense, in order to sow the evil of bondage in the colonies.[58] Evans's own *Sentinel* and his *Working Man's Advocate* took more radical antislavery positions. Evans's denunciations of slavery in these papers were for a time more uncompromising than the articles by William Lloyd Garrison that Evans also reprinted.

In 1831 and 1832, Evans repeatedly supported an end to slavery and even full rights for freed Black people. He opposed any use of colonization as a scheme to deport troublesome free Blacks, or even 'the surplus of slaves', because such policies could be used to make slaves more easily managed. 'We are by no means convinced', Evans wrote, 'that anything but *fear* or compulsion will effect the abolition of slavery.'[59] The debates on abolition in Virginia in the early thirties excited Evans's interest and moved him to stand in support of abolition for reasons of 'justice and humanity'. Evans again and again described slave insurrectionists, including Nat Turner, as fighters for freedom and as the natural result of the slave system, likening the rebels to the Polish patriots who were fighting for liberation.[60] Evans predicated his opposition to a standing army in large part on the troops' role in suppressing slave revolts, 'in other words to prevent the practice of the principle of our government – "All men are created equal".'[61] He likewise opposed anti-Indian policies, regarding the standing army as an instrument for the oppression of native Americans and backing self-determination for the Cherokees.[62]

As militant abolitionism matured, the *Advocate* paid far less attention to the rights of people of color. Evans did defend the civil rights of abolitionists but, as early as 1833, he also denounced their 'fanaticism'. Surely the revivalism and sabbatarianism of the abolitionists offended the freethinking Evans, but it is also worth noting that almost from the start Evans's defense of slaves and of Indians had proven easily subordinated to national unity and Democratic party politics.[63] His editorials and news columns, amidst support for slave rebels and Indian rights, gave political backing to the Tennessee slaveholder and Indian fighter Andrew Jackson and promoted the career of Kentucky slaveholder and Indian fighter Richard Johnson as Jackson's heir apparent. Evans could unblushingly write that Jackson stood for 'Liberty against slavery', without pausing to add 'for whites alone'. By 1833, the *Advocate* ran articles pronouncing that there was 'a very small shade of difference indeed' between Northern and Southern 'slaves' and two years later it was pioneering in the usage of *white slavery*. The ten-point programs in the *Advocate* said nothing of Black or Indian rights; nor did such subjects appear among the many toasts at Tom Paine commemorations.[64]

When Evans returned to labor editing in the 1840s, he clearly con- nected his diminished emphasis on slavery with his growing appreciation of the extent of oppression among whites. He wrote to the abolitionist Gerrit Smith in 1844, 'I was formerly, like yourself, sir, a very warm advo- cate of the abolition of slavery. This was before I saw that there was *white* slavery.'[65] This logic was almost word for word the same as that defended by such other land and labor reformers as Robert Dale Owen and Horace Greeley in the 1840s.[66] The position taken by Evans and his National Reformers marked the first time that it was systematically argued that the oppression of people of color could be addressed only if white class oppression were first addressed. Without land reform, the National Reformers argued, Black slaves could only gain freedom to starve if eman- cipated. Therefore abolitionists not supporting free homesteads were really 'substitutionists'.[67] The utopian socialists of the Associationist movement made the similar argument that only the success of com- munalism could end 'all slavery'.[68]

Evans's stance infuriated the Garrisonian abolitionists, with Garrison running the Reformers' views in the 'Refuge of Oppression' column of *The Liberator*.[69] Even so, Evans and his cothinkers did not argue for white supremacy – at times they bravely supported equal rights – but instead assumed that the position of white workers was central in any reform movement. Sometimes Evans and Greeley briefly justified this stance simply because white slavery was 'closer to home'. At other junctures they held that Black slaves were not yet 'sufficiently sensible' of their oppres- sion.[70] The key to social justice thus lay among the white workers who, if they could be dissuaded from fruitless strikes, could unite with small employers and deliver a decisive blow for freedom.[71] The emancipation of

79

whites, it was further hoped, would set an example for Southern slaveholders.[72]

Given this prioritizing of struggles by whites, Evans and his followers could take astonishingly antiracist positions but support these positions quite inconsistently. The National Reform press, for example, not only regarded Indians as having been illegally dispossessed but as having more advanced ideas about land than did white civilization. As part of the masthead of his paper, Evans during the forties long ran a quotation from the Indian leader Black Hawk asserting the Indians' right to land. But that same paper lavished far greater praise on Andrew Jackson, who presided over the conquest of Black Hawk.[73] Indeed, the National Reformers took the view that free homesteads for whites were a major reform for Indians, claiming that there was plenty of land for all and that land speculation, not white expansion, caused tensions with Indians. Evans's associate John Commerford even argued that the Indians' having been robbed of their land was an argument for letting not only them but 'the whole family of the American people, enjoy it.'[74]

Similarly, Evans could insist that there was not 'another individual in the United States … more sincerely desirous of abolishing slavery' than himself but still build a National Reform organization that long ignored chattel slavery in its program and that included or supported such prominent proslavery Democrats as Commerford, Mike Walsh and Ely Moore.[75] He could endorse civil rights for free Blacks, abolitionist candidates favoring land reform, and even the controversial admission of a Black delegate to the Industrial Congress convention. But he would still insist that laws requiring the return of freed slaves, though wrong, were of limited importance, since the escaped slave would not be free in the North anyway.[76] There was no room for oppression in Evans's world, but also no room for consideration of the special nature of the oppression of those victimized differently than his white constituency.

Free Labor, White Slavery and the Fate of Labor Abolitionism

By 1860, Evans and many of his fellow labor radicals had come to support the Republican party, where they were joined by a large number of abolitionists. Many of Evans's views became Republican positions. 'Free Soil' had been a labor reform slogan before it became an antislavery and Republican one. The Republican appeal 'Vote yourself a farm' came straight from an 1846 land reform handbill. But the question preceding it in that handbill – 'Are you tired of slavery – of drudging for others?' –

did not find its way into Republicanism.[77] Variations on the phrase *slavery of wages* still had some currency in novels and before Irish and German immigrant audiences,[78] but on the eve of the Civil War phrases like *free labor* and *free white labor* had proven far more common and meaningful, even among skilled workers and labor journalists who had pioneered in comparing hirelings and slaves.[79]

Amidst new peaks in the numbers of wage workers and amidst what Robert Fogel has described as a protracted, severe decline in the living standards of native-born workers, the metaphor *white slavery* dramatically gave way.[80] Horace Greeley's trajectory was not atypical, moving as he did from a utopian socialist conviction that Northern workers were 'slaves' to the wage system in the 1840s to a Republican defense of Northern *free labor* by 1860. Republicans continued to spill tremendous amounts of ink over the threat of white slavery, but it was seen as just that – a threat and not a reality. And the threat was increasingly seen as coming, not from capital, but from a conspiracy of slaveholders against the Republic.[81]

Historians have not probed this important shift in rhetoric, perhaps because it was short-lived. Eric Foner, who perceptively notes that slavery metaphors were 'eclipsed' in labor's language in the fifties, added that they rose like a 'phoenix' after the Civil War.[82] That the free labor coalition managed to defeat the Slave Power and helped bring about conditions for a much-energized labor movement probably made it less likely that scholars would agonize over the rhetoric of Republicanism. Nonetheless, a few writers, from Edward Bellamy to Alan Dawley, have speculated that without the sectional conflict, individuals like Greeley and even groups like the Lynn shoe workers, might have moved quickly to a socialist critique of the wage system.[83] Such intriguing counterfactual arguments are, for reasons explored below, not wholly satisfying, but they do focus attention on the fact that the critique of white slavery developed in the 1830s and 1840s did not and could not survive strongly in the 1850s. The ethnocultural conflicts of that decade help to explain why that was so, as do the prominence of the question of slavery in the territories and the real aggression of proslavery forces.[84] But also deserving consideration is the possibility that the case for white slavery suffered from serious weaknesses even during those years when it was put forward most aggressively. In examining those weaknesses we come to understand why it was exceedingly unlikely that any strong common movement against wages slavery and chattel slavery could emerge.

One overlooked reason for the hesitancy of many workers to call themselves slaves was that a significant minority of the Northern working class was abolitionist. The recent and exciting studies of John Jentz, Herbert

81

Aptheker, Herbert Shapiro, Edward Magdol and others have made a strong case that artisans and workers in shoe and textile factories formed a significant part of the abolitionist rank-and-file, probably out of proportion to their share of the population.[85] And we have long known that Black workers provided much of the energy of the abolitionist movement. It was, of course, possible to support abolitionism and to attack 'wage slavery' at the same time. Whites like John A. Collins, William West, Sarah Bagley, Horace Greeley, Nathaniel P. Rogers and Evans sought to attack 'all slavery', and some free Blacks even referred to themselves as slaves.[86] However, especially before the alliance of Evans and Gerrit Smith around a program of abolition and land reform in the late 1840s, a consistent lesson taught by abolitionism was that chattel slavery was a category of oppression much harsher than any other.

Escaped slaves made this point especially vividly. Frederick Douglass's first autobiography, an agitational work of the highest order, made it clear that after escaping slavery he could not get work in New Bedford's shipyards because of the color bar. Nonetheless, he gloried in freedom while denied work in the North but had chafed even when he had been allowed to hire himself out as a slave in Baltimore. Freedom, Douglass emphasized, was far more than an economic category.[87] Black abolitionists recounted telling stories about informing 'white slaves' that their former position on the plantation was open after their escape but never finding anyone eager to take the job.[88] The escaped slave and abolitionist William Wells Brown squarely confronted the chattel slavery/white slavery debate by reminding audiences that even in relatively antirepublican Britain, white workers were free to change employers, free to educate their children and free to make use of the judicial system. White abolitionists echoed these distinctions.[89]

And they were heard. Even labor papers making the case for the existence of white slavery printed arguments sharply calling the metaphor into question. The letter of 'A Factory Girl' to the *Voice of Industry* in 1845 came at the height of class struggle in the textile industry. It encouraged workers to listen to the 'eloquent appeals' of Frederick Douglass and to realize that there 'is a depth in *slavery* beyond the reach of any, but those who have been made the recipients of its horrors.' Its writer then considered specifics:

> ... contrast the condition of the slave with that of your own; while you enjoy the liberty of conscience, and possess all the natural and enduring relations of human existence, the slave who is made in the image of God [is] bought and sold like cattle – families scattered, and hearths made desolate – infants torn from [their] mothers and sold by the pound.[90]

Similarly, during the militant Lynn shoe strike in 1860, women workers carried banners promising that they would not be 'SLAVES'. But at the same time a worker wrote, 'You know we are not a quarter as bad off as the slaves of the South, though we are by our foolishness ten times as bad off as we ought to be. They can't vote, nor complain and we can.'[91]

Similar care to distinguish white workers from slaves came from many other sources who did not necessarily write from an abolitionist perspective. As early as 1836, a mechanic wrote that though it had been argued in Congress that 'the mechanical and laboring population' of the North was comparable to the South's slave population, he disagreed. 'So long ... as [the white working] class retains their power ... to right their wrongs peaceably through the ballot box', he reasoned, 'such assertions tend but to show the ignorance ... of those that give utterance to them.'[92] A *New England Offering* editorial in 1848 began by allowing that the 'Northern laborer has not its rightful privileges [that] in some things he suffers what a slave may never be called upon to endure [and] that poverty and dependence are thraldom.' But it added immediately that 'every freeman should repel with indignation' the white slavery metaphor. The editorial argued that this was necessary out of 'self-respect' and was required for the white worker to do 'justice to himself' as well as to do justice to the slave. To call the white worker a slave, according to the *Offering*, not only 'obliterate[d] nice distinctions' but 'detract[ed] from the dignity of the laborer.' The editorial then raised a series of vital questions to those who termed white workers slaves:

> Is his right to himself, to his family ... of so little worth? Is his hope for the future, his prospects for his children, for so slight a value? Is his liberty to acquire – perhaps fortune – it may be happiness – but at all events character – is this so small a treasure?[93]

It was when such questions were raised – when the debate moved away from stacking the material grievances of the slave against those of the white worker – that the white slavery metaphor collapsed. Information on slaves' standards of life as compared to those of white workers was vague enough to permit comparisons. Indeed the issue still remains controversial among historians. If, as was sometimes the case, writers on white slavery used the plight of the famine-striken Irish as a standard of comparison, the lot of Black slaves could look materially good.[94] But to defend the concept of white slavery on republican grounds was far more difficult. Only in the hottest moments of ten-hour campaigns could the case be made that the lack of time for intellectual life and for citizenship suffered by hireling labor subverted the Republic – that 'Liberty is incompatible with ignorance.' Only then could long hours therefore be said to have constituted a 'slavery of mind' that destroyed a 'FREEMAN'.[95]

The grounds for defending the white slavery metaphor were typically quite ill-connected to republican traditions. In one 1846 National Reform debate on slavery, for example, a speaker raised sharp objections to the phrase *slavery of wages*, pointing out that white workers could not be sold. True enough, came the reply, but the Black slave has 'attendance in sickness' not enjoyed by whites. A third speaker then added that such differences were as inconsequential as those 'twixt dweedledum and tweedledee.'[96] The exchange illustrates the tendency of those attacking 'all slavery' to liquidate the republican critique of hireling labor, to lose focus on the question of dependency, and to suggest, amidst fierce rhetoric, that liberal, even paternal, reforms could save the day. 'AMERICAN LADIES WILL NOT BE SLAVES' ran the motto of Lynn's striking shoe workers before concluding 'GIVE US A FAIR COMPENSATION AND WE LABOUR CHEERFULLY.'[97]

The prospect of speedy amelioration could not easily be discarded. Indeed, it was almost necessary if the white slavery comparison were to amount to anything more than a confession of defeat. If whites really were slaves, decade after decade and with little possibility of change, they had, in republican terms, proven themselves 'unworthy of the name FREEMAN'.[98]

That proslavery Southerners were also using the term *white slavery* highlighted the fact that the term could not lastingly justify itself in terms of the very *herrenvolk* republicanism that had initially given it life. Some white workers might ally themselves with Southerners like Calhoun for specific reasons, stressing common enemies. But the proslavery South was, not surprisingly, a very inconsistent ally, ultimately more ready and able to forge alliances with Northern merchant capital, especially in the labor movement center of New York City, than with workers. Suggestions that the United States embrace a *herrenvolk* labor system shunting all undesirable work onto Black slaves and 'freeing' whites for higher tasks were only episodically made.[99] In such a situation, to be called 'slaves' by lordly Southerners came to be seen as a considerable affront. That some Southerners argued that slavery was a superior way to organize society, and that ideally white workers should also be chattel, did not help matters. As some Southern writers on white slavery confessed, 'Free society! We sicken of the name'. The entire metaphor itself became disgraced. When proslavery Southerners characterized Northern workers as 'greasy mechanics' or 'menials' as well as white slaves, it became clearer that these were words of contempt, not of sympathy. In 1856, the Southern poet

William Grayson penned a book-length verse, titled, significantly enough, *The Hireling and the Slave*. In it he rhymed a case for regarding hired labor as worse off than slave labor and drew the conclusion that miserable white Northerners would 'freely … give' themselves to slavery to become 'secure to live'.[100]

As a badge of degradation, shorn of the possibility of quick dramatic change, the term *white slavery* could not survive as a phrase embraced by Northern white workers. Antislavery poets, especially James Russell Lowell, searingly mocked the politicians – North and South – who called workers 'witewashed [sic] slaves'.[101] Labor reformers, some of whom had used and were using *white slavery*, by the late 1840s began inching toward a defense of the free labor North and pointing to the particular degradation of white Southerners. The latter group was said to obey 'like bondmen' and to live in a society that, because it did not recognize that the mechanic's 'capital is his ingenuity and his sinews', attacked the workers' 'dignity as citizens, and their manhood as freemen.' According to Helene Zahler, the main appeals of the Republican party to workers in the 1856 election consisted of publicizing degrading comments made about Northern wage-earners by Southern proslavery figures.[102]

Bernard Mandel, in his seminal study of labor and slavery, has pointed out that, from the 1830s on, some white workers became angry when *others* called them slaves. He cited several examples of what he called early 'I can say it about myself but you can't' rejections of metaphors using slavery to describe white labor.[103] The process by which the term *white slave* came to be rejected by Northern workers when it came from Southerners suggests something of the same logic. But a deeper explanation – and one more able to account for the language and practice of Northern white workers all the way from the attacks on the word *servant* to the embrace of the term *free white labor* – would run: 'You can't say it and I can say it about myself only with great hesitation and trepidation.' That is, the term *white slavery* always fought an uphill battle in a nation in which racism, slavery and republicanism conspired to make it exceedingly hard to cast oneself as in bondage. To be a slave, even a white slave, was to be associated with degradation. Genteel factory women who rejected the term knew this, and knew that slavery implied sexual exploitation as well.[104] To be a slave also implied connection with blackness. Northern workers became angry not only when called *white slaves* by Southerners but also, and undoubtedly more so, when called *white niggers*. The proponents of the term *white slavery*, Republican advocates of free white labor cleverly charged in 1857, made the white 'the counterpart of the negro.'[105]

Both white slavery metaphors and working class abolitionism served to locate the position of hired labor within a *slaveholding* republic. Both failed because they could not do so unproblematically. Comparisons of white workers with slaves, which are too often considered as simply *class* expressions, were shot through with resonances regarding America's racial realities.[106] To ask workers to *sustain* comparisons of themselves and Black slaves violated at once their republican pride and their sense of whiteness. Since justifications for the metaphors tended to focus on the *treatment* of white workers, the republican critique of hireling labor as a threat to personal and political independence was generally not sharpened or advanced by comparisons to chattel slavery.

Working class abolitionism also takes on a different cast if we place it more squarely within the context of a slaveholding republic with an expanding wage labor force. The significant numbers of mechanics and of shoe and textile workers who supported abolitionism undoubtedly found reason to think about issues of oppression because they faced and feared oppression. There was a sense in which, as Herman Melville has a character in his novel *The Confidence-Man* say, 'Abolitionism ... expresses the fellow-feeling of slave for slave.'[107] But there was also another possible logic to working class support for abolitionism, one that perhaps helps to answer the critical question of why no distinct 'labor wing' of abolitionism developed. To take a radical antislavery position and to follow middle class leaders who emphasized the *differences* between positions of the self-reliant 'free' white mechanic and the Black slave was a way to distance oneself from slaves.

We know that many abolitionists were evangelical Christians who claimed control over their own moral and economic destiny. We know that mechanics and other workers were important parts of the mass base of abolitionism. We know that many mechanics joined the revivals and the temperance movement. In such a situation it is likely that only some of the mechanics supporting abolition were rebels also inclined toward trade unionism. In arguing for the importance of workers in early abolitionism, the antislavery leader Thomas Wentworth Higginson referred, for example, not to freethinkers but to those afire with 'the Second Advent delusion'.[108] Many were workers who, whatever their doubts and whatever their chances, sought to achieve independence through moral reform and steady habits.[109] They worried about being 'slaves to drink' or 'slaves to sin' but claimed the ability to change individually and to prosper.[110] In many ways, this worldview salvaged as much of the republican vision as the critique of white slavery did. But in a nation in which whiteness was so important and emancipation so hard to imagine, abolition was bound to be a minority movement within the working class as in the larger society. If the rhetorical framework of white slavery was limited because it asked white workers to liken themselves to Black slaves, working class abolitionism was limited because it asked white workers to organize energetically on the Black slave's behalf.

The defense of free white labor, around which the Republican party gained ground in the 1850s and to which opposing parties also sought to appeal, succeeded among white workers because it better appealed to the values of *herrenvolk* republicanism than did either the languages of white slavery or of abolitionism. It did not ask white workers to consider themselves slaves nor devote themselves to slaves. But a broader similarity among the various languages of labor should also be noted. All of the three approaches liquidated the question of hireling labor. The abolitionist and free labor analyses tended to regard the wage bargain as freely arrived at, and perhaps temporary. The white slavery position had to force the comparison it sought to make through hyperbole by chronicling the ill-treatment of white workers and often retreated from its criticisms at the first sign of liberalization.

All this suggests that David Brion Davis's provocative ideas concerning antislavery and the acceptance of wage labor need to be pushed further still. Davis has argued that attacks on chattel slavery made 'free labor' (that is, wage labor) more easily acceptable during the first half of the nineteenth century. But in looking at US working class history, it is clear that the existence of *slavery*, not just of antislavery, stalled the development of a telling critique of hireling labor – a critique that might have built on and transcended the republican heritage. It was not just the abolitionists and Republicans who failed to produce such a critique. Also failing were the often proslavery laborites who argued that workers were white slaves. As long as slavery thrived, any attempt to come to grips with wage labor tended to lapse into exaggerated metaphors or frantic denials of those metaphors. Only with Black emancipation could a more straightforward critique of wage slavery, and a fierce battle over the meaning of *free labor*, develop. By that time, the importance of a sense of whiteness to the white US worker was a long-established fact, not only politically but culturally as well.[111]

Notes

1. John R. Commons et al., *A Documentary History of American Industrial Society*, Cleveland 1910, 5:317–18.
2. Ibid., 5:317–18 and 6:315–18; Sean Wilentz, *Chants Democratic: New York City and the Rise of the American Working Class, 1788–1850*, New York 1984, 293. Compare *Working Man's Advocate* (New York) [*WMA*], 9 March 1833.
3. Marcus Cunliffe, *Chattel Slavery and Wage Slavery: The Anglo-American Context, 1830–1880*, Athens, Ga. 1979, 9–13; on France, see David Geggus, 'Racial Equality, Slavery and Colonial Secession during the Constituent Assembly', *American Historical Review* 94 (December 1989): 1291, and William H. Sewell, Jr., *Work and Revolution in France: The Language of Labor from the Old Regime to 1848*, Cambridge 1980; on Germany, I am indebted to Prof. Jonathan Sperber for discussing usages through 1848; on Britain, see Dorothy Thompson, *The Chartists*, London 1984, 226 and passim; Alfred Plummer, *Bronterre: A Political Biography of Bronterre O'Brien, 1804–1864*, London 1971, 194–97; Gareth Stedman Jones, *Languages of Class: Studies in English Working Class History, 1832–1982*, Cambridge 1983, 146.
4. Richard Hofstadter, *The Paranoid Style in American Politics and Other Essays*, New York 1966.
5. George Fredrickson, *The Black Image in the White Mind: The Debate over Afro-American Character and Destiny, 1817–1914*, New York 1971, 28–42 and 46–48; Herbert Shapiro, 'Labor and Antislavery: Reflections on the Literature', *Nature, Society and Thought* 2 (1989): 471–90.
6. David R. Roediger and Philip S. Foner, *Our Own Time: A History of American Labor and the Working Day*, London 1989, 19–42, esp. 32.
7. *WMA*, 12 March 1831 and 7 April 1832; Cunliffe, *Chattel Slavery and Wage Slavery*, 12–15.
8. *New England Artisan*, 21 June 1834; William Sullivan, *The Industrial Worker in Pennsylvania*, Harrisburg, Pa. 1955, 48–49.
9. Bernard Mandel, *Labor: Free and Slave: Workingmen and the Antislavery Movement in the United States*, New York 1955, 64.
10. M.M. Mathews, ed., *Dictionary of Americanisms, On Historical Principles [DA]*, Chicago 1951, 2:1120; *DAE*, 4:2479; Richard Henry Dana, *Two Years before the Mast*, Boston 1911 (reprints 1868 edition), 126.
11. *Mechanics' Free Press*, 17 January 1829.
12. Commons et al., *Documentary History*, 5:332.
13. *The Man*, 22 February 1834; Harriet H. Robinson, *Loom and Spindle: On Life among the Early Mill Girls*, New York 1898, 84.
14. Cunliffe, *Chattel Slavery and Wage Slavery*, 32–68; Roediger and P. Foner, *Our Own Time*, 50–53; *Young America* [*YA*], 18 October 1845 Edward Pessen, *Most Uncommon Jacksonians: The Radical Leaders of the Early Labor Movement*, Albany, N.Y. 1967, 163.
15. Richard Slotkin, *The Fatal Environment: The Myth of the Frontier in the Age of Industrialization, 1800–1890*, New York 1985, 146–50; Jonathan Prude, *The Coming of Industrial Order: Town and Factory Life in Rural Massachusetts, 1810–1860*, Cambridge, Mass. 1983, 100–24 and 133–57; quote from *The Man*, 8 March 1834. See also *WMA*, 2 March 1833.
16. *The Man*, 13 May 1834, as cited in Philip S. Foner, ed., *The Factory Girls*, Urbana, Ill. 1977, 14 n2.
17. Seth Luther, *Address to the Workingmen of New England*, Boston 1832, 32. See also pp. 11 and 17.
18. *The Man*, 13 May 1835.
19. Stephen Simpson, *The Working Man's Manual: A New Theory of Political Economy*, Philadelphia 1831, 16–17; Pessen, *Uncommon Jacksonians*, 77.
20. Simpson, *Manual*, 17, and 85–87.
21. Quoted in Anne Norton, *Alternative Americas: A Reading of Antebellum Political Culture*, Chicago 1986, 238; Cunliffe, *Chattel Slavery and Wage Slavery*, 22.

22. Quoted from *Factory Tracts No. 1: Factory Life as It Is*, Lowell, Mass. 1845, as in P. Foner, *Factory Girls*, 131.

23. *YA*, 7 June 1845.

24. *WMA*, 17 August 1844; 8 March 1845, and *YA*, 7 February 1846, for example.

25. Norman Ware, *The Industrial Worker, 1840–1860*, Gloucester, Mass. 1959 (1924), xv.

26. *Radical*, March 1841, 33; Barry Goldberg, 'Beyond Free Labor' (Ph.D. dissertation, Columbia University, 1978); S.B. Flexner and H. Wentworth, eds, *Dictionary of American Slang*, New York 1975, 577; *OED2*, 12:75.

27. Cunliffe, *Chattel Slavery and Wage Slavery*, 10.

28. On *slavery of wages* and *wages slavery*, see *WMA*, 8 March 1845, and *YA*, 24 May 1845 and 7 February 1846; Commons et al., *Documentary History*, 7:220; *Harbinger*, 26 June 1847; Mike Walsh in *Congressional Globe*, 33rd Cong., 1st. sess. 1854, pt. 2, 1232; *National Era*, 20 April 1848; *Liberator*, 19 March and 12 April 1847 and 21 April 1848; *New England Offering*, September 1848; *Voice of Industry*, 31 July 1845 and 7 May 1847. Thanks to Herbert Shapiro and Philip S. Foner for research materials on this point and others in this chapter.

29. *WMA*, 17 August 1844; YA, 6 February 1846; William Emmons, *Authentic Biography of Colonel Richard M. Johnson*, New York 1833, 29, 69, 72 and 92.

30. See Wilentz, *Chants Democratic*, and John Ashworth, *'Agrarians' and 'Aristocrats': Party Ideology in the United States, 1837–1846*, London 1983, 97–102.

31. The best discussion of the small master and self-employed craftsman is Wilentz, *Chants Democratic*, 42–48 and 251–53. See also Commons et al., *Documentary History*, 6:81–82 and 86, and Bruce Laurie, *The Working People of Philadelphia, 1800–1850*, Philadelphia 1980, 176–77.

32. Whitman, as quoted in Jean H. Baker, *Affairs of Party: The Political Culture of Northern Democrats in the Mid-Nineteenth Century*, Ithaca, N.Y. 1983, 144. See also Chapter 3.

33. Commons et al., *Documentary History*, 6:97–98; compare the reference to 'servile' overseers in *The Factory Girl*, 15 January 1843.

34. *WMA*, 17 August 1844; Ware, *Industrial Worker*, xiv.

35. On the 'coffin handbill', see Wilentz, *Chants Democratic*, 292. Uses of *white slavery* are far too frequent for complete citation, but see *WMA*, 25 July 1835; 7 February, 1 June, and 6 July 1844; 27 September 1845; *Radical*, March 1841, 35; Pessen, *Uncommon Jacksonians*, 162; Commons et al., *Documentary History*, 7:216–17, 220, 362; John Ashworth, 'The Democratic Review: A Study of a Radical Jacksonian Journal, 1837–1851' (M. Litt., University of Lancaster, 1973), 101–2; *Voice of Industry*, 19 February, 14 and 27 August 1847; *Harbinger*, 21 June 1845, 29–31; *National Labourer*, 9 April 1836; *National Anti-Slavery Standard*, 5 August 1847; *The Awl* (Lynn, Mass.), 4 September 1844; *The Mechanic* (Fall River, Mass.), 2 November 1844; Nashua (N.H.) *Gazette*, 1 October 1846; Theodore Sedgwick, *Public and Private Economy*, New York 1836, 254–55 and 263.

36. Eric Foner, 'Workers and Slavery', in Paul Buhle and Alan Dawley, eds, *Working for Democracy*, Urbana, Ill. 1985, 23.

37. Larry E. Tise, *Proslavery: A History of the Defense of Slavery in America, 1701–1840*, Athens, Ohio 1987, esp. 276 and 412; Thomas Man, *Picture of a Factory Village*, Providence, R.I. 1833, 7, 11 and 143.

38. Tise, *Proslavery*, 189; Pessen, *Uncommon Jacksonians*, 91–93; Fisk, 'An Oration Delivered … in the City of Charleston, S.C., July 4, 1837', n.p. n.d., 41; *WMA*, 25 July 1835.

39. Pessen, *Uncommon Jacksonians*, 92; Ashworth, *'Agrarians' and 'Aristocrats'*, 88–89; Philip S. Foner, *History of Black Americans from the Emergence of the Cotton Kingdom to the Eve of the Compromise of 1850*, Westport, Conn. 1983, 376 and 420.

40. Pessen, *Uncommon Jacksonians*, 93; P. Foner, *Black Americans*, 416 and 420; Norman Ratner, *Powder Keg: Northern Opposition to the Antislavery Movement, 1831–1840*, New York 1968, 20.

41. Joseph Dorfman, *The Economic Mind in American Civilization, 1606–1865*, New York 1946, 689–93; Mandel, *Labor: Free and Slave*, 81.

42. Mandel, *Labor: Free and Slave*, 81–82 and 105, includes Douglass quote; Wilentz, *Chants Democratic*, 334.

43. Quoted in Wilentz, *Chants Democratic*, 332–33.

44. Pessen, *Uncommon Jacksonians*, 95–96 and 162.

45. Ibid., 97; Wilentz, *Chants Democratic*, 333 n10; Walter E. Hugins, *Jacksonian Democracy and the Working Class: A Study of the New York Workingmen's Movement, 1829–1837*, Stanford, Calif. 1960, 90; *WMA*, 20 April and 8 May 1844; Ashworth, *'Agrarians' and 'Aristocrats'*, 244–45; David Herreshoff, *Origins of American Marxism*, New York 1973, 45; Michael A. Bernstein, 'Northern Labor Finds a Southern Champion: A Note on the Radical Democracy', in W. Pencak and C. Wright, eds, *Authority and Resistance in Early New York*, New York 1989.

46. Ratner, *Powder Keg*, 64; Leon F. Litwack, *North of Slavery: The Negro in the Free States, 1790–1860*, Chicago 1961, 157–59; P. Foner, *Black Americans*, 420; John M. Werner, *Reaping the Bloody Harvest: Race Riots in the United States during the Age of Jackson, 1824–1849*, New York 1986, esp. 286. Moreover, some labor leaders argued white Northern workers were already competing with Black slave labor; see Mandel, *Labor: Free and Slave*, 65.

47. Ashworth, *'Agrarians' and 'Aristocrats'*, 221–23 and passim. See also John Jentz, 'Artisans, 'Evangelicals and the City: A Social History of Abolition and the Labor Movement' (Ph.D. dissertation, City University of New York, 1977); Arthur Schlesinger, Jr., *The Age of Jackson*, Boston 1945.

48. Mandel, *Labor: Free and Slave*, 103–5.

49. P. Foner, 'Workers and Slavery', 22; *Radical*, March 1841, 35; Philip S. Foner, ed., *American Labor Songs of the Nineteenth Century*, Urbana, Ill. 1977, 104–5; *Voice of Industry*, 27 August 1847.

50. *The Mechanic*, 2 November 1844; *Voice of Industry*, 19 February 1847; *The Harbinger*, 10 July 1847, 82–83.

51. Quoted in Mandel, *Labor: Free and Slave*, 77; *WMA*, 6 July 1844, *YA*, 7 February and 4 September 1846. See also *Liberator*, 19 March and 12 April 1847; 21 April 1848; *National Laborer*, 9 April 1836, and *The Awl*, 4 September 1844, for views that, on balance, find the white slave's lot worse.

52. John Finch, *Rise and Progress of the General Trades Union of New York*, New York 1833, 19.

53. Orestes Brownson, 'The Laboring Classes, an Article from the *Boston Quarterly Review*', Boston 1840, 10; and Herreshoff, *American Marxism*, 43.

54. *WMA*, 22 June 1844; *The Awl*, 29 October 1845; *Congressional Globe*, 33rd Cong., 1st sess., 1854, pt. 2, 1232.

55. Commons et al., *Documentary History*, 7:216–17.

56. *WMA*, 22 June 1844.

57. See Shapiro, 'Labor and Antislavery', for a review of recent literature on these points.

58. *Free Enquirer*, 13 August 1831. The best account of Evans, labor and slavery in New York is Jentz, 'Artisans, Evangelicals and the City', esp. 210–19 and 251–54.

59. *Sentinel*, 2 June 1831; *WMA*, 2 December 1831, for the quote and also 4 June 1831; *Daily Sentinel and Working Man's Advocate*, 27 March 1830. The late Henry Rosemont's research notes were indispensable to my work on Evans.

60. *WMA*, 1 October 1831; 28 June 1832; *Sentinel*, reprinted in *The Liberator*, 1 October 1831; *WMA*, 8 March; 30 May; 9 July; 6 October; 12 and 19 November; 2, 12, 24 and 31 December 1831; Lause, 'Land, Labor and Race', forthcoming.

61. *WMA*, 4 August 1832.

62. *WMA*, 17 April 1830; 29 January 1831, and 4 August 1832.

63. *WMA*, 4 June 1831; 2 February 1833, and 14 June 1834; *The Man*, 19 July 1834; Eric Foner, 'Abolitionism and the Labor Movement', in *Politics and Ideology in the Age of the Civil War*, New York 1980, 65–66.

64. Quotes from *WMA*, 9 April 1834 and 9 March 1833. See also *Sentinel and Working Man's Advocate*, 22 June 1830; *WMA*, 23 June and 13 November 1830; 23 August and 10 October 1831; 16 March, 10 April, 8 November 1832, and 2 March 1833.

65. *WMA*, 6 July 1844.

66. Philip S. Foner, *American Socialism and Black Americans from the Age of Jackson to World*

War Two, Westport, Conn. 1977, 8–9; *Voice of Industry*, 21 August 1845; Commons et al., *Documentary History*, 7:211–13.

67. Quoted in Lause, 'Land, Labor and Race', forthcoming; *Young America*, 8 February 1851; *YA*, 4 September 1846. See also Herman Schlüter, *Lincoln, Labor and Slavery*, New York 1913, 61.

68. Commons et al., *Documentary History*, 7:207–17; *YA*, 28 June 1845.

69. E. Foner, 'Abolitionism and the Labor Movement', 72.

70. *YA*, 12 July 1845, and 26 April 1845; *Radical*, March 1841, 33; *Voice of Industry*, 2 July and 27 August 1847.

71. *WMA*, 11 May 1844, which enjoins workers not to strike 'against a master' but for land reform to do 'all the poor good and none of the rich harm.'

72. *WMA*, 17 August 1844; *Radical*, March 1841, 33–35.

73. For the National Reformers' antiracism, see n 70 above and esp. *WMA*, 25 October 1845, and Lause, 'Land, Labor and Race'. On Black Hawk, *WMA*, 4 May 1844; on Jackson, see *WMA*, 20 April 1844, and Ashworth, *'Agrarians' and 'Aristocrats'*, 97–99.

74. *WMA*, 6 April 1844. See also *WMA*, 27 July and 10 August 1844.

75. *WMA*, 5 October 1844, endorsed Moore and Commerford for office, both then Calhoun supporters. On Evans and Walsh, see Helene S. Zahler, *Eastern Workingmen and National Land Policy, 1829–1862*, New York 1941, 37 and 84n; on Evans's program, see *WMA*, 11 October 1845.

76. *New York Daily Tribune*, 3 June 1852; Lause, 'Land, Labor and Race'; *YA*, 8 February 1851.

77. Zahler, *Land Policy*, 73 n 37, 104 n 57, and 101–8; Commons et al., *Documentary History*, 7:306.

78. Wilentz, *Chants Democratic*, 333 and 385–86; Thomas Ainge Devyr, *The Odd Book of the Nineteenth Century; or, 'Chivalry' in Modern Days*, Greenpoint, N.Y. 1882, 103; Baker, *Affairs of Party*, 237; *Irish American*, 21 January 1860.

79. On free labor, the classic work remains Eric Foner, *Free Soil, Free Labor, Free Men: The Ideology of the Republican Party before the Civil War*, New York 1970, esp. 261–300. On free labor and free white labor, see William Forbath, 'The Ambiguities of Free Labor: Labor and the Law in the Gilded Age', *Wisconsin Law Review*, 4 (1985): 774; William Gienapp, *The Origins of the Republican Party, 1852–1856*, New York 1987, 355; Hinton Rowan Helper, *The Impending Crisis of the South: How to Meet It*, New York 1857, 87 and 156.

80. Robert W. Fogel, *Without Consent or Contract: The Rise and Fall of American Slavery*, New York 1989, 354–69.

81. Compare Commons et al., *Documentary History*, 7:213, and Roy M. Robbins, 'Horace Greeley, Land Reform and Unemployment, 1837–1862', *Agricultural History* 1 (January 1933): 38. On the threat of white slavery in the 1850s, see Gienapp, *Origins of the Republican Party*, 356–59; Johnson H. Jordan, 'An Address to the Free White Citizens of the Yet Free States', Washington, D.C. 1856, 8, and *A Bakepan for the Doughfaces, by One of Them*, Burlington, Vt. 1854, 14–16 and 63.

82. E. Foner, 'Abolitionism and the Labor Movement', 76.

83. Ibid., 74 and 75; Dawley, *Class and Community: The Industrial Revolution in Lynn*, — ✳ Cambridge, Mass. 1976, 238–39.

84. See E. Foner, *Free Soil, Free Labor, Free Men*; Gienapp, *Origins of the Republican Party*; Mandel, *Labor: Free and Slave*, 122–33.

85. Jentz, 'Artisans, Evangelicals and the City', passim; Shapiro, 'Labor and Antislavery', 471–90; Herbert Aptheker, *Abolitionism: A Revolutionary Movement*, Boston 1989, 35–49; Edward Magdol, *The Antislavery Rank and File: A Social Profile of the Abolitionist Constituency*, Westport, Conn. 1986.

86. Such figures are emphasized in Lause, 'Land, Labor and Race', and Shapiro, 'Labor and Antislavery', 482. On free Blacks, see *Colored American*, 25 November 1837, as cited in Mandel, *Labor: Free and Slave*, 228, n57.

87. Frederick Douglass, *Narrative of the Life of Frederick Douglass*, Wortley, near Leeds, 1846, 98 and 116.

88. *Liberator*, 28 April 1848. Thanks to Mark Lause for this reference.

89. P. Foner, *Black Americans*, 477–78; *Liberator*, 1 December 1837; *National Era*, 21 May 1857.

90. *Voice of Industry*, 25 September 1845.

91. Dawley, *Class and Community*, 82; P. Foner, *Labor Movement*, 1:274; see also Mary H. Blewett, *Men, Women and Work: Class, Gender and Protest in the New England Shoe Industry, 1780–1910*, Urbana, Ill. 1990, 128, for a leader's plea that Lynn strikers not let bosses 'make niggers of you', and 383 n60, for antiracist protests against her language.

92. Quoted in P. Foner, *Labor Movement*, 1:274.

93. *New England Offering*, September 1848; compare *Liberator*, 1 December 1837.

94. *Harbinger*, 10 July 1847; Fogel, *Without Consent or Contract*, is the latest, and surely not final, contribution to the standards of life debate.

95. *The Mechanic*, 10 July 1844.

96. *Young America*, 7 February 1844.

97. Dawley, *Class and Community*, 82.

98. *The Mechanic*, 20 July 1844.

99. Philip S. Foner, *Business and Slavery: The New York Merchants and the Irrepressible Conflict*, Chapel Hill, N.C. 1941; Mandel, *Labor: Free and Slave*, 104ff.; Robert Starobin, *Industrial Slavery in the Old South*, New York 1970; see also Matthew Estes, *A Defence of Negro Slavery*, Montgomery, Al. 1846, 168–70, for a striking, but curiously apologetic argument that slavery freed working class whites from 'drudgery' and enabled them to be free citizens.

100. Mandel, *Labor: Free and Slave*, 99 and 123–32; Wilfred Carsel, 'The Slaveholders' Indictment of Northern Wage Slavery', *Journal of Southern History* 6 (November 1940): 510–16.

101. Mandel, *Labor: Free and Slave*, 126 and 133.

102. *Voice of Industry*, 11 June 1847; Zahler, *Eastern Workingmen*, 102.

103. Mandel, *Labor: Free and Slave*, 228, n57.

104. Robinson, *Loom and Spindle*, 196–98, reprinting Clementine Averill's 'Letter From a Factory Girl to Senator Clemens' (1850); P. Foner, *Factory Girls*, 25 and 33.

105. *National Era*, 21 May 1857, reprinting from St. Louis *Democrat*, 7 May 1857.

106. Magdol, *Antislavery Rank and File*, 37 and 72–73; Mandel, *Labor: Free and Slave*, 76–95.

107. Herman Melville, *The Confidence-Man: His Masquerade*, New York 1971 (1857), 97.

108. Gilbert H. Barnes, *The Antislavery Impulse, 1830–1844*, New York 1964; Johnson, *Shopkeeper's Millennium*; Magdol, *Antislavery Rank and File*, 151; John R. McKivigan, *The War Against Proslavery Religion: Abolitionists and the Northern Churches, 1830–1865*, Ithaca, N.Y. 1984; Thomas Wentworth Higginson, *Cheerful Yesterdays*, Boston 1898, 115.

109. Wilentz, *Chants Democratic*, 281–84 and 306–14; Laurie, *Working People*, 119–24; Johnson, *Shopkeeper's Millennium*; Alan Dawley and Paul Faler, 'Working Class Culture and Politics in the Industrial Revolution: Sources of Loyalism and Rebellion', *Journal of Social History* 9 (June 1976): 466–80; Leonard L. Richards, *'Gentlemen of Property and Standing': Anti-Abolition Mobs in Jacksonian America*, Oxford 1970, 139–42; John S. Gilkeson, Jr., *Middle Class Providence, 1820–1940*, Princeton, N.J. 1986, 45–53.

110. Laurie, *Working People*, 90.

111. David Brion Davis, *Slavery and Human Progress*, New York 1984, 15 and 254; see also Thomas L. Haskell, 'Capitalism and the Origins of Humanitarian Sensibility, Part One', *American Historical Review* 90 (April 1985): 350 n59.

PART III

Work, Culture and Whiteness in Industrializing America

'The white man must no longer project his fears
and insecurities onto other groups, races and
countries. Before the white man can relate to
others he must forego the pleasure of defining
them. The white man must learn to stop viewing
history as a plot against himself.'

Vine Deloria

5

Class, Coons and Crowds
in Antebellum America

George Rawick, in his enormously suggestive conclusion to *From Sundown to Sunup*, argues that racism grew so strongly among the Anglo-American bourgeoisie during the years America was colonized because blackness came to symbolize that which the accumulating capitalist had given up, but still longed for. Increasingly adopting an ethos that attacked holidays, spurned contact with nature, saved time, bridled sexuality, separated work from the rest of life and postponed gratification, profit-minded Englishmen and Americans cast Blacks as their former selves. Racism, according to Rawick, served to justify slavery but also did more than that. Racists still pined for older ways, and even still practiced older styles of life, guiltily. All of the old habits so recently discarded by whites adopting capitalist values came to be fastened onto Blacks. As Rawick wonderfully puts it, Englishmen and profit-minded settlers in America 'met the West African as a reformed sinner meets a comrade of his previous debaucheries.' The racist, like the reformed sinner, creates 'a pornography of his former life. ... In order to insure that he will not slip back into the old ways or act out half-suppressed fantasies, he must see a tremendous difference between his reformed self and those whom he formerly resembled.' Blackness and whiteness were thus created together.[1]

During the last two decades, 'new labor historians' following in the footsteps of Herbert Gutman and E.P. Thompson have shown how dramatically capitalist labor discipline reshaped the lives of American workers in the period from the War of 1812 until the Civil War. Gutman and his students – and in a broad sense virtually all recent labor historians – have been his students – have chronicled capital's increasing demands for regular, timed and routinized labor and for 'industrial morality' off the job. Industrial capitalism and speedups in smaller shops joined cultural initiatives to eliminate holidays, divorce the worker from contact with nature, bridle working class sexuality, separate work from the rest of life and encourage the postponing of gratification. Even skilled workers in small shops and nominally self-employed artisans in the sweated trades were far from immune to such pressures.[2] Using and recasting the traditions of their crafts and their communities, workers often contested, and at some times successfully resisted, these new disciplines. But much of the new discipline was also internalized, both by those who used punctuality, regularity and habits of sacrifice to further labor organization and by those who saw the same values as necessary to accumulate wealth and move out of the ranks of wage labor.[3]

There was plenty of anxiety to go around. Those who sought to succeed by giving up traditional holidays and the 'social glass' surely were tempted to create 'a pornography of their former lives'. Those who continued to gamble, drink or take 'Saint Monday' off – the picturesque 'traditionalists' whom historians often have portrayed as holdouts resisting labor discipline – also had reason to fret. They faced social pressures, unemployment and even the poorhouse. Although historians try to draw lines between hard-plugging 'loyalists', hard-protesting 'rebel mechanics' and hard-drinking 'traditionalists', individual workers were pulled in all three directions, and changed categories often, especially during hard times. It was possible to feel guilty for taking a drink with a fellow journeyman at work on Monday and for refusing to do so on Tuesday.[4] The changes were staggering, as Sidney Pollard, a historian of the growth of industrial discipline in Britain, observes in a passage equally applicable to the United States:

> There was a whole new culture to be absorbed and an old one to be ... spurned, there were new surroundings, often a different part of the country, new relations with employers, and new uncertainties of livelihood, ... new marriage patterns and behavior patterns of children within the family and without.[5]

The ideas of Rawick and of Gutman have almost, but never quite, come together to inform an analysis of popular racism in the antebellum US. Historians have noticed the rise in racism in the urban North before the Civil War – a racism expressed in attacks on vestigial Black civil rights, in physical attacks on Blacks by white crowds, in the growth of racist invective, in color bars in employment and in the huge popularity of minstrel shows. They have argued that white workers often participated in racist mobs and constituted the mass audience for minstrelsy.[6] A few historical accounts, most notably Nathan Huggins's account of minstrelsy, have, like Rawick, described the tendency of racist entertainments of the period to project white male anxieties onto blackface characters. According to Huggins, the minstrel showgoers were themselves consumed by the struggle for success and by fears of cultural inferiority. They were knotted with repression, sexual and otherwise. 'Could the fantasies of such men', Huggins asks, 'have been other than the loose and undisciplined creatures of appetite of the minstrel stage?' But Huggins does not connect this anxiety and projection to the experiences of the working class men who formed so large a part of the minstrel show's audience. He tends to see the minstrel as reflecting the white American (male) character *in toto*, once adding the qualifier 'middle class'. Nor has anyone else yet fully placed Gutman's buffeted but resistant early white working class in front of the minstrel stage or in a crowd attacking Blacks, despite Gutman's suggestion in his seminal article on labor discipline that a consideration of racial diversity would need to occupy a 'central place ... in any comprehensive study of American work habits and changing ... working-class behavior.'[7]

This three-chapter section attempts to combine the insights of Rawick and Gutman. It treats the attractions of blackface, not just on the minstrel stage but also in popular crowds and even in racist language, as the result of the desire to project onto Blacks the *specific* behaviors that brought such conflicted emotions to whites during the formation of the first American working class. Gutman hints that anti-immigrant and inter-immigrant hostilities were in substantial measure conflicts between those recently (and perhaps uncertainly) disciplined to industrial morality and newly arriving preindustrial populations.[8] This chapter and the next two argue that the growing popular sense of whiteness represented a hesitantly emerging consensus holding together a very diverse white working class and that part of that consensus derived from the idea that blackness could be made permanently to embody the preindustrial past that they scorned and missed.

Language in Blackface

Just as the languages of class that developed in the United States in the early nineteenth century were shaped at every turn by race, so too did racial language reflect, in a broad sense, changes and tensions associated with class formation. In 1767, a featured Black performer in the first musical to be published in America sang a variation of what was to become 'Yankee-Doodle' as he portrayed a character called Raccoon, an

'old debauchee'.[9] Seventy years later, the white entertainer George
Washington Dixon had popularized Zip Coon as the blackface minstrel
embodiment of the irrepressible, irresponsible, dandified free Black in
the North. Seventy years after that, at the end of the nineteenth century,
the 'coon song' craze swept the nation, with individual racist songs selling as many as three million copies in sheet music. Probably the best-
known of the 'coon songs', Ernest Hogan's 'All Coons Look Alike to
Me', bore a title that suggested how thoroughly dehumanizing racist
stage stereotypes could be.[10]

And yet even amidst this lineage of seemingly unrelieved prejudice, the
'coon' image carried a substantial and striking complexity during most of
the years between 1767 and 1900. A song like 'All Coons Look Alike to
Me' could, quite simply, not have been written before 1848, because
human *coons* were typically *white* until that point. It is true that Zip Coon
and Raccoon strutted on early American stages, but the word *coon* referred
to a white country person, to a sharpster or, in phrases like a *pretty slick
coon*, to both.[11]

To complicate matters, the eagerness of the Whig party to identify
with rural white common people led it to adopt symbols like Davy
Crockett's coonskin cap and, in the 'log cabin and hard cider' presidential
campaign of 1840, to nail coonskins to supporters' cabin doors and to use
live coons as signs of party loyalty. Thus Whigs also became 'coons', especially in the speech of Democrats, who cursed Whigs in 'coongress' and
Whig 'coonventions', Whig 'coonism' and a lack of Whig 'coon-
sistency'.[12] The Whigs, to New York City Democrats, were a 'Federal
Whig Coon Party' – a slur that, though sometimes seen in historical writing as racist, probably had nothing to do with the Whigs' slightly greater
tolerance for antislavery. Instead, the accusation was that Whigs were sly
political manipulators, posturing in coonskin as friends of the common
man.[13]

Only gradually did *coon* emerge as a racial slur, with the first clear case
of such usage coming in 1848. That it first found racist use mainly on the
minstrel stage suggests that the slur evolved from Zip Coon, and in the
context of the many references to coon-hunting and eating coons in
blackface songs.[14] An alternative explanation is that *coon* derived from the
corruption of *barracoon*, from the Spanish *barracon*, which came into increasing use to describe the 'enclosures in which slaves [were] temporarily
enclosed after escape or during travel' in the years just before the Civil
War.[15] Whatever the derivation, all coons decidedly did not look alike in
the 1850s. Lewis Garrard's *Wah-to-Yah; or, The Taos Trail* of 1850, for example, introduces a frontiersman who says of himself, 'This coon ... had

made Injuns go under some.' He quickly adds, 'This child's no nigger.'[16]

The ambiguities of meaning in *coon* were not lost on Herman Melville, who brilliantly explored the mutability and the social construction of race, and even the deleterious effects of whiteness, in such works as *Benito Cereno*, *Moby Dick*, 'Paradise of Bachelors and Tartarus of Maids' and 'The Encantadas'. The racial dimensions of his work have received penetrating treatment from such scholars as Sterling Stuckey, Joshua Leslie and Carolyn Karcher. Karcher particularly observes that Melville's enigmatic masterpiece, *The Confidence-Man* (1857), mocks any firm distinction between black and white. She sees Melville's repeated characterization of the book's most disgusting character as a 'coon' as one key to the racial ambiguities of the novel.[17] The character, an outspoken antiabolitionist and probably a child molester, is of questionable color himself. 'My name is Pitch and I stick to what I say', he says at one point. By calling him a 'coon' Melville emphasizes the uncertainty as to his race.[18] If we add to Karcher's analysis the knowledge that *coon* itself was racially ambiguous in the 1850s and that it could in fact refer to a rural white or to a white confidence man, the layers of Melville's playfulness and seriousness become clearer.

Other racial slurs had similar histories. *Buck*, for example, was used to mean a 'dashing, young, virile man', presumably white, at the time of the American Revolution. As the nineteenth century wore on, *buck* came to signify a 'dandy' and a 'self-proclaimed fascinator of women'.[19] Only in 1835 does the first recorded usage of 'buck nigger' appear, and it is seven years later before *buck* is unambiguously cited as used as a noun to refer to a Black man. Paul Beale's *Dictionary of Slang* directs readers to see *'masher, dude* and *swell'* for a sense of British usages.[20] The term also found some antebellum applications to Indian men – as did *coon* in at least one instance – and gradually became a racial slur. By the early twentieth century, *Dialect Notes* would write of *buck*: 'Formerly a fop; now applied [almost] exclusively to male negroes.'[21]

Likewise possessed of a checkered past was the name Mose, which originally denoted the most interesting white male character type on the American stage. Mose was, in the late antebellum period, synonymous with the character of the 'B'hoy', the Irish and urban street pronunciation of *boy*, and one that denoted a particular type of tough, rowdy and often dandified urban white youth.[22] A low-comedy representative of young urban maleness – a fighter and a lover – Mose was typically an unemployed or apprentice artisan and a member of the volunteer fire departments whose disorderly behavior provoked the wrath of city fathers before the Civil War. When Mose appeared in 1848, according to one contemporary account, 'pit and galleries joined in the outcry' as many recognized themselves in his performance. He quickly became an American urban hero, a 'tough melon but sweet at the core', gracing the parades of artisan-based volunteer fire departments even in an outlying city like Nashville by the early 1850s.[23]

But by the time white Mose had made his way to Nashville, a blackface Mose was appearing in New York City. As early as 1852 the permanent minstrel companies there were performing the song 'Wake Up, Mose', in which the racial identity of the blackfaced hero changed from verse to verse. Tunes like 'De Darkey Fireman's Song' continued the confusion. The minstrel show's 'end men', coming into prominence during the last antebellum years, were, as Alexander Saxton has shown, part Zip Coon but also part Mose.[24] White Mose enjoyed a striking, but relatively brief, popularity. Scholars have blamed the steam engine and the professionalization of fire fighting for his demise. But Mose in blackface proved quite durable, incarnated as both an urban dandy and as a fatherly Southern Black. He became Aunt Jemima's husband in the ragdoll and salt-and-pepper shaker families of the twentieth century.[25]

Such words as *coon, buck* and *Mose* had more than ambiguous or multiple meanings: they had trajectories that led from white to black. More than that, each of them went from describing particular kinds of whites who had not internalized capitalist work discipline and whose places in the new world of wage labor were problematic to stereotyping Blacks. Rustics and con-men, fops and 'fascinators of women', brawlers and 'sentinels of the new army of the unemployed' – all of these proved easier to discuss when blacked up.[26] Such an evolution of language suggests that some use of the concept of projection is necessary to understand the growth of a sense of whiteness among antebellum workers, who profited from racism in part because it enabled them to displace anxieties within the white population onto Blacks. But the process of projection was not abstract. It took place largely within the context of working class formation and addressed the specific anxieties of those caught up in that process.

Mixed Multitudes, White Riots and Blackened Crowds

We have seen the considerable extent to which triumphant republicanism proved compatible with the casting of Blacks as 'anticitizens' to be excluded from civic affairs. For example, anyone the color of Crispus Attucks, the martyr of Boston's crowd before the

American Revolution, would have been barred from many Independence Day celebrations by the early nineteenth century.[27] And yet the reminiscences of theater manager Sol Smith suggest a curious gap in this tendency toward exclusion. Smith described how, in 1814, he and his fellow 'Republican boys' set out to attack the Massachusetts State House in Boston because the Federalists had illuminated the building to celebrate Napoleon's downfall. 'We didn't tear down anything at all', Smith continued, in a passage nicely reflective of how intertwined racism, rebelliousness and republicanism could be, 'but we chased all the niggers off the [Boston] Common, as was usually done on all occasions of gathering.' All occasions, Smith concluded, except 'what was termed nigger 'lection ... [when] the colored people were permitted to remain unmolested on Boston Common.'[28]

Indeed on *that* day, the 'Republican boys' of New England could probably be found marvelling at and imitating the music and dance of African-Americans. Negro Election Day, which began in the mid eighteenth century as an offshoot of more staid white New England election celebrations, initially took shape when slaves came to towns with voting whites and began to choose Black 'governors' and other officials amidst great African-influenced festivity. Over the years, Blacks consolidated a position of leadership within a hugely popular holiday that came to last four and even six days. No fewer than twenty-one New England cities left records of having celebrated the day, which was also marked to some extent in North Carolina.[29] Some of the flavor of the festivities emerges from the wonderful verses of a lament for the holiday by a Lynn poet after the discontinuance of Election Day in 1831 in Massachusetts. The poem amounts almost to a catalogue of the pleasures of preindustrial life:

> And is Election Day no more?
> Good Old 'Lection ...
> No more shall we go up
> To see 'Old Willis!'
> He has hung up his fiddle
> On the last peg.
> The days of old 'Lection are over,
> The glorious days of 'Landee John!'
> When 'Gid' use to hustle coppers,
> And the niggers play 'paw-paw',
> On Boston Common.
> No more shall we eat ''Lection cake',
> Or drink muddy beer,

Misnomered 'ale',
At 'Old Bly's'.
The days of dancing 'Suke' are done,
And fat 'Bet' shall shake her jolly sides no more
To the merry winding about
Of linked sweetness, long drawn out,
From old 'Pompey's fiddle'!
No more shall 'the Governor'
Sit in his great arm-chair,
To encounter the stare
Of the idle mixed multitude,
Black spirits and white
Blue spirits and grey ... [30]

In many other locales, similarly Black-led and African-influenced entertainments also drew in white participants. The Pinkster celebrations of New Jersey and New York slaves transformed a Dutch festival of spring into an African-American one that nonetheless had a strong white constituency in the late eighteenth and early nineteenth centuries. Pinkster was characterized, as James Fenimore Cooper shows in his novel *Satanshoe*, by a very languid sense of time. Its own length was indeterminate, with three or four days of celebration and a week of preparation common. The same amusements that characterized Negro Election Day prevailed at Pinkster, along with spectacular African dancing, the building of beautiful arbors and the crowning of a Black king. Cooper portrayed Blacks as 'beating banjoes, singing African songs and ... laughing in a way that seemed to set their very hearts rattling in their ribs.' He also portrayed hundreds of whites eagerly looking on. Pinkster further resembled Negro Election Day as being a time in which rural and urban populations mixed in cities under Black leadership.[31] In early nineteenth-century New Orleans, slave dances at Congo Square occurred more regularly, convening every Sunday and drawing considerable numbers of impressed white onlookers.[32]

Racially mixed and Black-led entertainments provoked the special wrath of the agents of the new industrial morality, who especially disliked the mixing of Blacks and working class whites. As the folklorist Melvin Wade observes regarding Black coronation festivals in New England, the growing popularity of the celebrations made 'white clergymen, politicians and other public figures [join] in a chorus of criticism.' An early historian of Lynn reflected the viewpoint of the reformers in arguing that the 'excesses of the negroes gave rise to the vile manner in which [Negro Election] was observed by some of the lower class of our own complexion.'[33] A New York opponent of Pinkster, writing in 1803 regarding the festivities in Albany, referred to them as 'periodic seasons of dissipation' drawing together 'the blacks and a certain class of whites, together with children of all countries and colors ... a motley group of thousands ... presenting to the eye of a moral observer, a kind of chaos of sin and folly, of misery and fun.'

By 1811, the Albany Common Council had forbidden food and alcohol stands, gambling, dancing and 'marching or parading, with or without any kind of music' during Pinkster. By 1831, Massachusetts had joined Connecticut in switching election days to colder months and robbing Negro Election celebrations of their springtime appeal. Enforcement of statutes against 'lewd and lascivious behavior' also helped to ensure that Negro Election joined Pinkster in decline.[34] Black-led, biracial celebrations seem to have survived longer in the South, where curbs on them were more often linked to fears of rebellion than to campaigns for industrial morality. Black election day festivities thrived in some North Carolina towns into the 1850s. New Orleans slave dances, though attacked on May Day 1808 and curbed for a time after Nat Turner's Rebellion, also persisted.[35] Meanwhile, in New York City authorities frequently singled out Black–white gatherings for attack.[36]

But as important as actions by the state to discourage racial mixing were, also critical were popular actions of whites in sharply curtailing such mixing by the 1830s. There seems, for example, to have been very little resistance to the curbs on Pinkster and Negro Election Day by white former participants.[37] Moreover, those at the bottom of society often vied with the industrial moralists and the police in creating color bars. Driving Blacks from celebrations was common. Popular attacks on public places known for mixing of the races were rife. New York City's African Grove Theatre, founded in 1821, offered the city a chance to see the young Ira Aldridge, destined to become one of the century's premier actors. It was open to Blacks and whites, though with a partition between the races. After arrests of the cast, shoutings-down of performers and a white riot, the theater closed and Aldridge went into artistic exile in Britain.[38] In Philadelphia in 1834 a mob of working class whites attacked a tavern with an interracial clientele and helped start a major race riot.[39] In Columbia, Pennsylvania that same year a 'committee of working men, and others favorable to their cause' met in the wake of an anti-Black riot to resolve that only the complete removal of Blacks from the town would bring lasting peace. Expulsion of the Black population was likewise the goal in at least ten other riots between 1829 and 1841.[40]

As late as the early 1800s, Black excellence in and centrality to popular entertainment was frequently remarked upon by white Americans. But that centrality could only be episodically asserted in the urban North on those occasions when the color line was not drawn. By the 1830s, Alexis de Tocqueville observed that, particularly in the North, Blacks did not 'share ... the recreations of whites'. Even so, the association of Blacks with preindustrial joys, with entertainment prowess and with 'natural humor' continued.[41] Blackface literally stepped in as a popular entertainment craze at the very moment that genuinely Black performers and celebrations were driven out.[42]

Nor was blackface confined to the minstrel stage. White crowds repeatedly colored *themselves*, replacing excluded Blacks from within their own ranks. Of course, some care must be exercised here. Body-painting is often a part of popular festivity. There is no shortage of examples of Africans painting themselves white ceremonially and, as George Lipsitz has shown, the African-American 'Mardi Gras Indians' of Louisiana have promiscuously crossed racial lines to create one of America's richest popular traditions. Within the Anglo-American tradition there was also a substantial tradition of blacking the skin or of dressing up as Indians on occasions of festivity, rebellion and 'misrule'.[43] The revolutionaries dumping tea into Boston harbor, Constance Rourke argues, combined racial disguise, revelry and revolt so thoroughly that 'it may well be a question whether the participants enjoyed more dumping the tea ... or masquerading in war paint and tomahawks.'[44]

Nonetheless, in the racially charged atmosphere of antebellum America, blacking up (or redding up) was not simply traditional, joyous or decorative. It also usually involved a conscious declaration of whiteness and white supremacy, even as it identified celebration and popular justice with adopting a racial disguise. Indian impersonation, common among volunteer fire companies, was also often a feature at militia days, where half the participants sometimes 'became' Indians to stage a mock battle from an anti-Indian war.[45] The antirent protesters in New York between 1839 and 1845 so frequently adopted 'redface' disguises as they drove off sheriffs and rent collectors that the state government outlawed dressing up as Indians. But the antirent rebels do not seem to have experienced the exhilaration Rourke imputes to the tea-dumpers of Boston harbor. Instead, their spokesmen apologized for having to wear Indian disguises and reassured listeners that 'although they were obliged to darken their faces they had hearts like their white brethren.'[46]

Nor were the rebelliousness and preindustrial joyousness of crowds in blackface separable from the (usually conscious) white supremacy pervading that form of masking. The context in which popular blackfacing emerged and the purposes to which it was directed ensured as much. Blackface crowds apparently came into prominence in the Age of Jackson, even as truly mixed popular celebrations were waning and as minstrelsy was taking off in popularity. According to the fullest local study, Susan G. Davis's superb account of 'street theater' in Philadelphia, blackened white crowds were overwhelmingly young, male and working class. They borrowed freely from the minstrel stage, moving in bands known as the 'Jim Crows' and the 'Strut-Some Guards'.[47]

The most marked use of blackface took place in two significant venues. The first were militia day gatherings at which, by 1835, blackface was added to the mismatched costumes, malformed horses and discordant 'rough music' with which the lower classes of Philadelphia mocked the hierarchy and compulsion associated with militia service. There is also evidence of blackface antimilitia protests in New York City.[48] In much of the North, militia days and artillery election days were closed to Black participation and sometimes even to Black observation from early in the nineteenth century. However, in parts of New England, 'nigger shows' quickly came to provide blackface at militia days where black faces were barred. Similarly, in Philadelphia blackfaced whites put in appearances at Independence Day festivities shortly after Blacks were forbidden to come.[49]

In the vast Christmas processions of antebellum Philadelphia, blackface spread rapidly to become the 'most common disguise' in the festival maskings shortly after its first use in 1829. The revelries of the holiday season were themselves growing during this period, transcending smaller German 'besnickling' and Anglo-American house visiting processions to become huge parades, replete with fun, mock militia troops, rough music and transvestism. Not a few young white toughs took advantage of the season to become blackened *Aunt Sallys* crossing lines of both gender and race.[50] At first Blacks participated in the expanded celebrations, which much resembled the spectacular, Black-led Jonkonnu (or John Canoe or John Kunering) festivals held at Christmastime in the Caribbean and just to the south of Philadelphia in the mainland US. Many Black Philadelphians, and some who were white, doubtless knew of the elaborate Jonkonnu traditions nearby and some genuinely Black traditions influenced the expanded white Christmas maskings.[51]

Nonetheless, the most common role for Black Philadelphians in antebellum Christmas maskings was as victims of blackfaced mobs. The scenario is as fascinating as it is tragic. The chief attraction of masking, as Davis observes, was that it offered a chance to 'act black' for a time. It also afforded the opportunity to move beyond gender boundaries and – in that

105

the processions often went to elite places of entertainment and sometimes attacked municipal watchmen – to mock the respectable, middle class, orderly and wealthy.[52] And yet the processions – like those by New York City's rowdy and at times blackfaced white 'callithumpian' bands – repeatedly ended the evening by engaging in the very traditional, white, male street activity of beating up free Blacks. In 1834, blacked-up Philadelphians attacked Blacks in a major race riot not connected to Christmas maskings. In 1840, Blacks celebrating the Christmas season as part of the street processions were set upon by attackers in blackface.[53] Such violence may have contributed to a decline, or even disappearance, of Black celebration of holiday masking until after the Civil War. But even when not celebrating on the streets, Blacks could not avoid attacks from those dressed as Jim Crow or Aunt Sally. Christmas racial clashes, initiated by blackface mobs, took place regularly between 1837 and 1848, with the last erupting into full-scale riot. Some of the violence involved white and Black gangs, but on other occasions, blacked-up mobs attacked African-Americans who were in church.[54]

However scattered and seasonal it was, this pattern of blackface-on-Black violence provides a useful entry into broader issues raised by antebellum popular mobbings of Blacks. While it is true that the Christmas maskers likely included some whites suffering from the seasonally high wintertime jobless rates in Northern urban areas, it is difficult to think of job competition with free Blacks as central to the yuletide attacks. To argue that the rituals and the blackface served literally to mask the labor market considerations of the rioters only delays confronting the insufficiency of job competition as an overarching explanation for the violence. If the struggle over jobs were so compelling, why was there a need for such sideshows?[55] Nor does the simple materialist explanation that the maskers put on blackface to hide their identities in order to commit crimes while celebrating enable us to exorcise the riddle of why people would both imitate and beat up Blacks on the same night.[56] Mere blacking up was hardly a foolproof disguise and may well have aroused the suspicion of the forces of law and order. In any case, a white skin was such a proven antebellum defense against prosecution for attacks on Blacks that adding a layer of burnt cork to the face was superfluous in that regard. Perhaps the fact that some whites *thought* blackface granted license is more impressive than the actual impact of the disguise.

A more convincing explanation, and one that opens onto insights regarding nonblackfaced racist mobs, would allow that Philadelphia's blacked-up Christmas maskers both admired what they imagined blackness to symbolize and hated themselves for doing so. In a backhanded

way, the very insistence on excluding Blacks from a range of p
celebrations may have reflected a perception that African-American style,
music and dance would have dominated mixed celebrations, as had happened with Pinkster and Election Day. David Dalby's reminder that many
slaves came from areas more aesthetically inclined, and perhaps accom-
plished, than was the society of their owners is a fascinating one. How far
his observation can be extended to illuminate comparisons of African-
American and Anglo-American urban working class culture in antebellum
Northern cities is worth asking. What is certain is that many urban whites
at the time credited Blacks with tremendous expressive power.[57] To some
– and this may also help explain the virtual exclusion of Blacks from the
antebellum minstrel stage – the choice may have seemed one between
all-white and Black-led entertainments.

Blackface served not only to identify the white crowd with the excellence of Black popular culture but also to connect its wearers with the
preindustrial permissiveness imputed to African-Americans. It reem-
phasized that the Christmas night or the militia day was a time of celebration and license, of looseness, drinking and promiscuity. But even in the
midst of revelry and even given the real desires of the crowds to 'act
black', the celebrants needed to underscore continually the point that they
were still white. That chimney sweeps were part of the crowds adds a
curious twist to this drama, in that sweeps faced the daily problem that
their occupation and the involuntary blacking up it entailed might lead to
their being identified with Blacks.[58]

So too did the presence of many Irish complicate matters. As we shall
see in Chapter 7, the Irish were frequently conflated with Blacks and
sometimes were themselves seen as the group symbolizing preindustrial
license. So much was this the case that rowdy, undisciplined behavior in
the 1830s was sometimes called 'acting Irish'.[59] Blackface masking defiant-
ly disregarded the charge of respectable society that sweeps and Irishmen
were 'like Blacks'. But late night attacks on actual Blacks underscored that
blackface was only an appealing disguise to be washed off in the morning.
The choice of targets in riotous revelry made the point that the mob
would neither be joined in common preindustrial celebration by people of
color nor allow Blacks to appear more self-disciplined than lower class
whites.

Other white mobs and callithumpian bands who, without blackface,
victimized Blacks, showed the same seemingly contradictory choice of targets. The crowds singled out places in which Blacks and whites took common sensual pleasures: brothels, taverns and the homes of interracial
couples. On the other hand, the most exalted and serious institutions of

the African-American community came in for attack: churches, West Indian emancipation celebrations and temperance halls. Some riots featured attacks on both the forces of disorder and order in the Black community. They demanded in essence that African-Americans remain in their places as 'anticitizens' at the separate, undisciplined bottom of urban society, as a touchstone against which a wide variety of ill-disciplined popular white behavior could be justified both to the respectable and to the rowdy fretting about respectability. Thus, the 1834 New York City riots found a mob breaking into a Black church, where they listened to one of their number speak 'in mock negro style' and 'struck up a *Jim Crow* chorus'. Race riots were, as a Cincinnati observer put it in 1843, a 'festival', a 'carnival' and an American 'Saturnalia'. But they had respectable targets.[60]

Projection played a vast role here, with the values inculcated by industrial morality being a special focus. The attacks on Black temperance halls came at a time when the drinking habits of the white working classes had come to be seen by reformers and by some workers as alarmingly undisciplined and at a time when the term *nigger drunk* (that is, 'very drunk') was finding its way into the language. The best evidence suggests than Black antebellum Northern urbanites were probably more temperate than whites, but neither popular language nor the mobs wanted to recognize that fact.[61]

Also striking is the extent to which antiamalgamation hysteria coincided with challenges to the traditional patriarchal expectations and sexual freedom of laboring males. On the one hand, as Christine Stansell's brilliant study of working women in New York City shows, the decreasing dependency of wage-earning single 'girls' made for a much more open-ended, if not egalitarian, pattern of gender relations in urban plebeian youth culture after 1830. Stansell finds these new relations embedded in a growing working class consciousness that 'undermined some features of eighteenth-century misogyny' but also 'vaunted' maleness and proved compatible with growing group-based sexual violence against women. Stansell wisely observes that the growing tendency of 'b'hoys' to protect 'their women' from sexually predatory 'gentlemen' expressed at once class consciousness, a new respect for working women *and* a 'fundamentally patronizing' new paternalism. The spectacular 1834 New York City race and antiabolitionist riots also featured white workers seeking to protect 'their women', but from amalgamation with Blacks, not with the wealthy. The riots in Columbia, Pennsylvania in the same year featured skilled workers waxing hysterical about the threat of interracial sex. These skilled workers may have accepted what Stansell regards as the typical pre-1860 urban working class standard, which allowed for sexual expression before marriage but may also have worried that perhaps the abstinence enjoined by revivalists and reformers was the path to success. That the Columbia rioters vividly imagined that abolitionists would somehow *make them* be the sexual partners of Blacks suggests that no small psychosexual anxiety ran through the mobs.[62]

One further reason that Philadelphia's maskers and many nonblackface white mobs attacked Blacks is that it was easy to do so. In antiabolitionist mobs, it was often possible to riot in a highly protected setting, in crowds led by conservative members of the city's older elite.[63] Given the choice, late at night, of turning for a last run through an area of posh clubs or a final thrust at the Black community, crowds knew that the forces of law and order would vastly prefer the latter. The decision of Sol Smith and his friends to abandon plans to attack the Massachusetts State House and instead to chase 'all the niggers off the Common' took the path of least resistance. When an 1835 Baltimore riot turned from an ambitious attack on bank directors' homes and instead savaged the Black community, it too had found the easier course. As David Grimsted has shown, the tendency to riot against asylums for Black orphans carried the singling out of the defenseless for attack to a chilling extreme.[64]

In New York City in 1834, rioters took rather more complicated but equally telling paths. After moving from attacks on symbols of 'race-mixing' and abolitionism the crowd turned to a white target, descending on and breaking into the Bowery Theater, which had employed a British actor who was reputedly an 'antirepublican' snob. The enterprising theater manager calmed the crowd by having an actor sing an immensely popular song. That it was a blackface minstrel number – 'Zip Coon' – suggests that while *herrenvolk* republican popular culture often combined antiaristocratic and racist protests, the former could overwhelm the latter.[65] Similarly, though racist street theater offered the chance to express resistance to the new industrial morality, it also tended to turn resentments against that morality away from both frank defenses of traditional habits and organized forms of labor protest.

The question of whether race riots expressed the values of white working class culture in antebellum America is a difficult one. On the one hand, working class communities clearly provided cover for the rioters, who were seldom identified and still less often found guilty of serious crimes by urban juries. The riots bespoke the anxieties – not just or mainly centering on fears of Black competition for jobs – of a working population experiencing new forms of industrial discipline. Race riots, especially those growing out of popular celebrations like Christmas maskings, also embodied the traditions and rituals of often newly urbanized working class communities.[66]

However, the composition of the mobs and the response of some within the labor movement suggest that anti-Black and antiabolitionist riots split the working class. Rioters tended to represent particular segments of the working class, with young, male, unskilled and apprentice workers especially prominent, though in some cases skilled artisans dominated. The apprentices were by the forties variously called 'b'hoys' to suggest their swagger and 'bound boys' to suggest their problematic unfreedom, as craft traditions of apprenticeship waned in a slaveholding republic.[67] In a society that prized being 'free, white and twenty-one' most rioters could only fully claim status based on the second of those qualifications. To the considerable extent that anti-Black rioters came to be Irish, in a nation still debating how to classify the Irish racially, even that claim was not fully secure. Moreover, the antiabolitionist mobs, and some antiblack ones, often gathered under the leadership of conservative older elites despised by generous sections of the working class.[68]

Thus, it is not surprising that racist mob activity often drew censure from labor writers and even at times from the urban artisan–based penny press. George Henry Evans's response to New York City's racist and antiabolition riots of 1834 consisted of an unstinting attack on 'mobites'. Though at the time hardly enamored of abolitionists, Evans defended their civil rights and the rights and humanity of free Blacks. William Leggett, the labor Jacksonian who edited the New York *Post*, similarly took a civil libertarian approach, backing off on his paper's earlier castigations of abolition and gradually coming to support the demand.[69]

These two extreme examples were rare but even the most inflammatory penny press papers – full before the riots of attacks on, in the blackfaced language of their parodies, 'Bobolition' – tended to recoil from the mob and, in several cases, to support reparations for mob victims. In New York City in 1834 a significant percentage of the rioters came from skilled crafts rapidly being marginalized, but they were portrayed in the press as the disreputable 'dregs of society'. As John Jentz has acutely observed, the reaction to the riots became a way to express tension between the radical but respectable 'labor empire' and the rowdy 'traditionalists' of street republicanism.[70] It might be added that even the more popularly rooted creations of urban artisan culture, such as the penny press, had considerable reservations about race riots, objecting not to the mob's racism but to its preindustrial disdain for respectability and discipline. Thus a *herrenvolk* republicanism of the streets was not sustainable, given the divisions within the working class between those who, to oversimplify deliberately, had and had not come to accept industrial discipline. But a *herrenvolk* republicanism of the stage was another matter.

Notes

1. George P. Rawick, *From Sundown to Sunup: The Making of the Black Community*, Westport, Conn. 1972, 132–33.

2. Herbert G. Gutman, *Work, Culture and Society in Industrializing America*, New York 1977, esp. 3–78; E.P. Thompson, 'Time, Work-Discipline and Industrial Capitalism', *Past and Present* 38 (December 1967): 56–97; Paul Faler, 'Cultural Aspects of the Industrial Revolution: Lynn, Massachusetts Shoemakers and Industrial Morality, 1826–1860', *Labor History* 15 (Summer 1974): 367–94; Bruce Laurie, '"Nothing on Compulsion": Life Styles of Philadelphia Artisans, 1820–1860', *Labor History* 15 (Summer 1974); David R. Roediger and Philip S. Foner, *Our Own Time: A History of American Labor and the Working Day*, London 1989, 2–42.

3. Paul Faler and Alan Dawley, 'Working Class Culture and Politics in the Industrial Revolution', *Journal of Social History* 9 (June 1976): 466–80; Paul Johnson, *A Shopkeeper's Millennium: Society and Politics in Rochester, New York, 1815–1837*, New York 1978; Barbara M. Tucker, '"Our Good Methodists": The Church, the Factory and the Working Class in Antebellum Webster, Massachusetts', *Maryland Historian* 8 (Fall 1977): 26–37.

4. Faler and Dawley, 'Working Class Culture', 466–80; Gutman, *Work, Culture and Society*, esp. 5 and 19–32; Bruce Laurie, *Working People of Philadelphia, 1800–1850*, Philadelphia 1980, 40–42, 116–19, 124, 139–47 and 201–2.

5. Quoted in Gutman, *Work, Culture and Society*, 14.

6. Jean H. Baker, *Affairs of Party: The Political Culture of Northern Democrats in the Mid-Nineteenth Century*, Ithaca, N.Y. 1983, 214–16; Laurie, *Working People*, 61–66, 124–25 and 155–57; Robert Toll, *Blacking Up: The Minstrel Show in Nineteenth Century America*, New York 1974, 32–33; Paul A. Gilje, *The Road to Mobocracy: Popular Disorder in New York City, 1763–1834*, Chapel Hill, N.C. 1987, 154–56.

7. Huggins, *Harlem Renaissance*, Oxford 1971, 253 and 252–57 passim. See also the short section on minstrels in George Lipsitz, *Time Passages: Collective Memory and American Popular Culture*, Minneapolis, Minn. 1990, 63–64, in which a connection to industrial discipline is briefly made; Gutman, *Work, Culture and Society*, 13, 17 n14 and 58–59 n41, but see also Mimi Rosenberg, 'An Unpublished Interview with Herbert Gutman on United States Labor History', *Socialism and Democracy* 10 (Spring-Summer 1990): 58.

8. Gutman, *Work, Culture and Society*, 68–70.

9. James H. Dorman, 'Shaping the Popular Image of Post-Reconstruction American Blacks: The "Coon Song" Phenomenon of the Gilded Age', *American Quarterly* 40 (December 1988): 451; Alan W.C. Green, '"Jim Crow", "Zip Coon": The Northern Origins of Negro Minstrelsy', *Massachusetts Review* 11 (Spring 1970): 385.

10. Dorman, 'Popular Image', 453 and 459.

11. The best source is Frederic G. Cassidy, ed., *Dictionary of American Regional English* [*DARE*], Cambridge, Mass. 1985, 1:763. But see also *DA*, 1:388–89; *DAE*, 1:611–12; *OED2*, 2:962 and *OED2* supplement (1972), 1:630–31.

12. Thomas B. Alexander, 'The Presidential Campaign in 1840 in Tennessee', *Tennessee Historical Quarterly* 1 (March 1942): 37; Alexander Saxton, *The Rise and Fall of the White Republic: Class Politics and Mass Culture in Nineteenth-Century America*, London 1990; *OED2*, 2:962. See also *AG*, 1:201–2. Crockett's own initial connection to coonskins in folklore may have resulted from the borrowing of a story originally connected to the Black Seminole John Horse. See Kenneth W. Porter, 'Davy Crockett and John Horse: A Possible Origin of the Coonskin Story', *American Literature* 15 (March 1943): 10–15.

13. Quoted, and loosely connected to racism, in Wilentz, *Chants Democratic*, 327.

14. See, for example, *DARE*, 1:763; *DA*, 1:388; *OED2*, supplement, 1:630–31; *Ethiopian Serenaders' Own Book*, Philadelphia 1857, 8, and 37; *Christy's New Songster*, New York n.d., 35; *Ethiopian Glee Book*, Boston 1849, 24, 72–73, 103, 160; *Howe's 100 Ethiopian Songs*, Boston and Chicago 1877, 224; Harold Wentworth and Stuart Berg Flexner, eds, *Dictionary of American Slang*, New York 1975, 122.

15. *OED2*, 1:679; Tamony Papers, University of Missouri–Columbia; Charles R. Shrum, quoted in 'Editorial Notes', *American Mercury* 9 (October 1926).

16. Lewis H. Garrard, *Wah-to-Yah; or, The Taos Trail*, Norman, Okla. 1955 (1850?), 117, 163, 208, 216, 226, 228, 238, and for the quote, 190. Compare Robert Montgomery Bird, *Nick of the Woods*, New York 1939 (1837), 84–85.

17. Karcher, *Shadow over the Promised Land*, Baton Rouge, La. 1980, 256–57; Joshua Leslie and Sterling Stuckey, 'The Death of Benito Cereno: A Reading of Herman Melville on Slavery', *Journal of Negro History* 67 (Winter 1982): 287–301.

18. Herman Melville, *The Confidence-Man: His Masquerade*, New York 1971 (1857), 101, 121 and 98–120 passim.

19. *DARE*, 1:405–06; *DAE*, 1:330; David Grimsted, *Melodrama Unveiled: American Theatre and Culture, 1800–1850*, Chicago 1968, 194; *The Negro Singer's Own Book*, New York and Philadelphia n.d., 154. See also *AG*, 1:107.

20. Paul Beale, ed., *Dictionary of Slang and Unconventional English*, London 1984, 143.

21. Quoted in *DARE*, 1:405–6.

22. *DARE*, 1:227; *DAE*, 3:1548 and 1:200.

23. On the Mose type and his popularity, see Grimsted, *Melodrama*, 192, which includes the quote; Richard M. Dorson, 'Mose, the Far-Famed and World-Renowned', Hershel Parker, ed., *American Literature* 15 (1943): 288–300; James Boyd Jones, Jr., 'Mose the Bowery B'hoy and the Nashville Fire Department', *Tennessee Historical Quarterly* 40 (Summer 1981): 170–81; and, most sentimentally, David S. Reynolds, *Beneath the American Renaissance: The Subversive Imagination in the Age of Emerson and Melville*, New York 1988, 463–66.

24. Alexander Saxton, 'Blackface Minstrelsy and Jacksonian Ideology', *American Quarterly* 27 (March 1975): 8–11; *The Ethiopian Glee Book: Containing the Songs Sung by the New Orleans Serenaders*, Boston 1850, 214.

25. Joseph Boskin, *Sambo: The Rise and Demise of an American Jester*, New York 1986, 140. See also Charles Townsend, *Negro Minstrels*, New York 1969, 12–B.

26. Wilentz, *Chants Democratic*, 301.

27. See Chapter 2, n62.

28. Sol Smith, *Theatrical Management in the West and South*, New York 1968, 12.

29. Melvin Wade, '"Shining in Borrowed Plumage": Affirmation of Community in the Black Coronation Festivals in New England, ca. 1750–1850', *Western Folklore* 40 (July 1981): 171–82; Joseph P. Reidy, 'Negro Election Day and Black Community Life in New England, 1750–1860', *Marxist Perspectives* 1 (Fall 1978): 102–17; Lorenzo J. Greene, *The Negro in Colonial New England*, Port Washington, N.Y. 1966, 245–48; Robert C. Kenzer, *Kinship and Neighborhood in a Southern Community: Orange County, North Carolina, 1849–1881*, Knoxville, Tenn. 1987, 62.

30. Reprinted in Paul G. Faler, *Mechanics and Manufacturers in the Early Industrial Revolution, Lynn, Massachusetts, 1780–1860*, Albany, N.Y. 1981, 128–29.

31. Sterling Stuckey, *Slave Culture: Nationalist Theory and the Foundations of Black America*, New York 1987, 80–81, 142 and 144; Shane White, 'Pinkster in Albany, 1803: A Contemporary Description', *New York History* 70 (April 1989): 191–99; and White 'Pinkster: Afro-Dutch Syncretization in New York City and the Hudson Valley', *Journal of American Folklore* 102 (January–March 1989): 71; James Fenimore Cooper, *Satanshoe*, New York 1845, 1:70 and 69–86 passim; A.J. Williams-Myers, 'Pinkster Carnival: Africanisms in the Hudson River Valley', *Afro-Americans in New York Life and History* 9: 7–17; Edwin Olson, 'Social Aspects of Slave Life in New York', *Journal of Negro History* 26 (January 1941): 71–72.

32. Gary A. Donaldson, 'A Window on Slave Culture: Dances at Congo Square in New Orleans, 1800–1862', *Journal of Negro History* 69 (Spring 1984): esp. 66–67.

33. Wade, '"Borrowed Plumage"', 178.

34. White, 'Pinkster', 71; and White, 'Contemporary Description', 192 and 196–97 for the quotation; Reidy, 'Negro Election', 112–13.

35. Kenzer, *Kinship and Neighborhood*, 62; Donaldson, 'Congo Square', 67; Dena J. Epstein, *Sinful Tunes and Spirituals: Black Folk Music to the Civil War*, Urbana, Ill. 1977, 90–99 and 132–36.

36. Alessandra Lorini, 'Festive Crowds in Early Nineteenth Century New York' (Paper presented at the Conference on Time, Space, Work and Leisure in Pre-Industrial America, University of Paris VII, June 1987). See also Vincent E. Powers, '"Invisible Immigrants": The Pre-Famine Irish Community in Worcester, Massachusetts, From 1820 to 1860' (Ph.D. dissertation, Clark University, 1976), 262–63.

37. White, 'Pinkster', 71–72; White, 'Contemporary Description', 192; Wade, '"Borrowed Plumage"', 178.

38. Russell Sanjek, *American Popular Music and Its Business*, New York 1988, 2:156–58; Herbert Marshall and Mildred Stock, *Ira Aldridge: The Negro Tragedian*, Carbondale, Ill. 1958, 32–48, and above Chapter 2, n62.

39. Laurie, *Working People*, 62.

40. Philip S. Foner and Ronald L. Lewis, eds, *The Black Worker: A Documentary History from Colonial Times to the Present*, Philadelphia 1978, 1:175–78; John M. Werner, *Reaping the Bloody Harvest: Race Riots in the United States during the Age of Jackson*, New York 1986, 286–87.

41. Boskin, *Sambo*, 69, which includes de Tocqueville's quote.

42. Marshall and Stock, *Aldridge*, 37.

43. Lipsitz, *Time Passages*, 233–53; Susan G. Davis, *Parades and Power: Street Theatre in Nineteenth-Century Philadelphia*, Philadelphia 1986, 77–111; Bryan D. Palmer, 'Discordant Music: Charivaris and White Capping in Nineteenth-Century North America', *Labour/ Le Travailleur* 3 (September 1973): 5–62, esp. 31 and 49.

44. Quoted in Albert Murray, *The Omni-Americans: Black Culture and the American Experience*, New York 1970, 15.

45. Telfer H. Mook, 'Training Day in New England', *New England Quarterly* 11 (December 1938): 689; Davis, *Parades and Power*, 145.

46. Donald B. Cole, *Martin Van Buren and the American Political System*, Princeton, N.J. 1984, 407–8; David Maldwyn Ellis, *Landlords and Farmers in the Hudson-Mohawk Region, 1790–1850*, Ithaca, N.Y. 1946, 242–50; *Working Man's Advocate*, 17 August 1844.

47. Davis, *Parades and Power*, 106 and 108.

48. Ibid., 77–101, esp. 86 and 96. See also Palmer, 'Discordant Music', 34.

49. Greene, *New England*, 247–48; Esther A. Peck, *A Conservative Generation's Amusements: A Phase of Connecticut's Social History*, Bangor, Me. 1938, 17–22; Davis, *Parades and Power*, 106 and Chapter 2, n62 above; Mook, 'Training Day', 687. See also *WMA*, 19 July 1845, for a 'nigger joke' in the labor press regarding militia service. The butt of the joke is a militia officer.

50. Susan G. Davis, '"Making Night Hideous": Christmas Revelry and Public Disorder in Nineteenth-Century Philadelphia', *American Quarterly* 34 (Summer 1982): 189, 193–94 and passim. Dutch traditions, known to an extent in parts of North America, connected the figure of Black Peter, St. Nicholas's helper, with Christmas pagaents. See Gerald Early, 'A New Reading of Herman Melville's *Benito Cereno*' in *Tuxedo Junction: Essays on American Culture*, New York 1989, 218–23.

51. Davis, *Parades and Power*, 104; Elizabeth A. Fenn, 'All Dance, Leap and Play: Jonkonnu, Slave Society and Black Dance', in American Dance Festival, *The Black Tradition in American Modern Dance*, Gerald E. Myers, ed., n.p. 1988, 9–10; Ira De A. Reid, 'The John Canoe Festival', *Phylon* 3 (1942): 349–70; Stuckey, *Slave Culture*, 68–73 and 104–6.

52. Davis, '"Making Night Hideous"', 193–94 and 188–97 passim.

53. Gilje, *Road to Mobocracy*, 254–60; Davis, '"Making Night Hideous"', 192; John Runcie, '"Hunting the Nigs" in Philadelphia: The Race Riot of August 1834', *Pennsylvania History* 39 (1972): 209.

54. Davis, '"Making Night Hideous"', 192, n32, and *Parades and Power*, 108.

55. On jobs and race riots, see the careful comments of Gilje, *Road to Mobocracy*, 164–67;

Laurie, *Working People of Philadelphia*, 63–66 and 157; Leon Litwack, *North of Slavery: The Negro in the Free States, 1790–1860*, Chicago 1961, 100–102; Runcie, 'Race Riot', 197.

56. Davis, *Parades and Power*, 108.

57. David Dalby, 'Jazz, Jitter and Jam', *New York Times*, 10 November 1970; Boskin, *Sambo*, 66–68.

58. Davis, '"Making Night Hideous"', 192; Gilje, *Road to Mobocracy*, 254.

59. Davis, *Parades and Power*, 77 and 143; Runcie, 'Race Riot', 194–95.

60. Quoted in John B. Jentz, 'Artisans, Evangelicals and the City: A Social History of Abolition and Labor Reform in Jacksonian New York' (Ph.D. dissertation, City University of, New York 1977), 249; Gilje, *Road to Mobocracy*, 155 and 162–69; Davis, *Parades and Power*, 46; Laurie, *Working People of Philadelphia*, 63–66 and 124; Litwack, *North of Slavery*, 102; David Grimsted, 'Ante-Bellum Labor: Violence, Strike and Communal Arbitration', *Journal of Social History* 19 (Fall 1985): 8; Werner, *Bloody Harvest*, 125, 130–40, 195–96 and 279–89. On 're-spectability', see also Davis, *Parades and Power*, 151. The stark conclusion of John Runcie's 'Race Riot' also deserves consideration in this connection. See pp. 217–18 for his observation that 'no account of the [1834 Philadelphia] riot should overlook the simple incontrovertible fact that "hunting the nigs" offered a welcome opportunity for certain people to ... get drunk, destroy property ... and generally enjoy themselves at the Negroes' expense.' On Cincinnati, see David Grimsted, 'Rioting in Its Jacksonian Setting', *American Historical Review* 77 (April 1972): 385.

61. *DA*, 2:1117; Donald Yacovone, 'The Transformation of the Black Temperance Move-ment, 1827–1854: An Interpretation', *Journal of the Early Republic* 8 (Fall 1988): esp. 297. See also *AG*, 2:605.

62. Christine Stansell, *City of Women: Sex and Class in New York 1789–1860*, New York 1986, 83–101; Richards, *Gentlemen of Property and Standing*, 152; Linda K. Kerber, 'Abolitionists and Amalgamators: The New York City Race Riots of 1834', *New York History* 48 (January 1967): 28–39. Werner, *Bloody Harvest*, 286; P. Foner and Lewis, *Black Worker*, 1:175–78.

63. See Richards, *Gentlemen of Property and Standing*.

64. Smith, *Theatrical Management*, 12; Baker, *Affairs of Party*, 246. See also Leonard P. Curry, *The Free Black in Urban America, 1800–1850*, Chicago 1981, 96–97.

65. Wilentz, *Chants Democratic*, 265.

66. Baker, *Affairs of Party*, 245–46; Davis, *Parades and Power*, 72–111; Runcie, '"Hunting the Nigs"', esp. 218–19; Iver Bernstein, *The New York City Draft Riots: Their Significance for American Society and Politics in the Age of the Civil War*, New York 1990, 342–43.

67. *AG*, 1:58 and 94; Jentz, 'Artisans, Evangelicals and the City', 234–69; Richards, *Gentlemen of Property and Standing*, 150–55; Davis, '"Making Night Hideous"', 192–95; Gilje, *Road to Mobocracy*, 143–70; W.J. Rorabaugh, *The Craft Apprentice from Franklin to the Machine Age in America*, New York 1986, 132–33, 140 and 167–71.

68. Richards, *Gentlemen of Property and Standing*, 131–55; Grimsted, 'Rioting', 392; Laurie, *Working People of Philadelphia*, 64–66; Albon Man, 'Labor Competition and the New York City Draft Riots of 1863', *Journal of Negro History* 36 (October 1951): esp. 394 and n67 above. On the 'race question' regarding the antebellum Irish, see Chapter 7 below.

69. Jentz, 'Artisans, Evangelicals and the City', 251–53; Werner, *Reaping the Bloody Harvest*, 129.

70. Jentz, 'Artisans, Evangelicals and the City', 234; Werner, *Reaping the Bloody Harvest*, 124–42; Richards, *Gentlemen of Property and Standing*, 152; Wilentz, *Chants Democratic*, 264; Alexander Saxton, 'Problems of Class and Race in the Origins of the Mass Circulation Press', *American Quarterly* 36 (Summer 1984): 232–33; Gilje, *Road to Mobocracy*, 167–68.

114

6

White Skins, Black Masks:
Minstrelsy and White Working Class
Formation before the Civil War

Mechanics Hall, New York City home to the celebrated Christy Minstrels, described in its name the social group that most influenced blackface entertainment's form and content. In other cities Mechanics Halls likewise hosted minstrel troupes.[1] Of the giants of the early minstrel stage, Billy Whitlock was a typesetter before blacking up and indeed set type by day and performed by night in the 1830s. Dan Emmett, composer of 'Dixie' and an early minstrel megastar, apprenticed as a printer. Thomas Dartmouth (Daddy) Rice, the first minstrel dancer to 'jump Jim Crow' on stage, had apprenticed as a woodworker.[2] Michael Hawkins, the composer of 'Back Side Albany', arguably the first important minstrel song, had trained as a coachmaker.[3]

However, to say that minstrel music was mechanics' music is to do more than illustrate the tendency for many of its leading lights to have been artisans or even to note that in many ways minstrelsy was itself a craft.[4] It is likewise to do more than to observe that the placement of theaters, the structure of pricing, the connections between minstrelsy and volunteer firemen, and the complaints of the elite suggest that urban common people were filling minstrel audiences.[5] It is to argue that the *content* of blackface performances identifies their particular appeals as expressions of the longings and fears and the hopes and prejudices of the Northern Jacksonian urban working class, especially the artisanate.[6]

In creating a new sense of whiteness by creating a new sense of blackness, minstrel entertainers fashioned a theater in which the rough, the

115

respectable and the rebellious among craft workers could together find solace and even joy. By so doing, the minstrel stage became a truly popular form of entertainment able to attract the immigrants, 'b'hoys' and unskilled of the city while also making special appeals to those in the West and some in the respectable middle classes and above. Minstrelsy was featured at President John Tyler's inauguration, and in performances before Queen Victoria. Abraham Lincoln stole away from the pressures of duty during the Civil War to see blackface shows.[7] But the energy and complexity of the minstrel stage came largely from below, and specifically from the uses of racial disguise not only to mask tensions between classes but also to mask tensions within the working class.

The blackface whiteness that delighted and unified the increasingly wage-earning urban masses was empty of positive content. If languages of class hinged on the quite vague definition of white workers as 'not slaves', the hugely popular cult of blackface likewise developed by counterpoint. Whatever his attraction, the performers and audience knew that they were *not* the Black dandy personified by Zip Coon. Nor were they the sentimentalized and appealing preindustrial slave Jim Crow. Blackface could be everything – rowdy, rebellious and respectable – because it could be denied that it was anything.

Blackfaced Whiteness: Roughness and Respectability

Lewis Erenberg has described the appeal of post–Civil War 'coon songs' as deriving from their ability to project onto Blacks values and actions that aroused both fear and fascination among whites. Such actions, he argues, could thus be 'experienced and condemned at the same time.'[8] This analysis also works well in considering antebellum minstrelsy, especially when combined with George Lipsitz's insight that 'the minstrel show "Negro" presented white society with a representation of the natural self at odds with the normative self of industrial culture.'[9] Minstrelsy's genius was then to be able to both display and reject the 'natural self', to be able to take on blackness convincingly and to take off blackness convincingly.

In no sense was the racial masking on stage simple. Minstrel entertainers both claimed to be pupils, or even kin, of the Blacks they mocked and as passionately made clear that they were white. Although scholars sharply debate the extent to which antebellum minstrel songs actually drew on African-American music, it is clear that early minstrels delighted in claiming to be a 'student of the negro' and therefore 'authentic' performers.[10] Audiences were occasionally addressed as 'my broder [brother] niggars', and one inventive parody of Shakespearean characters was titled 'Black and White Niggers'.[11] In a few instances there seems to have been genuine confusion among viewers as to the racial identity of blackface performers, and on at least one occasion a church agreed to let a troupe perform only on the condition that they not come as Blacks.[12] Minstrelsy did not steal Black material stealthily. It did so brazenly, acknowledging and emphasizing its Black roots, insisting, for example, on the banjo's African origins.[13]

Nor was Black music necessarily seen as quaint and primitive in its appeal. As Du Bois observed, in his chapter on the 'Sorrow Songs' in *Souls of Black Folk*, 'away back in the [1830s] the melody of these slave songs stirred the nation.' Walt Whitman found Negro dialect music, which he considered slave-connected, the basis for a national 'grand opera', while the composer John Philip Sousa compared the music of America's cotton fields to the works of great European composers.[14]

At the same time, blackface minstrels were the first self-consciously *white* entertainers in the world. The simple physical disguise – and elaborate cultural disguise – of blacking up served to emphasize that those on stage were really white and that whiteness really mattered. One minstrel pioneer won fame by being able to change from black to white and back in seconds. Playbills continually featured paired pictures of the performers in blackface and without makeup – rough and respectable, black and white. One showed the troupe 'As Plantation Darkeys' and, significantly, 'As Citizens'. Novelty whiteface acts such as the Four White Negroes or the Albino Minstrels emphasized the importance of color.[15] Songs repeatedly reminded the audience of its own whiteness by beginning 'Now, white folks ...'[16] Minstrels sentimentally highlighted their positions as 'the whitest of white folks' in verses like:

> There is not a man in the whole Minstrel Band,
> Who would ever go back on a friend;
> Tho' dark be his face, yet the black can't efface
> The kind deeds which through life him attend.[17]

Snappy jokes carried the point less laboriously, with performers proclaiming that they were 'like widows' in that they wore black only for a short time.[18]

The importance of a common whiteness under the blackface gave the minstrel stage the ability to foster astonishing ethnic diversity even during periods of anti-immigrant hysteria. As the African-American choreographer Leni Sloan has noted, many Irish immigrants performed brilliantly beneath black makeup.[19] Songs of Ireland, including Irish nationalist songs, took their places alongside Tyrolean warbling, yodelling, and Italian and Bohemian opera.[20] Among the many featured polkas were the 'African Polka' and one named for Jim Crow.[21] Songs of the western United States mixed with chorale harmonizing influenced by the abolitionist Hutchinson Family singers.[22]

This extreme cultural pluralism was at the same time a liquidation of ethnic and regional cultures into blackface and, ultimately, into a largely empty whiteness. Alan W.C. Green's study of minstrelsy argues that 'as various other types – particularly the Irishman and German – fused with native-born Americans, the Negro moved into a solo spot centerstage, providing a relational model in contrast to which masses of Americans could establish a positive and superior sense of identity.' Superior certainly, but it is difficult to see how the identity was positive, given that it was established by an infinitely manipulable negation comparing whites with a construct of a socially defenseless group. Like the doomed master in Hegel's celebrated essay 'Lordship and Bondage', blackfaced whites derived their consciousness by measuring themselves against a group they defined as largely worthless and ineffectual. Indeed, as Green himself shows, the trajectory of minstrelsy was to create an ersatz whiteness and then to succumb to a mere emphasis on the 'vulgarity, grotesqueness and stupidity' of the black characters it created.[23]

Blackface whiteness was not without its ethnic tensions, stereotypes and contradictions. Irish drinking and 'thickness' drew mockery from the minstrels, as did German speech. Ethnic types were recognizable under blackface. European music was burlesqued even as it was played. Some minstrel songsters end the blackface at a certain point and turn to mockeries of the Irish or even of rural whites. But in the main, all whites could easily participate in minstrelsy's central joke, the point of which remained a common, respectable and increasingly smug whiteness under the makeup.[24]

Just as the minstrel stage held out the possibility that whites could be 'black' for awhile but nonetheless white, it offered the possibilities that, via blackface, preindustrial joys could survive amidst industrial discipline. Even the 'rough' culture of young, rowdy traditionalist artisans and un-skilled workers could lie down with the 'respectable' norms of striving, upwardly mobile skilled workers.

To black up was an act of wildness in the antebellum US. Psychoanalytically, the smearing of soot or blacking over the body represents the height of polymorphous perversity, an infantile playing with excrement or dirt. It is the polar opposite of the anal retentiveness usually associated with accumulating capitalist and Protestant cultures. Painting oneself hearkened back to traditional popular celebrations and to paint oneself as a Black person, given American realities at the time, was to throw reason to the winds. It is no accident that the early minstrel show was sometimes called a 'nigger festival'.[25]

But performers on the minstrel stage were also often said to have been in the 'Negro business'.[26] The irrational bacchanalian act of blacking up was, as Melville makes clear at the beginning of *The Confidence-Man*, also an enterprise and even a scam.[27] The substantial salaries of minstrel entertainers engaged popular attention, as did the tendency of some highly successful performers and promoters (including P.T. Barnum) to do blackface for a time as prelude to fame and fortune elsewhere.[28] In a real sense, then, rubbing on blacking *was* an accumulating capitalist behavior. It may stretch a point to note that one of the first great minstrel hits bore the title 'Analisation',[29] but minstrels certainly did claim respectability off stage and did draw attention to the relationship between racial disguise and making money. 'Why is we niggas like a slave ship on de Coast of Africa?' one joke asked. 'Because', came the reply, 'we both make money by taking off the negroes.'[30]

Similarly assuaged was the tension between a longing for a rural past and the need to adapt to the urban present. The blackface wore rather thin when, for example, Irish minstrels sang laments by 'slaves' involuntarily removed from home and family. Other immigrants, migrants from rural to urban areas in the United States and migrants to the frontier, could likewise identify with the sentiments in 'Carry Me Back to Ole Virginny' or 'Dixie'.[31] So could almost any American involved in what Alexander Saxton has called the nation's 'endless outward journey' of expansion. Minstrelsy likewise idealized the preindustrial pastimes familiar to its white and often formerly rural audience. Hunting, especially of coons and possums, was a recurring delight during blackface performances, which also featured the joys of crabbing, eel catching, eating yellow corn, fishing and contact with animals not about to be killed. 'Niggas', one song had it, 'live on clover.'[32]

But the identification with tradition and with preindustrial joy could never be complete. It was, after all, 'niggers' who personified and longed for the past. Contradictions abounded. Even as they deplored American rootlessness, minstrels solidly supported American expansion. They strongly backed conquering Mexican areas occupied by 'yellow skins', for example.[33] Shows commonly switched abruptly from blackface paeans to pastoral life to having the entertainers perform, oddly enough, extended imitations of train sounds. Some minstrel venues even came to feature

119

mechanized blackface automatons.[34] A mythical Black South came to fill the role of an imagined haven standing against the deadening aspects of progress for popular Northern minstrel audiences, just as did a romanticized white South for the more solidly middle class readers of cavalier fiction. But the distance from full identification with those seen as resisting progress was greater on the minstrel stage because of their blackness.[35]

Most tellingly, lyrics in antebellum minstrel songs generally did not reflect the real success of Southern slaves at keeping preindustrial rhythms of work – indeed at uniting song and labor and using the former to pace the latter.[36] Instead, they assumed that the slave, except when 'given' a holiday by the master, worked all day in a manner not only hard but disciplined. The famous 'A Nigger's Life Is Always Gay' held that its title character 'work in field till set ob sun,/And den his work am always done.'[37] The songs seldom treated any preindustrial resistance to work, though they were perhaps somewhat more ready to broach the subject when discussing behavior clearly imputed to white workers than to slaves. Thus, the blackface 'History of the World', as distinctive as it was fanciful, revealed:

> De world was made in six days, and finished on de sebenth
> Kord in to de contract, it should a bin de lebenth
> But de carpenters got drunk, and de masons couldn't work,
> So de cheapest way to do it was to fill it in with dirt.[38]

Similarly, although blackface provided a mask behind which erotic longings could find expression, the break from the repressiveness of early Victorian America was far from complete. Not only did the racial form of the shows make it uncertain how far the audience was meant to empathize with – and how far it was mean to recoil from – the sexual freedoms portrayed, but the content of the shows also often bowed far in the direction of respectability and sentimentality.

Minstrelsy was a way for men to carouse after work in largely sexually segregated audiences. The theater's 'pits' were especially male preserves. Minstrelsy's popularity reflected the challenges to traditional plebeian concepts of maleness in the face of the declining household economy, of revivalist and reformist sexual purity drives, of the increase of women's paid labor, and of the rising uncertainty of ever attaining economic independence. For a young, single male to go out with the boys to see a minstrel show on a Saturday night meant foregoing courting that night.[39] It may have reflected the worries found in some minstrel shows over the expense of courtship or a fear of what Christine Stansell has called the 'expansive heterosexuality' between increasingly assertive single working women, living outside of households, and 'b'hoys' of antebellum cities. Stansell mentions a 'masculinism' that placed 'women on the sidelines' as a brake on heterosexual mingling. In minstrel theaters, women were usually not even on the sidelines. Given all this, as well as the antebellum cultural expectation that males would be sexually aggressive, the minstrel crowd seems to have combined hormones and anxiety in proportions conducive to appreciating entertainment based on sex and violence.[40]

The shows would not have wholly disappointed those seeking titillation. They of course transcended the bonds of decorum set by revivalists and propurity reformers, not to mention the male artisan–based Graham Society, whose devotees ate bland food to curb the flow of sexual juices and harness their energies for productive purposes.[41] Minstrelsy contained its full share of sexual puns, including homoerotic ones. It included very considerable transvestism – with troupes being almost universally all-male and with early minstrel stars gaining fame for 'looking the wench'. The content of the shows called gender identity into further question, as in the conundrum 'If a woman changes her sex what religion would she be?' – a line to which an end-man answered, 'A he-then.' Mild sexual bragging and references to promiscuity ran through songs of 'dandy coons' and 'lubly gals'. Some tunes, such as 'The Nigger Wench Fight', gloried in immorality: 'When de whites dey do go to bed,/The devil is working in de nigger's head.' A few were sexually graphic, such as 'Juliana Phebiana Constantiana Brown', whose title was paired in the chorus with 'Den up and down my darkies, oh! gently up and down.' On balance, songs showing promiscuous Black women were probably more popular than those emphasizing the sexuality of Black men, with the fairly ribald 'wench' song 'Lucy Long' being among the most performed antebellum minstrel tunes.[42]

But surviving antebellum minstrel lyrics and jokes certainly did not rival the sexuality and erotic punning in the works of contemporary literature by Melville or in the pulp fiction of the immensely popular George Lippard. Indeed, minstrelsy was probably not as sexually charged as most abolitionist writing.[43] Most blackface contact between men and women occurred in happy, but decorous, love songs or in sentimental laments for loves lost. The violent and sexually menacing black male of the post–Civil War 'coon song' is largely absent from early minstrelsy.[44]

As the music historian Robert Winans has remarked, antebellum minstrelsy provided at best a short 'respite' from the prevailing sentimentality of the period. Marian Mair's comments on 'black' sexuality in British blackface shows of the 1850s in the main apply equally well to the United States. Such sexuality, she argues, was 'over-enthusiastic, undignified and misguided but ultimately safe.'[45] When it was not safe, as when the Temple of Muses theater in New York City brought in minstrels who were actually female and 'indecent' to boot, 'a furious melee developed between offended customers and offending [performers].'[46]

The sexual tameness of the minstrel stage resulted in part from its accommodation of both the roughness and the respectability within male working class culture. The pre–Civil War 'coon song' guides for amateur minstrels so stressed decorum and cleanliness that they left little doubt that many who appreciated the shows wished to be respectable.[47] On the other hand, the limited sexual adventuresomeness of antebellum minstrels also derived in part from the fact that their audiences were sufficiently close to a preindustrial past to long for a range of broadly *erotic* pleasures – such as laughter, unfettered movement and contact with nature – rather than narrowly defined *sexual* fulfillment. But in blackface it was easy for erotic desire to find its way into becoming what bourgeois culture tended to make it – first, mere sentimentalism and, later, sentiment plus mere carnality.[48]

The desires animating the minstrel stage – however much they were originally more playfully erotic than nakedly pornographic – could find full expression only beneath a racial disguise. That disguise homogenized cultural oppositions so facilely that it could express the ethos of both respectable and rowdy working class culture at once, or perhaps so facilely that it could fully express the ethos of neither. A marvelous description of a minstrel performance from the *London Illustrated News* caught the power and limits of blackface whiteness perfectly in this connection:

> Yet out of all of this nonsense, ... there somehow arises a humanizing influence which gives an innocent recreation a positive philanthropic sentiment. This sentiment connects itself with them as a colored troupe. With white face the whole affair would be intolerable. It is the ebony that gives the due and needful color to the monstrosities [and] the breaches of decorum.[49]

Militant Minstrels? The Fate of Oppositional Culture in Blackface

Some intriguing recent studies have focused less on the issue of whether the early minstrel show was rowdy or respectable and more on the extent to which it was a *rebellious* cultural form that subverted class and even racial hierarchies. Sean Wilentz has found minstrelsy in the capital of blackface, New York City, to have expressed plebeian, even working class, culture. But he cautions against seeing only white supremacy as the message of blackface. 'The shows', Wilentz has written, 'took racism for granted. As the form developed, the real object of scorn ... was less Jim Crow than the would-be aristo[crat] – either the white interlocutor or the dandified black.' Wilentz further suggests that minstrelsy historically moved from anti-Black caricature to subtle class criticism, describing the turn 'from racist humor to mocking the arrogance, imitativeness and dim-wittedness of the upper class in "permissible" ways.' Wilentz concludes that the blackface stage produced social criticism in the atmosphere of a 'kind of carnival' – an image used by nineteenth-century observers and one picked up by modern historians of blacking up to point out the ways in which blackface humor had the same tendency to level social distinctions and to deflate social pretensions that Mikhail Bakhtin so brilliantly described in precapitalist carnivals.[50]

Wilentz's analysis suffers from the obvious drawback that it is difficult to identify a time when minstrel entertainments moved away from 'racist humor'. Most scholars have in fact found that blackface stereotyping became more crude and vicious between 1830 and 1900.[51] Another line of argument, most clearly developed by William F. Stowe and David Grimsted, attempts to circumvent this objection. Stowe and Grimsted contend that blackface entertainments, though they reflected the racist culture from which they grew, subverted *both* racism and social hierarchies among whites. Minstrelsy thus featured 'complexity in comic portrayal' of Blacks and 'questioned, teased and contradicted, as well as confirmed' white supremacist attitudes. Moreover, according to Stowe and Grimsted, the black mask helped allow 'deep expressions of emotions of loss and longing, as well as ridicule of social and intellectual platitudes and the discrepancies between American dreams and American realities' *among whites*.[52]

The cases made by Wilentz and by Stowe and Grimsted for viewing minstrelsy as a kind of oppositional, contestatory culture ultimately fail, but in such a broadly revealing way as to make this brief excursion into historiography worthwhile. Both approaches stand out because they rightly acknowledge that blackface entertainment was not merely about race relations but also about social relations among whites. Both interpretations fail in large part because they depend on the assumption that the racial content and the class content of minstrelsy can be neatly separated. Wilentz takes this position straightforwardly in arguing for a 'turn' away from humor based on race. Stowe and Grimsted reproduce this illusion at another level. When arguing that racism was subverted by the variety of images of minstrel entertainers – the beautiful, graceful, the ignorant, the savvy, the lonely, the wronged and the villain – they put aside the extent

to which audiences knew that these were white entertainers, playing thin-
ly blacked-up white stock characters. When arguing that blackface was a
slight veneer providing the 'distance' necessary to do effective social
satire, they minimize the extent to which the mask seemed real to the
audience and subverted the social criticism being expressed.[53]

Any rounded analysis of the minstrel mask would have to admit and
even emphasize considerable ambiguity, including the presence of sub-
texts and the simultaneous identification with, and repulsion from, the
blackfaced character. But if there is reason to suspect that the identification mitigated the repulsion toward the stage character in blackface, there
is little evidence that it mitigated white hostility toward real Blacks. Just
as calling oneself a white slave did not necessarily imply sympathy with
the Black slave, watching comedians in blackface did not imply solidarity
with Black Americans. And blackface-on-Black violence suggests that just
the opposite logic – one of hatred toward the object of desire – could
prevail.

Amidst great complexity, two facts about the racial politics of the
minstrel stage before 1870 stand out. First, with very minor exceptions
coming mainly in the realm of dance, white entertainers never crossed the
color line on stage.[54] Second, blackface performances tended to support
proslavery and white supremacist politics. Certainly some songs evoked
the horrors of slavery, especially of being sold and taken away from home.
But countless others painted a paternal plantation and contented slaves.
What varied far less was that when political chips were down, minstrelsy
could speak directly for specific anti-Black policies in a way that it could
not for egalitarian ones. Minstrels ridiculed 'bobolashun', joined Southern
expansionist elements in supporting the war against Mexico, argued that
escaped slaves wanted to go back to slavery, and dismissed British antislavery appeals by observing, 'They had better look at home, to their own
white slaves.'[55] When *Uncle Tom's Cabin* proved an antislavery popular success, minstrels replied with proslavery versions, featuring tunes like
'Happy Are We, Darkies So Gay', and performances by such major stars
as T.D. Rice.[56] The Civil War brought an outpouring of minstrelsy, most
of whose political content was given over to attacking emancipation, the
use of Blacks as troops, taxation to pay for Freedmen's Bureau activities,
Black civil rights, and alleged favoritism toward 'the nigger'.[57]

All these specifically reactionary racial references should not surprise
us. They took place within the context of a form that implicitly rested on
the idea that Black culture and Black people existed only insofar as they
were edifying for whites and that claims to 'authentic' blackness could be
put on and washed off at will. Thus it was possible to sing heart-rending

songs of slave children sold away from their parents and to draw no, or even proslavery, political conclusions. As Alexander Saxton has written:

> The ideological impact of minstrelsy was programmed by its conventional black-face form. There is no possibility of escaping this relationship because the greater the interest, talent, complexity and humanity embodied in its content, the more irresistible was the racist message of its form.[58]

When we turn to discussing whether minstrelsy, whatever its racism, was nonetheless a form of oppositional culture *among whites*, we cannot entirely put its anti-Black form and proslavery content aside. After all, race and slavery were tremendously important antebellum political issues and were the ones to which minstrelsy spoke most consistently. In the minstrel mecca of New York City, it should added, the proslavery cultural politics of the minstrel stage was not in opposition to, but in rough congruence with, the stance taken by the city's mercantile elite.[59]

Moreover, the racial logic of minstrelsy was replicated in framing discussions of the second most commonly addressed issue, women's rights. Minstrels claimed the right to turn Black for as long as they desired and to reappear as white. They forcefully denied Blacks that right, parodying fancy dress, 'l'arned' speech, temperance and religion among Blacks as ridiculous attempts to 'act white'. Mockeries of Black political activity and claims to civil rights sometimes literally turned on the impossible vision of activist Blacks wishing to turn literally white.[60] Similarly, minstrels claimed the right to be female for as long as they liked and then to reappear as male. But they necessarily denied women the same right to cross gender boundaries. Blacked-up whites appeared in drag on stages where 'bloomerism' – the wearing of trousers by women – was, Robert Toll argues, 'the minstrels' greatest concern'. The standard minstrel 'Women's Rights Lectures' denounced political rights for women, but a more immediate fear was that white male control over masks and symbols might be breached by 'Bloomerizical' women:

> When women's rights is stirred a bit
> De first reform she bitches on
> Is how she can wid least delay
> Just draw a pair ob britches on.[61]

In addressing divisions among white males, blackface entertainers did not speak to any political question with the regularity with which they addressed racial and gender issues. They sometimes did take strong populist stances, as in 'Dat Gits Ahead of Me', which asks

How is it banks suspend and break
and cause such awful times?
The [bank] President's allowed to take
And pocket all the dimes.[62]

Similar scattered protests against politicians generally, profiteering merchants, sexually predatory gentlemen, taxes, corruption and hypocritical,
fashion-conscious religion found a voice. However, the shows seldom
spoke even obliquely to conflicts between labor and capital, though after
the Civil War siding with 'the poor' against 'the rich' and even against
'blood-sucking, thieving employers' found some expression.[63]

By far the most common rebellious feature of antebellum minstrelsy
was a partly cultural and partly political air of defiance toward authorities,
snobs and condescending moralists. The extent to which this stance, or
posture, was compromised by its blackface form has already been discussed in considering the rowdiness and respectability of the minstrel
stage. Worth adding here is that, although white leaders of organized
religion did have some reason for their dislike of minstrels, most satire of
authority figures was doubly distanced from 'seriousness' by race.[64] The
ridiculous and comically named politician, preacher or temperance advocate was of course in blackface. Beyond that convention, the minstrel
stage offered a choice as to whether the character would speak in a 'Black'
accent – that is, in an extravagant dialect – or in an 'American' or immigrant accent, indicating that he was on some level white. The moralist or
politician of the minstrel stage generally had his blackface identity reinforced by his being 'Brudder Bones' or 'Jacobus Snowball' and by his out-
landish speech, which was capable of describing Adam and Eve's expulsion
from Eden with 'so de Lor' cotch 'em boff and he throw dem over de
fence, an' he tole 'em, "Go work for your libin!"'[65] Stowe and Grimsted
have commented that the 'distance' provided by blackface made for social
and cultural criticism able to present 'truths ... which would have been
profoundly troubling or socially dangerous if presented or taken in serious
form.' Sometimes the distancing was very elaborate indeed.[66]

The huge numbers of blackface 'hashes' of Shakespeare present the
issue of cultural rebellion in great complexity and sharp relief. These
parodies have been portrayed as egalitarian attacks on pretentious, elitist
and European culture, much like the burlesques of opera by 'niggeretto'
songs.[67] However, as Lawrence Levine has shown, Shakespeare was a *mass*
favorite in the early nineteenth century, and the idea that his plays were
'high culture' developed only slowly and unevenly.[68] The role of minstrelsy in the development of a split between high and low culture remains to
be studied, with the questions of race and the treatment of Shakespeare

being central. The very fact of parody implied a certain familiarity with the originals, and just as certainly, as one cultural historian has written, Shakespeare 'could take such ribbing.' The parodies often did display a decidedly anarchical spirit and, as in the story of Hamlet and Egglet, considerable inventiveness.[69]

But they were also highly racialized and featured extremely thick 'Black' accents. *Othello* predictably presented particular opportunities to place sexuality, violence and high art within the nonthreatening confines of sentiment and of a hyper-emphasized blackface mask. As the Black American actor Ira Aldridge gained fame for his performances of Othello in exile, blacked-up performers in the US sometimes 'jumped Jim Crow' after doing the play. One plot summary referred to 'thick-lip Othello, that nagur-faced fellow.' His tragic romantic affair with Desdemona – focused squarely enough on race in the original – was transformed, minstrel-style: 'He didn't lub her very long bekase she wasn't yailer.' A conundrum pointed out that Desdemona was 'like a ship … when she was Moored.'[70] Who was humbled? Cultural snobs? Black Americans? Or the popular masses themselves, who were heirs to a far richer tradition of appreciating of both the humor and the artistry of Shakespeare? The questions admit more than one answer.

Minstrelsy made a contribution to a sense of popular whiteness among workers across lines of ethnicity, religion and skill. It achieved a common symbolic language – a unity – that could not be realized by racist crowds, by political parties or by labor unions. Blackface whiteness meant respectable rowdiness and safe rebellion. It powerfully addressed the broadest tensions generated by the creation of the first American working class. By and large, it did so by racializing conflict more than by directly articulating class grievances. The 'Knights of the Burnt Cork' were far more compelling when they attacked aristocrats than employers and were still more so when they attacked Blacks. Calvin C. Hernton's comment that 'the racist visits his own essence upon the Negro – but it is not a way that leads out', applies in a sad and double sense to antebellum minstrelsy, which 'led out' neither to antiracism nor to a tenable assertiveness among white workers.[71] To ask whether it might have been different is surely to run the risk of being branded a utopian. It is frankly in that spirit that this chapter closes by counterfactually wondering how America, for African-Americans and for working class whites, might have turned out differently if the same social energies and creativity poured into blackface entertainments had somehow gone instead into the preservation and elaboration of Negro Election Day?

Notes

1. E.L. Rice, *Monarchs of Minstrelsy: From 'Daddy' Rice to Date*, New York 1911, 17; Carl Wittke, *Tambo and Bones: A History of the American Minstrel Stage*, Durham, N.C. 1930; 50–51; Jean H. Baker, *Affairs of Party: The Political Culture of Northern Democrats in the Mid-Nineteenth Century*, Ithaca, N.Y. 1983, 217.

2. Rice, *Monarchs*, 12; James H. Dorman, 'The Strange Career of Jim Crow Rice', *Journal of Social History* 3 (Winter 1970): 109; Hans Nathan, *Dan Emmett and the Rise of Negro Minstrelsy*, Norman, Okla. 1962, 104.

3. William J. Mahar, '"Backside Albany" and Early Blackface Minstrelsy: A Contextual Study of America's First Blackface Song', *American Music* 6 (Spring 1988): 2–3; Russel Sanjek, *American Popular Music and Its Business: The First Four Hundred Years*, New York 1988, 2:161.

4. See Rice, *Monarchs*, and, for a sense of lineage, Olive Logan, 'The Ancestry of Brudder Bones', *Harper's New Monthly Magazine* 58 (1879): 687–98.

5. Wittke, *Tambo and Bones*, 58–65; Robert C. Toll, *Blacking Up: The Minstrel Show in Nineteenth-Century America*, New York 1974, 10–13; Vera B. Lawrence, ed., *Strong on Music: The New York Music Scene in the Days of George Templeton Strong, 1836–1875*, New York 1988, 2:372.

6. Alexander Saxton, 'Blackface Minstrelsy and Jacksonian Ideology', *American Quarterly* 27 (March 1975): 9–11, and *The Rise and Fall of the White Republic: Class Politics and Mass Culture in Nineteenth-Century America*, London 1990. Saxton regards the most important early minstrel innovators as of middle class background, however. See 'Blackface Minstrelsy', 6.

7. William F. Stowe and David Grimsted, 'White–Black Humor', *Journal of Ethnic Studies* 3 (Summer 1975): 81; Sanjek, *Popular Music*, 172; John Lair, *Songs Lincoln Loved*, New York 1954, 39–52; Daily Paskman, *'Gentlemen, Be Seated!' : A Parade of the American Minstrels*, New York 1976, 14.

8. Lewis A. Erenberg, *Steppin' Out: New York Nightlife and the Transformation of American Culture, 1890–1930*, Chicago 1981, 73.

9. George Lipsitz, *Time Passages: Collective Memory and American Popular Culture*, Minneapolis, Minn. 1990, 64.

10. For the debate on whether African-American influence on minstrels was pronounced, see Joseph Boskin, *Sambo: The Rise and Demise of an American Jester*, New York 1986, 80–81; Constance Rourke, *American Humor: A Study of the National Character*, New York 1961, 263–69; Mahar, '"Backside Albany"', esp. 10–13; Toll, *Blacking Up*, 40–51; Sanjek, *Popular Music*, 173; Howard L. Sacks and Judith R. Sacks, 'Way Up North in Dixie: Black–White Musical Entertainment in Knox County, Ohio', *American Music* 6 (Winter 1988): 418–27; Sam Dennison, *Scandalize My Name: Black Imagery in American Popular Music*, New York 1982; Alan W.C. Green, '"Jim Crow", "Zip Coon": The Northern Origins of Negro Minstrelsy', *Massachusetts Review* 11 (1970): 385–97. With the exception of Dennison, most recent accounts tend to credit to at least some degree Rourke's contention that interaction with Blacks shaped minstrel music. The most extreme recent statement of this viewpoint is Robert Cantwell, *Bluegrass Breakdown: The Making of the Old Southern Sound*, Urbana, Ill. 1984, 259–64. Clearly, 'authenticity' was claimed and prized by minstrels. See Rice, *Monarchs*, 87; Toll, *Blacking Up*, 42, 46 and 50.

11. *Christy's New Songster*, New York 1863?, 75; *Nigger Melodies*, St. Louis n.d., 113–14. See also Frank Dumont, *Burnt Cork; or, The Amateur Minstrel*, New York 1881, 15–16.

12. Lawrence, *Strong on Music*, 555; Robert B. Winans, 'Early Minstrel Show Music, 1843–1852', in Glenn Loney, ed., *Music Theatre in America*, Westport, Conn. 1984, 80; Toll, *Blacking Up*, 32.

13. Paskman, *'Gentlemen, Be Seated!'* 28–30; 'Jordan Is a Hard Road to Travel', New York 1854, sheet music. It is worth noting that several minstrel songs directly burlesque spirituals.

14. W.E.B. Du Bois, *The Souls of Black Folk*, Chicago 1903, 251; Rourke, *American Humor*, 273; Lawrence W. Levine, *Highbrow/Lowbrow: The Emergence of Cultural Hierarchy in America*, Cambridge, Mass. 1988, 237.

15. Rice, *Monarchs*, 115; Winans 'Minstrel Show Music', 80; Lawrence, *Strong on Music*, 344–492, esp. 345; for typical playbills and sheet music covers, see *Christy's Melodies as Composed and Sung by Them*, New York n.d., in Newberry Library; Toll, *Blacking Up*, 39.

16. *Christy's New Songster*, 95; Nelse Seymour, ed., *Nelse Seymour's Big Shoe Songster*, New York 1863, 61–62; *The Negro Singer's Own Book*, Philadelphia and New York n.d., 132; Elias Howe, ed., *Howe's 100 Ethiopian Songs*, Boston and Chicago 1877, 222–23; *The Ethiopian Seranader's Own Book*, Philadelphia 1857, 107.

17. Rice, *Monarchs*, 185; see also Logan, 'Brudder Bones', 688.

18. Baker, *Affairs of Party*, 219.

19. See 'Irish Mornings and African Days on the Old Minstrel Stage: An Interview with Leni Sloan', *Callahan's Irish Quarterly* 2 (Spring 1982): 49–53. See also Rice, *Monarchs*, 38, 39, 54, 79, 123, 131, 144, 151 on Irish stars.

20. Paskman, *'Gentlemen, Be Seated!'*, 16; Winans, 'Minstrel Show Music', 72 and 95; *Christy's Bones and Banjo Melodist*, New York 1864, 57; Wittke, *Tambo and Bones*, 121 and 200; Rice, *Monarchs*, 23.

21. Rice, *Monarchs*, 185; *The Ethiopian Glee Book*, Boston 1849, 89.

22. Winans, 'Minstrel Show Music', 228; Lawrence, *Strong on Music*, 228.

23. Green, 'Northern Origins', 395; G.W.F. Hegel, *The Phenomenology of Mind*, J.B. Baillie trans., London 1910, 1:175–88.

24. Dumont, *Burnt Cork*, 55–59 and the advertisement for *Bones* in back; Wittke, *Tambo and Bones*, 121; Rice, *Monarchs*, 185; Toll, *Blacking Up*, 173–80; Gary D. Engle, ed., *This Grotesque Essence: Plays from the Minstrel Stage*, Baton Rouge, La. 1978, xxvii; Lair, *Songs Lincoln Loved*, 44; *Handy Andy's Budget of Songs*, n.p. n.d., 67; Winans, 'Minstrel Show Music', 95 and the shrewd comments on minstrelsy in Amiri Baraka [Leroi Jones], *Blues People: Negro Music in White America*, New York 1970, 83–84.

25. Sandor Ferenczi, 'The Origins of Interest in Money', in Richard C. Badger, ed., *Contributions to Psychoanalysis*, Boston 1916; Otto Fenichel, 'The Drive to Amass Wealth', *Psychoanalytical Quarterly* 7 (1938).

26. Rice, *Monarchs*, 23; *DA*, 2:1120; Wittke, *Tambo and Bones*, 60.

27. Herman Melville, *The Confidence-Man: His Masquerade*, New York 1971 (1857), 7–14.

28. Paskman, *'Gentlemen, Be Seated!'*, 17–18; Lawrence, *Strong on Music*, 554; Ralph Keeler, 'Three Years as a Negro Minstrel', *Atlantic Monthly* 24 (July 1869): 75.

29. Wittke, *Tambo and Bones*, 19.

30. *Negro Singer's Own Book*, 196, with a similar joke on p. 197. See also Keeler, 'Three Years', 76, on respectability. Erenberg, *Steppin' Out*, 18–20, presents a similar analysis.

31. 'Interview with Leni Sloan', 49–53.

32. Saxton, 'Blackface Minstrelsy', 28 and 12; *The Ethiopian Glee Book: Containing the Songs Sung by the New Orleans Serenaders*, Boston 1850, 182.

33. Saxton, 'Blackface Minstrelsy', 13–14; Robert W. Johannsen, *To the Halls of the Montezumas: The Mexican War in the American Imagination*, New York 1985, 230; Rourke, *American Humor*, 272.

34. Lawrence, *Strong on Music*, 232–33 and 286.

35. William R. Taylor, *Cavalier and Yankee: The Old South and American National Character*, New York 1961.

36. W.E.B. Du Bois, *The Gift of Black Folk: The Negroes in the Making of America*, New York 1970, 29–30; Eugene D. Genovese, *Roll, Jordan, Roll: The World the Slaves Made*, New York 1975, 285–324.

37. Seymour, *Big Shoe Songster*, 8; *Christy's Negro Songster*, 10–11; Dumont, *Burnt Cork*, 7; *Christy's Bones and Banjo Melodist*, 28–29; *Nigger Melodies*, 34; *Ethiopian Glee Book: Containing the Songs Sung by the New Orleans Serenaders*, 198; *Buckley's Song Book for the Parlor*, New York 1855, 25. For an important exception, see *Ethiopian Glee Book* (1849 version), 119.

38. *Handy Andy's Budget of Songs*, 29.

39. It is worth noting in this connection that just after the Civil War popular use of the term *nigger night* to mean Saturday night is recorded, and that the term was said in the North to have been connected with the custom of courting on Saturday evenings. See John S.

Farmer, *Americanisms – Old and New*, London 1889, 391; Wittke, *Tambo and Bones*, 124; John B. Jentz, 'Artisans, Evangelicals and the City: A Social History of Abolition and Labor Reform in New York City' (Ph.D. dissertation, City University of New York, 1977), 248; Erenberg, *Steppin' Out*, 18; Christine Stansell, *City of Women: Sex and Class in New York, 1789–1860*, New York 1986, 1–62 and 76–102.

40. *Buckley's Parlor Songster*, 58; Stansell, *City of Women*, esp. 96–97 and 83–86 and n41 below.

41. Stephen Nissenbaum, *Sex, Diet and Debility in Jacksonian America: Sylvester Graham and Health Reform*, Chicago 1980, 143–45 and passim. Generally, see John D'Emilio and Estelle B. Freedman, *Intimate Matters: A History of Sexuality in America*, New York 1988, 39–170.

42. Keeler, 'Three Years', 77; Paskman, *'Gentlemen, Be Seated!'*, 85; Dumont, *Burnt Cork*, 63; *Ethiopian Glee Book*, 184–85; Howe, *100 Ethiopian Songs*, 201; Saxton, 'Blackface Minstrelsy', 12; Wittke, *Tambo and Bones*, 180; Newman I. White, 'The White Man in the Woodpile', *American Speech* 4 (February 1929): 212; *Ethiopian Glee Book* (1849 version), 34; Winans, 'Minstrel Show Music', 91. Lawrence, *Strong on Music*, 286, gives an account of an odd 1844 performance using women, noting it as the first to do so.

43. Herman Melville, *Moby Dick; or, The Whale*, New York 1967 (1851), and George Lippard, *The Quaker City; or, The Monks of Monks Hall*, New York 1970 (1845). See also David S. Reynolds, *Beneath the American Renaissance: The Subversive Imagination in the Age of Emerson and Melville*, New York 1988, 216–22. On the sexual content of abolitionist literature, see Ronald Walters, 'The Erotic South: Civilization and Sexuality in American Abolitionism, *American Quarterly* 25 (May 1973): 177–201.

44. Erenberg, *Steppin' Out*, 18–20; Wittke, *Tambo and Bones*, 124–25; Dorman, 'Shaping the Popular Image', 455; Paskman, *'Gentlemen, Be Seated!'*, 85.

45. Winans, 'Minstrel Show Music', 93; Marian Mair, 'Black Rhythm and British Reserve: Interpretations of Black Musicality in Racist Thought since 1750' (Ph.D. dissertation, University of London, 1987), 134.

46. Lawrence, *Strong on Music*, 556, n38.

47. Dumont, *Burnt Cork*, 6.

48. Dorman, 'Shaping the Popular Image', 455; Nancy M. Goslee, 'Slavery and Sexual Character: Questioning the Master Trope in Blake's *Daughters of Albion*, *ELH* 57 (Spring 1990): 123. On eros and sexuality, see Herbert Marcuse, *Eros and Civilization: A Philosophical Inquiry into Freud*, Boston 1954, 197–237, and *One-Dimensional Man: Studies in the Ideology of Advanced Industrial Society*, Boston 1964, 71–79.

49. Quoted in Wittke, *Tambo and Bones*, 54.

50. Wilentz, *Chants Democratic*, 259. See also Mikhail Bakhtin, *Rabelais and His World*, trans. Helene Iswolsky, Cambridge, Mass. 1968.

51. Dorman, 'Shaping the Popular Image', 455 and passim; Green, 'Northern Origins', 395.

52. Stowe and Grimsted, 'White–Black Humor', 80–81 and 83; Boskin, *Sambo*, 81.

53. Stowe and Grimsted, 'White–Black Humor', 78–96, esp. 89; Wilentz, *Chants Democratic*, 259.

54. Toll, *Blacking Up*, 195; Baker, *Affairs of Party*, 218. For exceptions, see Toll, *Blacking Up*, 195; Rice, *Monarchs*, 42 and 48; Lawrence, *Strong on Music*, 555.

55. *The Negro Forget-Me-Not Songster*, Baltimore n.d., 11–12. For the range of portrayals of slavery, see Saxton, 'Blackface Minstrelsy', 18–21; William L. Van Deburg, *Slavery and Race in American Popular Culture*, Madison, Wis. 1984, 39–48; Toll, *Blacking Up*, 73–97; Baker, *Affairs of Party*, 229–31; Stowe and Grimsted, 'White–Black Humor', 89–96. See also *Negro's Own Book*, 336, and Gumbo Chaff, ed., *The Ethiopian Glee Book: A Collection of Popular Negro Melodies*, Boston 1848, 2, on 'bobulashun' . On returning to slavery, see J. Wade, ed., *Christy's Minstrels' New Songs with Choruses*, London n.d., 17; *Christy's Negro Songster*, New York 1855, 15.

56. Van Deburg, *Slavery and Race*, 46–48.

57. See Chapter 8 and Baker, *Affairs of Party*, 231–38; Toll, *Blacking Up*, 104–28; Saxton,

'Blackface Minstrelsy', 22; Wittke, *Tambo and Bones*, 191–92; Seymour, *Big Shoe Songster*, 27–28.

58. Saxton, 'Blackface Minstrelsy', 27; *Ethiopian Glee Book*, 186; Anna C. Mowatt, 'Fashion; or, Life in New York,' in David Grimsted, ed., *Notions of the Americans, 1820–1860*, New York 1970, 171–72; *Handy Andy's Budget of Songs*, 5.

59. Philip S. Foner, *Business and Slavery: The New York Merchants and the Irrepressible Conflict*, Chapel Hill, N.C. 1941.

60. Baker, *Affairs of Party*, 251 and 258; Toll, *Blacking Up*, 162; Howe, *100 Ethiopian Songs*, 222; *Minstrel Gags and End Men's Handbook*, Upper Saddle River, N.J. 1969 reprint, 18 and 102; Wittke, *Tambo and Bones*, 168–71.

61. Toll, *Blacking Up*, 162–63; Dumont, *Burnt Cork*, 46–49; Stowe and Grimsted, 'White–Black Humor', 89.

62. Seymour, *Big Shoe Songster*, 20–21.

63. Toll, *Blacking Up*, 185 and 180–87 passim; Baker, *Affairs of Party*, 234; Saxton, 'Blackface Minstrelsy', 21.

64. Wittke, *Tambo and Bones*, 22; Lawrence, *Strong on Music*, 555.

65. Toll, *Blacking Up*, 162 and 182; *Minstrel Gags*, 18 and 102.

66. Stowe and Grimsted, 'White–Black Humor', 83.

67. Engle, *This Grotesque Essence*, xxvii; *Negro Singer's Own Book*, 63. The fullest study remains Ray B. Browne, 'Shakespeare in American Vaudeville and Negro Minstrelsy', *American Quarterly* 12 (Fall 1960): 374–91, esp. 376. See also Charles Haywood, 'Negro Minstrelsy and Shakespearean Burlesque', in Bruce Jackson, ed., *Folklore and Society*, Hatboro, Penn. 1966, 77–92.

68. Levine, *Highbrow/Lowbrow*, 1988, 4, 15 and passim.

69. David Grimsted, *Melodrama Unveiled: American Theater and Culture, 1800–1850*, Chicago 1968, 239–40; Levine, *Highbrow/Lowbrow*, 15.

70. Browne, 'Shakespeare', 377 and 380–81; Seymour, *Big Shoe Songster*, 41–42; Christy, *Christy's Bones and Banjo Melodist*, 7; Marshall and Stock, *Aldridge*, 164, 167 and 258–59.

71. Wittke, *Tambo and Bones*, 210; Calvin C. Hernton, *Sex and Racism in America*, New York 1965, 112.

7

Irish-American Workers and White Racial Formation in the Antebellum United States

Low-browed and *savage, grovelling* and *bestial, lazy* and *wild, simian* and *sensual* – such were the adjectives used by many native-born Americans to describe the Catholic Irish 'race' in the years before the Civil War.[1] The striking similarity of this litany of insults to the list of traits ascribed to antebellum Blacks hardly requires comment. Sometimes Black/Irish connections were made explicitly. In antebellum Philadelphia, according to one account, 'to be called an "Irishman" had come to be nearly as great an insult as to be called a "nigger".' George Templeton Strong, a Whig patrician diarist living in New York City, considered Irish workmen at his home to have had 'prehensile paws' rather than hands. He denounced the 'Celtic beast', while maintaining that 'Southern Cuffee seems of a higher social grade than Northern Paddy.'[2] Nativist folk wisdom held that an Irishman was a 'nigger', inside out. But by no means did nativists, who more typically developed a 'moral' rather than a 'racial' critique of the Irish, corner the market on calling the whiteness of the Irish into question. A variety of writers, particularly ethnologists, praised Anglo-Saxon virtues as the bedrock of liberty and derided the 'Celtic race'.[3] Some suggested that the Irish were part of a separate caste or a 'dark' race, possibly originally African. Racial comparisons of Irish and Blacks were not infrequently flattering to the latter group.[4] The Census Bureau regularly collected statistics on the nation's 'native' and 'foreign' populations, but kept the Irish distinct from even the latter group. Political cartoonists played on the racial ambiguity of the Irish by making their stock 'Paddy' charac-

133

ter resemble nothing so much as an ape.[5] In short, it was by no means clear that the Irish were white.

There were good reasons – environmental and historical, not biological – for comparing African-Americans and the Irish. The two groups often lived side by side in the teeming slums of American cities of the 1830s. They both did America's hard work, especially in domestic service and the transportation industry. Both groups were poor and often vilified. Both had experienced oppression and been wrenched from a homeland.[6] Many Northern free Blacks who lived alongside Irish-Americans not only knew that their families had been torn from Africa by the slave trade but had also themselves experienced the profound loneliness, mixed with joy, that Frederick Douglass described as the result of escaping North from slavery, leaving loved ones behind. Longing thus characterized both the Northern Black and Irish-American populations, and members of neither group were likely return home again. When Douglass toured Ireland during the famine of 1845–46 he heard in the 'wailing notes' of Irish songs echoes of the 'wild notes' of the sorrowful songs he had heard in slavery and was 'much affected'.[7] In 1829, Blacks and Irish were the co-victims of a Boston 'race' riot.[8]

Shared oppression need not generate solidarity but neither must it necessarily breed contempt of one oppressed group for the other. For some time there were strong signs that the Irish might not fully embrace white supremacy. In cities like Worcester and Philadelphia, Blacks and Irish lived near each other without significant friction into the early 1830s.[9] They often celebrated and socialized together, swapping musical traditions and dance steps. Even as late as the immediate post–Civil War years Lafcadio Hearn described Black and Irish levee workers in Cincinnati as sharing a storehouse of jokes and tales, of jigs and reels and even of dialect words and phrases. Love and sex between Black men and Irish women were not uncommon.[10] In the 1834 anti-Black, antiabolitionist New York City riots, Irish militiamen helped to restore order. Indeed, the antiabolition riots of the 1830s generally drew little Irish participation.[11]

Most promisingly, abolitionists noted little popular racism, and much sympathy for the plight of the slave, in Ireland. In 1842, 70,000 Irish in Ireland signed an antislavery address and petition, which called on Irish-Americans to '*cling by the abolitionists*' in seeking not just the end of slavery but of racial discrimination as well. The address advised: 'Irishmen and Irishwomen! treat the colored people as your equals, as brethren.'[12] Though much abolition agitation in Ireland was initiated by the Dublin Quakers, the most celebrated Irish abolitionist was Daniel O'Connell, who also led the massive Repeal campaign for Irish freedom through an end to union with Britain. Called 'The Liberator', O'Connell sponsored the 1842 petition knowing that his words would alienate some Irish-Americans and cut financial contributions to the Repeal struggle. Nonetheless, the very firmness of the politically sophisticated O'Connell's stance on Irish America and abolition suggests that he was optimistic that many in the US would ultimately stand with him.[13] Another of Ireland's greatest mass leaders, the temperance organizer Father Theobald Mathew, joined O'Connell in sponsoring the petition drive.[14] Men who knew a great deal about how to move large numbers of Irish people believed it quite possible that Irish-Americans, whom O'Connell saw as having much in common with all colonized people, might become critics of white supremacy.[15]

The radical abolitionist followers of William Lloyd Garrison – including two of the Garrisonians most concerned with the white working class, Wendell Phillips and John A. Collins[16] – busily organized for unity between the supporters of the 'repeal' of British colonialism and the 'repeal' of American slavery. The Garrisonians could claim a strong record of supporting Irish nationalism and rebuking American nativism, and their campaign began auspiciously when an overflow crowd of more than five thousand packed Boston's Faneuil Hall to receive the petition and to pass resolutions for Black and Irish freedom.[17]

But it quickly became apparent that the Irish 'peasants' who heartily applauded at Faneuil Hall were atypical of Irish-American opinion on slavery and race. The meeting had hardly occurred when a mob of Philadelphia Irish attacked Blacks gathering to celebrate West Indian emancipation – a cause dear to O'Connell – near the hall from which Blacks promoted temperance, Father Mathew's passion.[18] By 1843, the British Owenite traveller John Finch would report to London readers the 'curious fact' that 'the democratic party and particularly the poorer class of Irish emigrants, are greater enemies to the negro population ... than any portion of the population in the free states.'[19]

O'Connell's pleas and threats achieved nothing. Irish-American and Catholic newspapers, some of which had originally argued that the petition and address were fakes, soon began to attack O'Connell. They portrayed him as at best misinformed and at worst a meddler who associated with religious skeptics who threatened the unity of the United States. Irish-American contributions to the Repeal campaign were jeopardized, but O'Connell refused to move from his outspoken abolitionism, though he did distance himself somewhat from the religious unorthodoxy of some of the Garrisonians. Even O'Connell's pointed threat to read proslavery Irish-Americans out of the nationalist struggle failed to rally his erstwhile followers to the banner of abolition. 'Dare countenance the system of slavery', he warned, and 'we will recognize you as Irishmen no more.'[20]

But Irish-Americans had already made their reply: they had refused to recognize O'Connell. An important and typical Irish-American answer to O'Connell, written by miners in New York, answered his call with a sharp denial that Blacks were 'brethren' of Irish-Americans and an unequivocal statement of their loyalty as Americans who were full 'CITIZENS of this great and glorious republic'. The statement condemned O'Connell's address as the interference of an outsider, and declared that no cooperation with abolitionists would be forthcoming. From 1843 until 1854, Garrisonians and O'Connell's followers separately pushed unsuccessfully against the 'proslavery' position of Irish-Americans.[21] They failed, succeeding only in weakening Repeal forces in both Ireland and the United States. When Father Mathew toured America in 1849, he rejected any cooperation with abolitionists, contenting himself with fighting 'slavery' to alcohol.[22]

Nor did the tremendous influx of desperate Irish emigrants fleeing the results of famine after 1845 produce significant amelioration in Irish-American attitudes toward Blacks. If the emigrants had antislavery and antiracist convictions in Ireland – and even there abolition fell on hard times after O'Connell's death in 1847 – they did not express those convictions in the New World. Irish-Americans instead treasured their whiteness, as entitling them to both political rights and to jobs. They solidly voted for proslavery Democrats and opposed abolition as 'niggerology'.[23] Astonishingly, for a group that easily furnished more immigrants to the United States than any other between 1828 and 1854, the Irish in New York City reportedly went to the polls in 1850 shouting not only 'Down with the Nagurs!' but also 'Let them go back to Africa, where they belong.' Similarly, Irish immigrants became leaders of anti-Chinese forces in California.[24] Even before taking a leading role in the unprecedentedly murderous attacks on Blacks during the 1863 Draft Riot in New York City, Irishmen had developed a terrible record of mobbing free Blacks on and off the job – so much so that Blacks called the brickbats often hurled at them 'Irish confetti'.[25] In 1865 the British worker James D. Burn observed, 'As a general rule, the people in the North have a lively feeling of dislike to men of colour, but it is in the Irish residents that they have, and will continue to have, their most formidable enemies: between these two races there can exist no bond of union except such as exists between the hind [deer] and the panther.'[26]

Having refused to take the path that O'Connell had charted, Irish-Americans went far in the other direction. Instead of seeing their struggles as bound up with those of colonized and colored people around the world, they came to see their struggles as against such people. Frederick Douglass, the Black abolitionist whose own quest for freedom had been substantially aided by the advice of a 'good Irishman' on Baltimore's wharves in the 1830s, could only wonder 'why a people who so nobly loved and cherished the thought of liberty at home in Ireland could become, willingly, the oppressors of another race here.' Or again he asked how a people 'so relentlessly persecuted and oppressed on account of race and religion' could take the lead among Americans in carrying 'prejudice against color to a point ... extreme and dangerous.'[27]

The making of the Irish worker into a white worker was thus a two-sided process. On the one hand, much to the chagrin of George Templeton Strong, Irish immigrants won acceptance as whites among the larger American population. On the other hand, much to the chagrin of Frederick Douglass and Daniel O'Connell, the Irish themselves came to insist on their own whiteness and on white supremacy. The success of the Irish in being recognized as white resulted largely from the political power of Irish and other immigrant voters. The imperative to define themselves as white came but from the particular 'public and psychological wages' whiteness offered to a desperate rural and often preindustrial Irish population coming to labor in industrializing American cities.

Ireland and the Origins of Irish-American Whiteness

'It was not in Ireland', thundered Daniel O'Connell to proslavery and white supremacist Irish-Americans, 'you learned this cruelty.'[28] He was right. However much the record of abolitionism in Ireland was exaggerated by American abolitionists and subsequent historians – the movement there was short-lived and much connected to O'Connell's own charisma and commitments[29] – the Irish were not race-conscious in the sense that Irish-Americans would be. There was some noting of regional color differences in Ireland though most residents had seen no one of African descent. Ireland probably shared in the longstanding Western European tradition of associating blackness with evil. There is some evidence of folk belief that the devil could turn people black, or turn people inside-out, thus making them black.[30] Irish-American folklore, down to the recent past, includes stories of ancestors who jumped off the boat in horror on arriving in America and seeing a Black person for the first time, thinking it was the devil. But the very fact that these stories survive so tenaciously in the United States should warn us that they may speak as much of the attitudes of later generations of Irish-Americans as of arriving Irish emigrants. The evil 'race' that plagued the Irish Catholic imagination was white and British, not Black and African.[31]

Some accounts have suggested that Ireland nonetheless set the stage for Irish-American racism in more indirect ways. Abolitionists complained, with good reason, that the Catholic Church hierarchy offered at best highly muted criticisms, and at worst racist defenses, of slavery. They charged that the Irish were particularly loyal to priests. Modern scholarship has even suggested that religious obedience left the Irish in a state of 'moral childhood'.[32] Aside from reminding us of the proximity of anti-Black and anti-Irish stereotypes, such a view fits poorly with the historical facts. The 'devotional revolution' in Ireland took hold rather late, after the onset of the potato famine, and after much emigration had occurred. Between 1815 and 1844, Catholic identity in Ireland had at least as much political as devotional content, and the mass nationalist politics in which Catholics participated had strong secular elements. Many Irish Catholics in the United States, even as late as 1855, were of the 'anonymous' (or nonpracticing) kind traditionally typical of south and west Ireland. They were little exposed to priestly influence on race relations or other matters, though their hatred of Protestant revivalists may have predisposed them to oppose abolitionism.[33]

More cogent, but still problematic, is the argument that the Irish Catholic past imparted so fierce a hatred of things British that it was natural, and even nationalist, for Irish-Americans to oppose abolitionism for its British connections. The ease with which Irish-Americans denounced 'Benedict Arnold' Garrison as a co-conspirator of the British supports this view, as does their readiness to accept the argument that blame for American slavery lay with the British, who had forced the institution onto the American colonies.[34] However, at least during the period of O'Connell's abolitionist influence, there were alternative nationalist positions that as strongly indicted Britain for creating slavery through its colonialism, but also claimed that much of the credit for British emancipation went to Irish legislators in Britain's Parliament and connected the plight of the Irish with that of other victims of colonialism, including slaves. In denouncing O'Connell, his Irish-American critics somewhat distanced themselves from the nationalist movement, standing as Americans who resented the influence of 'foreigners' on their affairs. The emphasis of Irish-Americans on the common whiteness they wished to be recognized as sharing with other Americans may, as Frank Murray argues, have sped their assimilation.[35]

What the Irish background surely did impart was a sad and particular context, enshrouded in both gloom and mist, in which Irish-American whiteness took shape. By the early 1830s, when the annual immigration of Irish Catholics passed that of Irish Protestants, agricultural misery, landlordism and dislocation in the handicrafts in Ireland had combined to produce an increasingly poverty-stricken stream of Catholic migrants. Migrants in the decade and a half before the Great Famine began in 1845 tended to have enough resources to exercise a limited but real choice about where to settle and what kind of work to take. Some achieved 'independence' from laboring for others, the goal that had animated their migration. Evidence suggests, according to Kerby Miller, that 'a substantial minority' of those migrating managed to set up as farmers. Local studies show substantially greater opportunities to become skilled workers for those arriving in prefamine years than for migrants coming after the famine. But hard and usually unskilled wage work was nonetheless the typical experience of the prefamine Irish Catholic immigrant, with the group being far poorer, less skilled and more urban compared with native-born Americans or with other European immigrants.[36]

The Great Famine turned these tendencies almost into iron rules. Between 1845 and 1855, Ireland lost over two million emigrants – a quarter of her population – with famine-associated deaths taking over a million more. The evictions of 1849, 1850 and 1851 alone forced a million Irish from their homes. Roughly three in four Catholic Irish famine-era migrants came to the United States, now seeking only survival. Without savings, they had small choice in where to settle. Without marketable skills, they served, carried and hauled when they could get work and sometimes held 'skilled' but low-paying jobs as outworkers or apprentices. The most decidedly preindustrial and little Anglicized parts of Ireland – the South and the isolated West – came to furnish many migrants. These were often Gaelic speakers who had previously resisted emigration as a kind of *deoraí*, or 'banishment', but now left Ireland dolefully, if perhaps also with an air of release. Although the poorest famine and eviction victims went to Britain, or died, the Irish emigrants to the US were nonetheless destitute and often nearly despairing. Recently peasants, now overwhelmingly laborers and servants, they settled in slums and shantytowns in cities in the United States, where large nativist political movements resented their religion, their poverty and their presence.[37] They often came with only their weakened bodies and their memories, the latter horribly bitter but capable of being kindled into a deeply nostalgic glow. Their numbers afforded them the political possibility to become white. The desperate nature of their labor and their longings ensured that they would embrace that possibility to the fullest.

Irish Votes, Democratic Votes and White Votes

Coming into American society at or near the bottom, the Catholic Irish sorely needed allies, even protectors. They quickly found them in two institutions that did not question their whiteness: the Catholic Church and the Democratic party. Although the former proved more open to promoting Irishmen to positions of power – most bishops in the United States were Irish by the 1850s – the Democratic party was far more powerful as a national institution and more consistently proslavery and white supremacist in its outlook. The church did reflect the racial attitudes of its members, with Kentucky Catholic newspapers carrying advertisements for the return of runaway slaves. New York church publications hinted at, and then spelled out, the view that the 'negro is what the creator made him – not a rudimentary Caucasian, not a human in the process of development but a negro.' The official Catholic paper in New York City meanwhile advised that emancipated slaves moving North be 'driven out, imprisoned or exterminated'. However, these strong and unpalatable Catholic stances, which existed alongside softer calls for amelioration of the slave's plight, at most reproduced existing white supremacist attitudes without challenging them.[38] The Democratic party did more.

Jean Baker, a leading historian of the Democrats between the Age of Jackson and the Civil War, has acutely observed that the Democratic party reinvented whiteness in a manner that 'refurbished their party's traditional links to the People and offered political democracy and an inclusive patriotism to white male Americans.' This sense of white unity and white entitlement – of white 'blood' – served to bind together the Democratic slaveholders and the masses of nonslaveholding whites in the South. It further connected the Southern and Northern wings of the Democracy.[39] But less noticed by scholars has been the way in which an emphasis on a common whiteness smoothed over divisions in the Democratic ranks within mainly Northern cities by emphasizing that immigrants from Europe, and particularly from Ireland, were white and thus unequivocally entitled to equal rights. In areas with virtually no Black voters, the Democrats created a 'white vote'.

From the earliest days of the American republic, Irish immigration to the United States had caused political division. The 'wild Irish', a term that invoked images of both 'semi-savage' Catholics and political rebels who were sometimes Protestants, excited particular concern among conservative Federalist politicians. Defense of immigration by the Jeffersonian Democrats helped to create a lasting preference for the

Democracy among newcomers, though party lines blurred considerably.[40] In any case, how immigrants voted was of small importance nationally through 1830, when only one ballot in thirty could come from the foreign-born. By 1845, that figure was to rise to one in seven, with the Great Famine exodus still to produce, between 1845 and 1854, by far the greatest decade of immigration in antebellum American history. Immigration largely meant Irish immigration, with between 43 percent and 47 percent of migrants each year between 1820 and 1855 coming from Ireland.[41]

By the early 1830s, the pattern of a strong Catholic Irish identification with the Democratic party, and with Andrew Jackson specifically, had strongly taken hold in urban centers like New York City. Although the existing urban Democratic political machines took time to inch away from the suspicion of immigrants felt by many of their artisan followers, Irish Catholics were welcomed as voters, party members and political muscle, though not typically as officeholders, by Democrats before the Civil War.[42] The Catholic Irish, the immigrant group most exposed to nativist opposition, accepted protection from Democrats. Lacking a nationalist tradition of agitation for land redistribution in Ireland, too poor to move West and perhaps soured on farm life after the famine, the Catholic Irish were particularly immune to late antebellum Free Soil criticisms of Democratic opposition to homestead laws. Democrats and Irish-American Catholics entered into a lasting marriage that gave birth to new ideologies stressing the importance of whiteness.[43]

From the 1830s, Democrats appreciated the ways in which the idea that all Blacks were unfit for civic participation could be transmuted into the notion that all whites were so fit. Pennsylvania Democrats, for example, solidified white unity by initiating the movement to codify the disfranchisement of the state's Blacks via constitutional amendment. Conflict with Mexico, and to some extent the rise of Chinese immigration, made it possible in the 1840s and 1850s for leading Democrats to develop racial schemes unequivocally gathering all European settlers together as whites against the 'colored' races. At a time when most Democratic theorists were coming to accept polygeniticist ideas regarding the separate creations of the 'black' and 'white' races, they were also defining 'white' in such a way as to include more surely the Irish and other immigrants.[44] Thus, James Buchanan contemptuously branded the Mexicans as a 'mongrel' race unfit for freedom but was glad that 'Americans' were a 'mixed' population of English, Scotch-Irish, French, Welsh, German and Irish ancestry. Missouri's Thomas Hart Benton wrote of a 'Celtic-Anglo-Saxon race', superior to, in descending order, the yellow, brown and red 'races'. Caleb Cushing aroused the Massachusetts legislature by announcing late in the 1850s that he admitted 'to an equality with me, sir, the white man, – my blood and race, whether he be a Saxon of England or a Celt of Ireland.' He added, 'but I do not admit as my equals either the red man of America, or the yellow man of Asia, or the black man of Africa.'[45]

The most celebrated racial exchanges of the nineteenth century remain Democratic leader Stephen A. Douglas's stalkings of Abraham Lincoln as a race-mixer during the 1858 Lincoln–Douglas debates. The debates came hard on the heels of the 1856 elections – the first in which the great mass of famine immigrants were voters – when national candidates had vied to best articulate the interests of the 'white man' by preventing 'white slavery'.[46] In those elections Know-Nothings threatened the Democracy by running, in Millard Fillmore, a trained artisan commanding substantial loyalty from native-born workingmen who feared immigrant culture and immigrant debasement of the crafts.[47] Douglas sought to make points among Illinois voters but also to speak to the needs of the Democracy as a national, and particularly Northern, party. He decided, in the words of a recent biographer, that 'Negro inequality made up the platform on which he would stand in the ensuing years.'[48] Mixing sex and politics, Douglas spoke for 'preserving not only the purity of [white] blood but the purity of the government from any . . . amalgamation with inferior races.' He added, drawing lessons from the Mexican conflict, that the results of 'this amalgamation of white men, and Indians and negroes, we have seen in Mexico, in Central America, in South America and in all the Spanish-American 'states.' Douglas promised that Mexican War veterans could back his claims regarding the effects of racial 'impurity'. He further protested that Lincoln's belief that the Declaration of Independence applied to people of color would make the debate's listeners, who sometimes chanted 'White men, White men' during his speeches, the equals of Fiji Islanders.[49] Significantly, he meanwhile also argued that Americans' ancestors were 'not all of English origin' but were also of Scotch, Irish, German, French, and Norman descent, indeed 'from every branch of the Caucasian race.'[50]

Douglas spoke in the highly racialized political language increasingly common among Democrats, and to some extent among their opponents. Since Blacks wielded virtually no political power, to mobilize the white vote it was useful to declare white opponents and their ideas to be Black. Discussing Republican support in Illinois, Douglas found that 'the creed is pretty black in the north end of the State; about the center it is pretty good mulatto and it is almost white when you get down to Egypt [Southern Illinois].'[51] The Republicans became, in Democratic propaganda and especially in appeals from or directed at Catholic Irish Democrats, the 'Black Republicans'. Irish Democrats often scored the perfidy of the German 'Black Dutch' or of 'red' Germans in league with 'Black' Republicans.[52]

Lincoln's studied replies to Douglas's race-baiting stressed that a belief in natural rights applied to Blacks did not imply a desire to intermarry, that Republicans better protected the 'white man's' interests than Democrats did, and that slaveholders, not Republicans, practiced racial amalgamation. Other Republican propaganda was much uglier, branding the Democracy a 'nigger party' by virtue of its association with slavery and connecting its proslavery and pro-Irish policies. German opponents of Irish Democrats similarly cast doubts on the race of their adversaries.[53]

Reginald Horsman's careful study of American 'racial Anglo-Saxonism' shows that 'politicians of Irish or Scotch-Irish ancestry' were especially prominent in challenging ideas of Anglo-Saxon superiority and in arguing for the existence of a new and improved 'American race' of white men.[54] Catholic Irish immigrants were also the best consumers of Democratic appeals that equated 'white men' and 'workingmen'. As Dale T. Knobel observes in *Paddy and the Republic*, 'Irish-Americans were sure to be enthusiastic about any treatment of American nationality that stressed the relevance of 'race' while putting the Irish safely within the Anglo-Celtic racial majority.' The aptly named Democratic New York City *Caucasian* particularly won Irish-born readers to its view that defense of the 'white working class' during the Civil War was best carried forward by attacking abolition.[55]

Democratic paeans to whiteness must have seemed a godsend to Irish Catholics, especially amid hardening anti-Irish attitudes after 1845. By the time of the famine, it could be argued – and was argued by Irish-Americans themselves – that longstanding British oppression had kept the Irish in political 'slavery' and brought utter economic dependency. Irish-Americans were deeply offended in the 1856 campaign when a remark by Buchanan implied that England had *not* made 'slaves' of the Irish. But to make this argument, and to compare Irish and African oppression, forfeited any claim of Irish-Americans to be qualified for freedom by republican criteria. Past and present, their history seemed to be one of degradation. As John Ashworth has perceptively put it, since Irish-Americans were in many cases as economically dependent as free Blacks, no 'empirical' case could be made that the immigrants had shown themselves fit for freedom, and Blacks by comparison had proven themselves unfit to be 'true Americans'.[56]

Nativists were somewhat constrained by the historic American acceptance of Irish immigrants, by the cultural proximity of Irish Catholics with clearly assimilable Celtic Protestants from Ireland, Scotland and Wales, and by the ease with which Irish Catholics could pass as mainstream 'white' Americans. Anti-immigrant politicians therefore generally did not dwell on the popular ethnological theories that identified the Celts as genetically inferior. They instead concentrated on Irish subservience to religious authority and Irish degradation, loosely arguing at times that the famine itself had helped produced an Irish 'race' incapable of freedom. Some unfavorably compared the Irish with free Blacks, not so much as racial types as in terms of their alleged records of fitness to function as republican citizens.[57] Black leaders like Frederick Douglass generally avoided anti-Catholicism but charged that the ignorance and intemperance of the Irish and their roles as 'flunkeys to our gentry' made it certain that Irish Catholics were not more desirable than Blacks as citizens of a republic.[58]

The Democratic emphasis on natural rights within a government 'made by the white men, for the benefit of the white man' appealed to Irish Catholics in large part because it cut off questions about their qualifications for citizenship.[59] Under other circumstances, Irish-American Catholics might not have accepted so keenly the 'association of nationality with blood – but not with ethnicity', which racially conflated them with the otherwise hated English. They might not have so readily embraced a view of 'American nationality that stressed the relevance of "race" while putting the Irish safely within an Anglo-Celtic racial majority.'[60] But within the constrained choices and high risks of antebellum American politics such a choice was quite logical. The ways in which the Irish competed for work and adjusted to industrial morality in America made it all but certain that they would adopt and extend the politics of white unity offered by the Democratic party.

'Slaving like a Nigger': Irish Jobs and Irish Whiteness

In 1856, Henry C. Brokmeyer, then a wage-earning immigrant German molder in St. Louis, wrote in his diary a question posed about one of his German-American friends: 'Why doesn't he learn ... a trade; and he wouldn't have to slave like a nigger?' Brokmeyer, who was to become not only independent of wage work but eventually lieutenant governor of Missouri, had picked up a pattern of usage common in American English since the 1830s.[61] Not only was *nigger work* synonymous with hard, drudging labor but to *nigger it* meant 'to do hard work', or 'to slave'.

144

'White niggers' were white workers in arduous unskilled jobs or in subservient positions.[62]

But not all European immigrants had the same prospects to 'learn a trade', let alone to acquire independence from 'slaving like a nigger', by owning a workshop or a farm. English and Scandinavian immigrants were especially likely to achieve such mobility, while the Irish and Germans faced most directly the question of how and whether their labor was different from 'slaving like a nigger'. But the Irish confronted the question much more starkly. Both before and after the famine, they were far more likely than the Germans to be without skills. The famine Irish infrequently achieved rural land ownership. Within large cities Irish-American males were skilled workers perhaps half as often as German-Americans, and were unskilled at least twice as often. Although frontier cities, perhaps attracting Irish migrants with more resources and choices, showed less difference between Irish and German occupational patterns, the Irish stayed at the bottom of white society.[63]

In larger Eastern cities the divergence was great. In Boston in 1850, according to Oscar Handlin, 22 percent of the German-born and 6 percent of the Catholic Irish-born worked in nonmanual jobs. 57 percent of the Germans were in skilled trades, as against 23 percent of the Irish. 47 percent of the Irish and only 12 percent of the Germans were unskilled. Handlin in fact argued that free Blacks were for a time both economically and socially more secure in late antebellum Boston than were the Irish. In New York City in 1855, Germans were about twice as likely to do nonmanual labor as the Irish, and the Irish were nearly five times as likely to be without skills. In Jersey City in 1860, over half of Catholic Irish-American workers, and only one German-American in eight, did unskilled labor.[64] In addition, many skilled and 'independent' Irish-Americans were only nominally or precariously so. Concentrated in declining artisanal crafts, often as outworkers or as highly exploited apprentices, Irish artisans and petty employers in some areas experienced significant downward mobility as they aged. Irish stevedores frequently descended into the ranks of employed longshoremen, and small Irish building trades contractors into the ranks of laborers, from year to year.[65]

The prominence of Irish workers, especially women, in jobs involving service in households became especially pronounced. Christine Stansell's work shows a dramatic 'Irishization' of such jobs, so that in New York City by 1850 three serving women in four were Irish-Americans. Faye Dudden's *Serving Women* details the same trends in a broader study. Travellers took note of the change as one that placed Irish Catholics in servile positions. Thomas Hamilton, writing in 1834, found that 'Domestic service ... is considered degrading by all [Americans] untainted with the curse of African descent.' He bet that Andrew Jackson could 'not find one of his constituents, who, for any amount of emolument, would consent to brush his coat.' The Scottish and British migrants quickly came to share this republican view, according to Hamilton. The Irish, he added, took servile jobs.[66]

With the coming of the Irish into dominance in household work, much of the *herrenvolk* republican practice of avoiding the term 'servant' for whites fell into disuse. From the Age of Jackson, reformers in New York City set out to reshape the behavior of often Irish 'domestic servants'. Thomas Hamilton's account echoed this usage and, as Dudden observes, even when the term *domestic* came to be used by itself, *servant* was implied. An 1859 traveller found that native-born Americans still avoided calling domestic workers of the same background servile names but reasoned, 'Let negroes be servants and, if not negroes, let Irishmen. ... ' 'Help', Dudden comments, 'were likely to deny the name of servant, while domestics usually had to accept that title.'[67]

Irish-American workers also suffered an association with servile labor by virtue of their heralded, and at least sometimes practiced, use as substitutes for slaves within the South. Gangs of Irish immigrants worked ditching and draining plantations, building levees and sometimes clearing land because of the danger of death to valuable slave property (and, as one account put it, to mules) in such pursuits. Frederick Law Olmsted's widely circulated accounts of the South quoted more than one Southerner who explained the use of Irish labor on the ground that 'niggers are worth too much to be risked here; if the Paddies are knocked overboard ... nobody loses anything.'[68]

Irish youths were also likely to be found in the depleted ranks of indentured servants from the early national period through the Civil War. In that position they were sometimes called 'Irish slaves' and more frequently 'bound boys'. The degraded status of apprentices was sometimes little distinguishable from indenture by the 1840s and was likewise increasingly an Irish preserve.[69] In New York City, Irish women comprised the largest group of prostitutes, or, as they were sometimes called in the 1850s, 'white slaves'.[70] Given all this, the tendency to call Irish workers 'Irish niggers' is hardly surprising.

Irish-Americans needed 'nigger work'. As the Southern historian U.B. Phillips put it, the dangerous jobs in which Irishmen substituted for slaves 'attracted those whose labor was their life; the risk repelled those whose labor was their capital.' The same might be said about indentured servitude, domestic service by married women, prostitution and other hard jobs for which Irish-Americans desperately competed. Irish-Americans could not simply say, as many other white Americans could, that Blacks were suited to menial or subservient jobs. They bitterly resented comments by some of the elite that Blacks made better servants. As Hasia Diner has remarked, even after the Civil War Irish anti-Chinese agitation was predicated in large part on the need to defend Irish domestic servant women from competition from Chinese males.[71]

Job competition has often been considered the key to Irish-American racism. From Albon Man to Bruce Laurie, historians have emphasized that Irish workers, especially on the docks and shipyards in cities like Cincinnati, Philadelphia, Baltimore, and above all New York City, fought to keep away Blacks as job competitors and as strikebreakers. Many such direct incidents of Irish violence to intimidate Black workers did occur, especially during the Civil War, and there is some justification for Laurie's view that in Philadelphia Irish gangs undertaking racist violence were exercising job control.[72] But to go from the fact that Irish workers really fought with Blacks over jobs on occasion to the proposition that Irish racism was really a cover for job competition is an economic determinist misstep that cuts off important parts of the past. Why, for example, when Irish Catholic immigrants said that they feared the 'amalgamation of labor' should historians hearken to their emphasis on labor and not to their emphasis on amalgamation?[73]

Moreover, to say that Irish-Americans acted as militant white supremacists because of job competition only invites the further question: why did they choose to stress competition with Black workers instead of with other whites? In 1844, Philadelphia Irish Catholics who mobbed Blacks to clear them from dockworking jobs had themselves recently been removed from handloom weaving jobs via concerted actions by Protestant weavers.[74] Why did they not mob the Protestants? In most cities, even when we consider only unskilled work, the Irish had far more German-American competitors than Black ones. Why was the animus against working with Blacks so much more intense than that of against working with Germans? Indeed, as Harold Brackman has argued, the main competitors of the Irish for unskilled work were other arriving Irish.[75] Why, given the strength of 'countyism' in Ireland and the patterns of intra-Irish factional fighting for canal-building jobs in the 1830s, did race and not time of emigration or county or even kin network become the identity around which Irish dockworkers in New York City could mobilize most effectively in the 1850s and during the Civil War?[76]

By and large, free Blacks were *not* effective competitors for jobs with the Irish. A small part of the urban labor force, negligible in most Midwestern cities, they at best held on to small niches in the economy and small shares of the population, while the immigrant population skyrocketed in the 1840s and 1850s. Discrimination of the 'No Irish Need Apply' sort hurt Irish opportunities. Sometimes, as in an 1853 New York *Herald* ad reading 'WOMAN WANTED – To do general housework … any country or color will answer except Irish. … ', such job prejudice was scarcely distinguishable from racial discrimination.[77] But what was most noteworthy to free Blacks at the time, and probably should be most noteworthy to historians, was the relative ease with which Irish-Americans 'elbowed out' African-Americans from unskilled jobs. By 1850, for example, there were about twenty-five times as many Irish-American serving women in New York City as Black serving women.[78]

One obvious reason that the Irish focused so much more forcefully on their sporadic labor competition with Blacks than on their protracted competition with other whites was that Blacks were so much less able to strike back, through either direct action or political action. As Kerby Miller has argued, Irish Catholic immigrants quickly learned that Blacks in America could be 'despised with impunity'. They also learned that free Blacks could be victimized with efficacy. Even the wholesale wartime atrocities against Blacks in the 1863 draft riots did not draw any opposition for assembled crowds nor vigorous prosecutions by municipal authorities. The attempt of Irish-American dockworkers in New York to expel *German* longshoremen from jobs under the banner of campaigning for an 'all-white waterfront' – perhaps the most interesting and vivid antebellum example of the social construction of race – reflects in part ill-fated Irish attempts to classify Germans as of a different color. But it also suggests how much easier it was for the Irish to defend jobs and rights as 'white' entitlements instead of as Irish ones.[79]

Had the Irish tried to assert a right to work because they were Irish, rather than because they were white, they would have provoked a fierce backlash from native-born artisans. As it was, in major cities North and South immigrants comprised a majority or near-majority in artisanal jobs by the 1850s. Despite their concentration in unskilled labor, Irish-Americans were also a large percentage of the artisan population and of the factory-based working class, especially in sweated and declining trades.[80] Native-born artisans often complained that Irish and German immigrants undermined craft traditions and sent wages down by underbidding 'American' workers. Historians as diverse in approach as Robert Fogel and W.J. Rorabaugh have held that the native-born workers were at least partly right in connecting the immigrants with a downward spiral of wages and a loss of control over work. Similar arguments have linked Irish immigration with the lowering of wages and the undermining of a promising labor movement of native-born women textile workers.[81] By no means is the case connecting Irish immigration with the degradation of native-born workers the only one that can be made. Edward Everett Hale observed at the time that with the coming of the Irish, 'Natives [were] simply pushed up into Foremen … , superintendents, … machinists' and other skilled occupations. Hale's view has some defenders among modern historians, but the important issue here is that many native-born artisans, rightly or wrongly, paired the arrival of the Irish with unfavorable changes in their crafts and wages and participated in both anti-immigrant riots and anti-immigrant political movements. By casting job competition and neighborhood rivalries as racial, rather than ethnic, the Irish argued against such nativist logic.[82]

Thus, the struggle over jobs best explains Irish-Americans' prizing of whiteness if that struggle is considered broadly, to include not only white–Black competition but white–white competition as well. Similarly, we must widen the focus from a struggle over jobs to include an emphasis on the struggle over how jobs *were to be defined* to understand more fully why the Irish so embraced whiteness. Specifically, the spectre of 'slaving like a nigger' hung over the Irish. In Ireland, peasants with small holdings had commonly described loss of a parcel as a descent to 'slavery'.[83] Irish-Americans did not mind referring to Britain's 'enslavement' of Ireland. Sometimes, as in the 1856 presidential campaign, they insisted on it. Would-be friends of Irish-Americans as diverse as Edward Everett Hale, Orestes Brownson and the labor reformers of the *Voice of Industry* all alluded to the British imposition of slavery or worse on Eire. Irish-Americans were also receptive to appeals from Democratic politicians who emphasized the threat of 'white slavery' in the United States and were cool to Republican attempts to portray talk of 'white slavery' as reckless and demeaning to white workers.[84]

But there were few specific attempts by the Irish or their friends to talk about a specifically Irish-American 'slavery' – a distended metaphor, as Frederick Douglass pointed out, but considerably less so than the generalized concept of 'white slavery', which was used. Immigrants, so hopeful of escaping slavery in Ireland, were hesitant to acknowledge a specifically ethnic defeat in the Promised Land, and real differences between the suffering in Ireland and that in America discouraged use of 'Irish slavery' to describe both situations.[85]

Most important, Irish-American Catholics did not want to reinforce popular connections of the Blacks and the Irish. If they could live with being called 'white slaves', it was harder to abide being called 'Irish niggers'. When Irishmen repeated jokes about slaves complaining that their masters treated them 'like Irishmen', the laughter had a decidedly tense edge.[86] But it was difficult to get out from under the burden of doing unskilled work in a society that identified such work and (some craft jobs) as 'nigger work'. If they were to sever this connection, the Irish could not just achieve a favorable labor market position vis-à-vis Blacks. They had to drive all Blacks, and if possible their memories, from the places where the Irish labored. Frederick Douglass warned the Irish worker of the possibility that 'in assuming our avocation he also assumed our degradation.' Irish workers responded that they wanted an 'all-white waterfront', rid of Blacks altogether, and not to 'jostle with' African-Americans.[87] They thought that, to ensure their own survival, they needed as much.

Industrial Discipline, Sexuality and Irish Whiteness

An analysis centering on Democratic politics and the struggles to secure and redefine the jobs of Irish-American Catholics provides important explanations for that group's embrace of whiteness. But by itself such an analysis makes the unthinking decision to insist on being white seem altogether too utilitarian. Neither political nor psycho-economic calculations can quite explain why some Irish-American Catholics would, for example, mutilate the corpses of the free Blacks they lynched in the 1863 Draft Riot in New York City. Neither can such factors by themselves explain why many other Irish immigrants looked with fascination at these crimes nor why members of the community on subsequent days fought to keep authorities from retrieving the corpses.[88] The psychological wages of Irish whiteness were sometimes of the sort based on rational, if horribly constrained, choices. But as frequently they were the products of what Frantz Fanon called 'the prelogical thought of the phobic' – the fevered thinking in which the racist nurtures his hatred as he 'project[s] his own desires onto the Negro' and behaves 'as if the Negro really had them.'[89]

But what desires? And why should the projections of Irish-American Catholics onto Blacks have been accompanied by such great ferocity? Fanon's further insights are valuable in considering these questions, in that his work is a model of both a refusal to reduce white racism to its sexual dimensions and of a refusal to shrink from discussion of these sexual dimensions. Fanon argues that racism places Blacks within the category of the 'biological', defining them as sexual but also as without

150

[handwritten annotations: "emasculation of Black in contrast to culture/society as male"; "nature vs. culture"]

history and as natural, erotic, sensual and animal.[90] Whiteness took shape against the corresponding counter-images, shunting anxieties and desires regarding relationships to nature and to sexuality onto Blacks.

For Irish-American Catholics, the anxieties and the desires resulting from a loss of a relationship with nature were particularly acute. Though gang labor, cottage industry and putting-out systems had some substantial currency in mid-century Ireland, no antebellum European immigrant group experienced the wrenching move from the preindustrial countryside to full confrontation with industrial capitalism in an urban setting with anything like the intensity of Irish Catholics. The German-American population, the most comparable group, was one that did develop significant splits within its ranks regarding slavery and white supremacy.[91] German-Americans often came to the United States after experiences as 'wandering' artisans, encountering urban life and wage labor gradually and while still having ties to the countryside. Within the US, German-Americans were far less urbanized than the Irish and more able to preserve familiar work rhythms and measures of craft control on the job, both because of the presence of German-dominated craft union locals and because of the significant numbers of German-American employers using German labor processes.[92]

Irish Catholics, especially but not only during the Great Famine, tended to emigrate directly from rural areas in which place mattered tremendously, contributing to a relationship with the past, to a sense of kinship and even to religious faith.[93] Torn from their homes, they resettled in places remarkably different from Ireland. Not only relocated in cities, but in the most crowded quarters of them, Irish-Americans maintained only the most tenuous of ties to nature. Their efforts to preserve the right to keep pigs in cities – continuing into the 1850s in New York City – and their success in gaining jobs involving butchering and the care of horses should not obscure the general trajectory of Irish-American Catholics – from the Ould Sod to no sod at all in a very short time. One New England factory worker recalled that factory management turned to Irish-American Catholic labor in part because 'not coming from country homes but living as the Irish do, in the town, they take no vacations, and can be relied on at the mill all year round.' It would have been more exact to say 'coming from country homes but not in this country.'[94]

[handwritten margin note: "this is Handlin's argument of industrial displacement of rural immigrant culture"]

[handwritten margin note: "he says earlier that Irish bitter memories may have made it undesirable to go rural."]

Of course, the time discipline and routinization of work demanded by industrializing America were not uncontested by Irish immigrants. Direct actions influenced by the Irish background – from banshee yelling to terror – shaped working class protest in the United States, especially after the Civil War.[95] Moreover, many Irish migrants defended preindustrial styles of life through informal actions, refusing or failing to become sober and disciplined workers. As Bruce Laurie has observed, the arrival of so many Irish Catholics 'changed the ethnic base of traditionism.' That is, the antebellum Irish were especially noted for drinking, for promiscuity, for brawling and for irregular work habits at a time when employers, educators and reformers actively attacked such vices as both immoral and inefficient.[96]

But it is vitally important to avoid romanticizing such informal resistance. To work – and the Irish desperately needed work – in an urban capitalist environment required conformity with time discipline and work discipline. If to some extent the Irish immigrants were 'insulated' from being directly bossed by their tendency to labor as outworkers, they also tended to work in settings very much subject to 'hurry and push' styles of management: in construction, in longshoring and carting, in service and in unskilled factory labor.[97] Young Irish indentures, apprentices and child laborers in mills often suffered a psychological battering from Protestant employers bent on reforming the children, sometimes in front of their parents.[98] Contemporary observers stressed not only 'uproarious' Irish working class behavior of the traditionalist sort but also the subservience, loyalty to employers and even the asceticism of the Irish.[99]

Not only were the opportunities for traditionalist resistance on the job circumscribed, but when Irish-American Catholics flouted Protestant and industrial capitalist standards regarding alcohol consumption and sexuality they often did so guiltily, knowing that their own standards were also being violated. If the Irish Catholics drank heavily in the United States and organized politically around a hatred of temperance reformers, they did not do so in mere continuation of preimmigration patterns of life. Though drinking was a central part of social life for males in Ireland, per capita alcohol consumption there in the early nineteenth century trailed that of the United States.[100] Moreover, the Irish who came to the United States in such great numbers came from a society with a tremendous mass temperance movement. Led by the legendary Father Mathew, that movement swept whole counties, inducing the poor as well as middle class Irish to take a temperance pledge and succeeding in reducing at least the visibility of alcohol consumption. Father Mathew enjoyed wide popularity among Irish American Catholics as well.[101] The connections between temperance and Protestantism, nativism and antislavery in the United States made Catholic Irish immigrants opponents (and targets) of the political movements against alcohol consumption.[102] However, drinking was far from being an unproblematic symbol of Irish-American Catholic resistance to Protestantism or to industrial discipline. Those downing the drinks may well have considered themselves backsliders more often than they considered themselves traditionalist opponents of Protestantism and industrial morality.

More tortured still were Irish-American Catholic expressions of sexuality. The reformer Charles Loring Brace worriedly described Irish immigrants in New York City as experimenters with the doctrines of 'Free Love'.[103] But Irish-American sexuality was at least as guilt-ridden as it was adventuresome. Gender relations took shape within an immigrant population in which men frequently far outnumbered women. As avoidance of service occupations by single women and of wage work by married women became a badge of American respectability, Irish daughters and wives labored for the family's survival, often in other people's homes and – to a degree little noticed by historians – often in the households of native-born skilled workers. Men frequently left their families to look for work and sometimes never came back. Wives and husbands advertised in newspapers for the return of their spouses. Need, not desire, drove immigrant women into prostitution. At the least, sexual experimentation occurred under highly unfavorable conditions.[104]

Moreover, the Irish background hardly nurtured a tradition of sexual freedom. Even before the mid-nineteenth-century Devotional Revolution in Ireland, attitudes toward extramarital sexuality were extremely negative, in part because of the importance of family and inherited land. Callithumpian bands in Ireland exposed the impure and ridiculed them with 'rough music' serenades. Such rituals continued in the United States, and newspapers with Irish-American Catholic readerships shared the concerns of Protestant reformers that 'sin, debauchery and crime [had] destroyed all natural and truthful perceptions' of the roles of 'the white woman'.[105] One dance hall and house of prostitution in a largely Irish section of antebellum New York City gave away Bibles to its customers. The same simultaneous defense of 'traditionalist' behavior and belief that such behavior was indefensible characterized much of Irish immigrant culture.[106]

George Rawick's argument that the typical early bourgeois racist constructed whiteness by imagining 'a pornography of his former life' and projecting it onto Blacks might be expanded in order to consider the racism of working class Irish-American Catholics who at times created a pornography of their *present* lives and at other times of their past.[107] The Irish immigrants addressed their own divorce from connections with land and nature's rhythms in part by attempting to define preindustrial behavior, and even longing for the past itself, as 'Black' behavior. When Irish immigrant minstrel entertainers sang 'Carry Me Back to Old Virginny', they both expressed feelings of loss and exile and at the same

153

time distanced themselves from those same feelings through blackface.[108] Irish immigrants consistently argued that African-American workers were lazy, improvident and irresponsible. The immigrants were used to hearing such characterizations applied to themselves, and not only by political enemies but also by their own newspapers, which fretted over the need to develop a 'work ethic' among the newly arrived.[109]

When free Blacks dramatically violated the Irish-American view of them as undisciplined and preindustrial – when they mounted temperance parades, for example – immigrant mobs stood ready to attack. But similarly mobbed were places in which Black and Irish people drank, schemed, played, made love and lived together. In part this pattern of crowd behavior reflected the violence of the urban underworld and the fact that crime and vice were arenas in which the races mixed with relative freedom.[110] But the riotous Irish-American attacks on the common pleasures of Blacks and of fellow Irishmen – the 1863 New York City mob directed its ire not only in the murdering of African-Americans and the destruction of houses of prostitution but also in the smashing of musical instruments – also suggest how fragile and artificial was the Irish insistence on defining Blacks as preindustrial 'others'.[111]

But the more frantically that Irish immigrants sought to distance themselves from Blacks, the more it became apparent that fascination mixed with repulsion in their attitudes toward African-Americans. The constant Civil War refrain of pro-Irish, Democratic politicians charged that Republicans and abolitionists had 'nigger on the brain'.[112] But appeals to and by Irish immigrants betrayed a monomaniacal focus on race, and particularly on race-mixing, that the antislavery forces could not match. The failure to institute color bars to keep free Blacks away from 'white' jobs presaged not just integrated workplaces to worried Irish-American Catholics but the sexual 'amalgamation of labor'.[113] Similarly, any application of natural rights to Blacks or advocacy of freeing the slaves was denounced as 'political amalgamation'. John H. Van Evrie's *New York Day Book*, which appealed to an Irish-American audience as *The Caucasian* and as 'The White Man's Paper', advised readers in the 'producing classes' that to cut their children's throats at once was preferable to handing them over to 'impartial freedom' and a consequent 'amalgamation with negroes'.[114]

Sometimes Democratic biracial sexual fantasies focused on antislavery leaders. Horace Greeley, Charles Sumner, Lincoln and the beautiful young abolitionist orator Anna Dickinson were special objects of fascination to pamphleteers and minstrel performers. An extended advertisement in the *New York Day Book* for the 1864 pamphlet *Miscegenation; or, The*

154

Millennium of Abolition conveys several common features of such propaganda. These include the idea that emancipation would reverse racial positions and enslave poor whites, and that antislavery Germans had broken their ties with the white race.[115] Above all, the passage shows the voyeuristic delight produced by reflection on Black sexuality and eroticism. It is alternately languid and fevered in describing a scene in which

> Sumner is introducing a strapping 'colored lady' to the President. A young woman (white) is being kissed by a big buck nigger, while a lady lecturer [Dickinson] sits upon the knee of a sable brother urging him to come to her lectures, while Greeley, in the very height of ecstatic enjoyment, is eating ice-cream with a female African of monstrous physique. ... In the background is a carriage, negroes inside, with white drivers and footmen; a white servant girl drawing a nigger baby and a newly arrived German surveying the whole scene exclaiming, 'Mine Got, vot a guntry!'[116]

Another fantasy appeared with equal frequency. In it, the goal of the antislavery forces, from Lincoln to Henry Ward Beecher to Hinton Rowan Helper, was to require interracial sex, and particularly Black–Irish sex. In part, this fantasy was used to explain real Black–Irish liaisons. The *Day Book*, for example, blamed 'Black Republicans' for the existence of 'the sexual conjunction of a Negro and a white woman', a relationship that was 'lust, but diseased, monstrous, hideous lust'. It reported that in the largely Irish Five Points area 'whites, negroes and mongrels readily "intermarry"', while blaming such relationships on the influence of the 'Abolition idea'.[117]

More broadly, the idea of an antislavery plot to force intimacy between the Irish and Blacks enabled political conspiracy theorists to reproduce, in highly sexualized form, the appeal of minstrelsy. It was possible to reflect on Black–Irish similarities, and even on Irish desires to recapture that part of themselves they had defined as 'Black', while vigorously denying any affinity to African-Americans. One could imagine anything – as illustrated by the example of a New York *World* editorial that held that the 'logical outgrowth of ... extravagant negrophilism' was the breaking of the incest taboo – and lay all guilt at the door of Blacks and 'Black Republicans'.[118]

The process by which the word *miscegenation* entered American usage to become a pivotal issue in the 1864 presidential campaign is most revealing in this connection. Coining the term were the Irish immigrant Democrat D.G. Croly and his coauthor, George Wakeman, who produced a sensational 1863 pamphlet titled *Miscegenation: The Theory of the Blending of the Races, Applied to the American White Man and Negro.*

Croly and Wakeman combined the Latin words *miscere* ('to mix') and *genus* ('race') in a neologism designed to replace the older term *amalgamation*.[119] Miscegenation's scientific ring gave it advantages, as did its success in conjuring up the 'mongrelization' of the United States as a political issue. By racist Democratic logic, Republican policies in 1864 threatened literally to establish a 'miscegen' nation. But Croly and Wakemen did not claim credit for this linguistic creativity. They instead anonymously wrote the pamphlet as an elaborate hoax, posing as pro-Republican abolitionists who saw mixing of the races as a 'rich blending of blood'. Croly then sent copies to prominent antislavery leaders. He hoped to secure their endorsements for theories that could then be used to embarrass the Republicans in the coming elections.[120]

As Sidney Kaplan's able discussion of the pamphlet has shown, 'the specific relationship of the Irish working-people and the Negro' formed the core of the hoax. The authors of *Miscegenation* purported to believe that Black–Irish mixing was already rife. They especially stressed 'connubial relations ... between the black men and white Irish women ... pleasant to both parties.' When a 'melaleuketic union' of Blacks and Irish took place, they added, it would 'be of infinite service to the Irish ... a more brutal race and lower in civilization than the negro.'[121]

Miscegenation succeeded briefly as a political dirty trick designed to produce a backlash among Irish and other white workers. Its effectiveness rested on Croly and Wakeman's understanding that their audience was not only ready to believe in Republican plots but was also fascinated by the prospects of Black–Irish sexuality. In a curious twist, Croly attacked his own unsigned pamphlet in a editorial in the New York *World*, holding that it showed that 'any man who chooses can write and cause to be printed whatever freak may come into his head' and that anonymity can protect designing authors.[122] It should be added that in constructing images of Blacks, opportunities abounded for Irish immigrants and for whites generally to indulge 'whatever freak' desire they imagined or to express perfectly understandable longings, without claiming authorship of those sentiments as their own.

Notes

1. Dale T. Knobel, *Paddy and the Republic: Ethnicity and Nationality in Antebellum America*, Middletown, Conn. 1986, 82–99; Herbert G. Gutman, *The Black Family in Slavery and Freedom, 1750–1925*, New York 1976, 298–301 and 303; William E. Gienapp, *The Origins of the Republican Party, 1852–1856*, New York 1987, 31.

2. For the 'Irishman' and 'nigger' quote, see Carl Wittke, *The Irish in America*, Baton Rouge, La. 1956, 125. Compare Matilda Houstoun, *Hesperos; or, Travels in the West*, London 1850, 1:179. On Strong, see Knobel, *Paddy and the Republic*, 87, and George Templeton Strong, *The Diary of George Templeton Strong: The Civil War, 1860–1865*, Allan Nevins and Milton Halsey Thomas, eds, New York 1952, 342 and 345. See also Harold David Brackman, 'The Ebb and Flow of Conflict: A History of Black–Jewish Relations Through 1900' (Ph.D. dissertation, University of California at Los Angeles, 1977), 232–34.

3. Ira Berlin and Herbert G. Gutman, 'Natives and Immigrants, Free Men and Slaves: Urban Workingmen in the Antebellum South', *American Historical Review* 88 (December 1983): 1187.

4. Reginald Horsman, *Race and Manifest Destiny: The Origins of American Racial Anglo-Saxonism*, Cambridge, Mass. 1981, 131; Knobel, *Paddy and the Republic*, 123–24 and 129–30; [David Goodman Croly and George Wakeman], *Miscegenation: The Theory of the Blending of the Races, Applied to the American White Man and Negro*, New York 1863, 29–31; Brackman, 'Ebb and Flow', 233.

5. *Harper's Weekly* 12 (5 September 1868): 568; Knobel, *Paddy and the Republic*, 90, and cartoons between pp. 156 and 157; Iver Bernstein, *The New York City Draft Riots: Their Significance for American Society and Politics in the Age of the Civil War*, New York 1990, sixth page of cartoons between pp. 124 and 125.

6. Kerby A. Miller, 'Green over Black: The Origins of Irish-American Racism', (Unpublished paper, 1969), 2–16; Miller's excellent paper has greatly enriched this chapter. Leon F. Litwack, *North of Slavery: The Negro in the Free States, 1790–1860*, Chicago, 1961, 155; Robert Ernst, *Immigrant Life in New York City, 1825–1863*, New York 1949, 66–67; Paul A. Gilje, *The Road to Mobocracy: Popular Disorder in New York City, 1763–1834*, Chapel Hill, N.C. 1987, 160–61.

7. Frederick Douglass, *Narrative of the Life of Frederick Douglass, An American Slave*, New York 1973 (1845): 14 and 106; Douglass, *My Bondage and My Freedom*, Chicago 1970 (1855), 76: thanks to Sterling Stuckey for the latter reference.

8. Oscar Handlin, *Boston's Immigrants: A Study in Acculturation*, New York 1977, 186.

9. Vincent Edward Powers, '"Invisible Immigrants": The Pre-Famine Irish Community in Worcester, Massachusetts, From 1826 to 1860' (Ph.D. dissertation, Clark University, 1976): 262–63; Dennis Clark, 'Urban Blacks and Irishmen: Brothers in Prejudice', in Miriam Ershkowitz and Joseph Zikmund II, eds, *Black Politics in Philadelphia*, New York 1973, 20–21; Berlin and Gutman, 'Natives and Immigrants', 1196.

10. Robert Cantwell, *Bluegrass Breakdown: The Making of the Old Southern Sound*, Urbana, Ill. 1984, 259; Alessandra Lorini, 'Festive Crowds in Early Nineteenth Century New York' (Paper presented at the Conference on Time, Space, Work and Leisure in Pre-Industrial America, University of Paris VII, June 1987); Powers, '"Invisible Immigrants"', 262–63; '"Irish Mornings and African Days": An Interview with Leni Sloan', *Callahan's Irish Quarterly*, 2 (Spring 1982): 49–53; Miller, 'Green over Black', 72–73.

11. John Barclay Jentz, 'Artisans, Evangelicals, and the City: A Social History of the Labor and Abolitionist Movements in New York City' (Ph.D. dissertation, City University of New York, 1977), 246; Leonard L. Richards, *Gentlemen of Property and Standing: Anti-Abolition Mobs in Jacksonian America*, Oxford 1970, 143.

12. Daniel O'Connell, *Daniel O'Connell upon American Slavery*, New York 1860, 38–40, emphasis original; Gilbert Osofsky, 'Abolitionists, Irish Immigrants and the Dilemmas of Romantic Nationalism', *American Historical Review* 80 (October 1975): 889–97.

13. Osofsky, 'Romantic Nationalism', 892–903; Joseph M. Hernon, Jr., *Celts, Catholics*

and Copperheads: Ireland Views the American Civil War, Columbus, Ohio 1968, 59–64.

14. Madeleine Hooke Rice, *American Catholic Opinion in the Slavery Controversy*, New York 1944, 81–82.

15. Osofsky, 'Romantic Nationalism', 893.

16. Ibid., 893, 894 and 897; Eric Foner, 'Abolitionism and the Labor Movement in Antebellum America', in *Politics and Ideology in the Age of the Civil War*, New York 1980, 67–71.

17. Osofsky, 'Romantic Nationalism', 899–901.

18. Bruce Laurie, *Working People of Philadelphia, 1800–1850*, Philadelphia 1980, 124.

19. John R. Commons et al., *A Documentary History of American Industrial Society*, Cleveland 1910, 7:60–61.

20. Osofsky, 'Romantic Nationalism', 905 and 897–906 passim.

21. Ibid., 902 and 899–905 passim; Handlin, *Boston's Immigrants*, 133; Hernon, *Celts, Catholics and Copperheads*, 62–65.

22. John Francis Maguire, *Father Mathew: A Biography*, London 1864, 470–72.

23. Hernon, *Celts, Catholics and Copperheads*, 64; Handlin, *Boston's Immigrants*, 132; Kerby A. Miller, *Emigrants and Exiles: Ireland and the Irish Exodus to North America*, New York 1985, 328–31.

24. Quoted in Litwack, *North of Slavery*, 163; Knobel, *Paddy and the Republic*, 13–14; Miller, *Emigrants and Exiles*, 197–204; Ralph Mann, 'Community Change and Caucasian Attitudes toward the Chinese: The Case of Two California Mining Towns, 1850–1870' in Milton Cantor, ed., *American Workingclass Culture: Explorations in American Labor and Social History*, Westport, Conn. 1976, 410 and 416–17.

25. Laurie, *Working People*, 124–25 and 156–58; Albon P. Man, Jr., 'Labor Competition and the New York City Draft Riots of 1863', *Journal of Negro History* 36 (October 1951): 376–405; Brackman, 'Ebb and Flow', 325 and Chapter 5 above.

26. James D. Burn, *Three Years among the Working Classes in the United States during the War*, London 1865, xiv.

27. Douglass, *Narrative*, 44; Douglass, as quoted in Albon P. Man, Jr., 'The Irish in New York in the Early Eighteen-Sixties', *Irish Historical Studies* 7 (September 1950): 97–98; Douglass, *The Life and Times of Frederick Douglass: Written by Himself*, New York 1962 (1881): 546.

28. Quoted in George Potter, *To the Golden Door: The Story of the Irish in Ireland and America*, Boston 1960, 372.

29. Hernon, *Celts, Catholics and Copperheads*, 62 and 67; Osofsky, 'Romantic Nationalism', 907–08; David Brion Davis, *Slavery and Human Progress*, New York 1984, 185.

30. Miller, *Emigrants and Exiles*, 235, 248 and 305; Miller, 'Green over Black', 10 and 90 n24.

31. Potter, *Golden Door*, 373; Jo Ellen McNergney Vinyard, 'The Irish on the Urban Frontier: Detroit, 1850–1880' (Ph.D. dissertation, University of Michigan, 1972), 220; Miller, *Emigrants and Exiles*, 305.

32. Osofsky, 'Romantic Nationalism', 906 and 908; Rice, *American Catholic Opinion*, 25–109; Miller, 'Green over Black', 23–25; Paul Blanshard, *The Irish and Catholic Power*, Boston 1953, 14–27 and 168–69.

33. Jay P. Dolan, *The Immigrant Church: New York's Irish and German Catholics, 1815–1865*, Baltimore 1975, 58; Miller, *Emigrants and Exiles*, 247, 291, 327; Potter, *Golden Door*, 374–76; Osofsky, 'Romantic Nationalism', 893; Emmet Larkin, 'The Devotional Revolution in Ireland, 1850–1875', *American Historical Review* 77 (June 1972): 625–52.

34. Florence E. Gibson, *The Attitudes of the New York Irish Toward State and National Affairs, 1848–1892*, New York 1951, 52–53 and 117; Rice, *American Catholic Opinion*, 103–4, n. 61.

35. Frank Murray, 'The Irish and Afro-Americans in US History', *Freedomways* 22 (First Quarter 1982): 27–28; Osofsky, 'Romantic Nationalism', 892–93; Potter, *Golden Door*, 372. See also Dennis Clark, *Hibernia America: The Irish and Regional Cultures*, New York 1986, 93–116, but esp. p. 112 n20 for commentary on how the desire to avoid being confuted with slaves 'imparted a special individualism' to the behavior of Irish workers in the South.

36. Miller, *Emigrants and Exiles*, 198–201 and 263–75, quoted from 1981; Carol Groneman Pernicone, 'The "Bloody Ould Sixth": A Social Analysis of a New York City Working Class Community in the Mid–Nineteenth Century' (Ph.D. dissertation, University of Rochester, 1973), 114–15; Vinyard, 'Irish on the Urban Frontier', 38–41; Laurie, *Working People*, 147; Powers, '"Invisible Immigrants"', 286–429.

37. Handlin, *Boston's Immigrants*, 43–46; Rorabaugh, *Craft Apprentice*, 133 and 167–71.

38. Wittke, *Irish in America*, 127; quotes from Miller, 'Green over Black', 25; Brackman, 'Ebb and Flow', 317; John C. Murphy, *An Analysis of the Attitudes of American Catholics toward the Immigrant and the Negro, 1825–1925*, Washington, D.C. 1940, 40–41, 50–51; see also Rice, *American Catholic Opinion*, passim.

39. Jean Baker, *Affairs of Party: The Political Culture of Northern Democrats in the Mid–Nineteenth Century*, Ithaca, N.Y. 1983, 180; George M. Fredrickson, *The Black Image in the White Mind: The Debate on Afro-American Character and Destiny, 1817–1914*, New York 1971, 90–91.

40. Miller, *Emigrants and Exiles*, 188–90; Dennis Clark, *The Irish in Philadelphia*, Philadelphia 1973, 15.

41. A.T. Lane, *Solidarity or Survival?: American Labor and European Immigrants, 1830–1924*, New York 1987, 27; David Montgomery, 'The Irish and the American Labor Movement', in David Doyle and Owen Edwards, eds, *America and Ireland, 1776–1976*, Westport, Conn 1980, 205.

42. Miller, *Emigrants and Exiles*, 328–31; Clark, *Philadelphia*, 117.

43. Eric Foner, 'Class, Ethnicity and Radicalism in the Gilded Age: The Land League and Irish-America', in *Politics and Ideology in the Age of the Civil War*, New York 1980, 153–61; Miller, 'Green Over Black', 19.

44. Lee Benson, *The Concept of Jacksonian Democracy: New York as a Test Case*, New York 1961, 318–20; Litwack, *North of Slavery*, 84–87; Gunther Barth, *Bitter Strength: A History of the Chinese in the United States*, Cambridge, Mass. 1964, 133–34; Baker, *Affairs of Party*, 179; Fredrickson, *Black Image*, 90–91.

45. Horsman, *Race and Manifest Destiny*, 250–53, including the quotations.

46. See Bernard Mandel, *Labor: Free and Slave*, New York 1955, 151–53; Joseph Rayback, 'The American Workingman and the Antislavery Crusade', *Journal of Economic History* 3 (1943): 161–62, and Chapter 4, n102.

47. W.J. Rorabaugh, *The Craft Apprentice from Franklin to the Machine Age in America*, New York 1986, 168–71; Michael Holt, *The Political Crisis of the 1850s*, New York 1978, 176.

48. Robert W. Johannsen, *Stephen A. Douglas*, New York 1973, 571.

49. Paul M. Angle, ed., *Created Equal: The Complete Lincoln–Douglas Debates of 1858*, Chicago 1958, 22–23, 64 and 156.

50. Quoted in Horsman, *Race and Manifest Destiny*, 251.

51. Quoted in Johannsen, *Douglas*, 726.

52. Rice, *American Catholic Opinion*, 101; Steven Rowan and James Neal Primm, eds, *Germans for a Free Missouri: Translations from the St. Louis Radical Press*, Columbia, Mo. 1983, 194; Ronald P. Formisano, *The Birth of Mass Political Parties: Michigan ,1827–1861*, Princeton, N.J. 1971, 287–88; Forrest G. Wood, *Black Scare: The Racist Response to Emancipation and Reconstruction*, Berkeley 1970, 18; Handlin, *Boston's Immigrants*, 145; Carl Wittke, *Refugees of Revolution: The German Forty-Eighters in America*, Philadelphia 1952, 207; Holt, *Political Crisis*, 187; Vinyard, 'Irish on the Urban Frontier', 224; Bernstein, *Draft Riots*, 33.

53. Indeed, so much of late antebellum politics revolved around proving one's whiteness that the recent and cogent calls by Eric Foner and others for a political history that considers how class interacted with the ethnocultural variables should be supplemented by an appeal for a consideration of ow race came to symbolize both ethnocultural and class positions. See Eric Foner, 'Causes of the American Civil War: Recent Interpretations and New Directions', in *Politics and Ideology in the Age of the Civil War*, New York 1980, 17–19; Richard N. Current, ed., *The Political Thought of Abraham Lincoln*, Indianapolis, Ind. 1967, 48, 91 and 105; Hinton R. Helper, *The Impending Crisis of the South*, New York 1857, 169 and 173; Formisano, *Political Parties*, 303, n32; Eric Foner, 'Racial Attitudes of the New York Free Soilers', in *Politics and*

Ideology in the Age of Civil War, New York 1980, 82–83; Kathleen Conzen, *Immigrant Milwaukee: Accommodation in a Frontier City, 1836–1860*, Cambridge, Mass. 1976, 216.

54. Horsman, *Race and Manifest Destiny*, 250.

55. Knobel, *Paddy and the Republic*, 178–179; Baker, *Affairs of Party*, 180; Wood, *Black Scare*, 23.

56. John Ashworth, *'Agrarians' and 'Aristocrats': Party Political Ideology in the United States, 1837–1846*, New York 1983, 221–23; Gibson, *New York Irish*, 86–89.

57. Knobel, *Paddy and the Republic*, Chapter 5, esp. 154–64; Thomas F. Gossett, *Race: The History of an Idea in America*, Dallas, Tex. 1964, 96–97. On the ability of Irish Catholics to 'pass' as non-Catholics, see Reverend John O'Hanlon, *The Irish Emigrant's Guide for the United States*, Boston 1851, 174. On expressions of preference for Blacks over Irish as citizens, see also Marvin E. Gettleman, *The Dorr Rebellion: A Study of American Radicalism, 1833–1849*, New York 1973, 130.

58. See Jay Rubin, 'Black Nativism: The European Immigrant in Negro Thought, 1830–1860', *Phylon* 39 (1978): 193–203, with Douglass quoted on p. 199.

59. The quoted passage is from Stephen A. Douglas, as in Johannsen, *Douglas*, 642.

60. Potter, *Golden Door*, 239–40; Miller, 'Green over Black', 30–31; Knobel, *Paddy and the Republic*, 156 and 178–79.

61. Henry C. Brokmeyer, *A Mechanic's Diary*, Washington, D.C. 1910, 33. See also p. 112.

62. *DA*, 2:1120 and 2:1867; *DAE*, 4:2479; Wittke, *Irish in America*, 125; Berlin and Gutman, 'Natives and Immigrants', 1188; Ira Berlin, *Slaves without Masters: Free Blacks in the Antebellum South*, New York 1974, 234–40.

63. Nora Faries, 'Occupational Patterns of German-Americans in Nineteenth-Century Cities', in Harmut Keil, ed., *German Workers' Culture in the United States, 1850 to 1920*, Washington, D.C. 1988, 37–51, esp. 39; Conzen, *Immigrant Milwaukee*, 73.

64. See n63 above and Handlin, *Boston's Immigrants*, 59, 69–70, 133 and 250–52; Robert Ernst, *Immigrant Life in New York City*,, New York 1949, 214–17.

65. See Susan E. Hirsch, *Roots of the American Working Class: The Industrialization of the Crafts in Newark, 1800–1860*, Philadelphia 1978, 47; Rorabaugh, *Craft Apprentice*, 133 and 140; Laurie, *Working People*, 159; Pernicone, 'The "Bloody Ould Sixth"', 114–16; Bernstein, *Draft Riots*, 118–19.

66. Christine Stansell, *City of Women: Sex and Class in New York, 1789–1860*, New York 1986, 156–61; Faye Dudden, *Serving Women: Household Service in Nineteenth Century America*, Middletown, Conn. 1983, 5–6; Thomas Hamilton, *Men and Manners in America*, Edinburgh 1834, 1:104–7; William Hancock, *An Emigrant's Five Years in the Free States of America*, London 1860, 41.

67. Dudden, *Serving Women*, 5–6; Hamilton, *Men and Manners*, 1:104–7; Charles Mackay, *Life and Liberty in America*, London 1859, 1:243; Stansell, *City of Women*, 164; Ernst, *Immigrant Life*, 65; Handlin, *Boston's Immigrants*, 61; Formisano, *Political Parties*, 181.

68. Roger W. Shugg, *Origins of Class Struggle in Louisiana*, Baton Rouge, La. 1968, 90–93; Cedric A. Yeo, 'The Economics of Roman and American Slavery', *Finanzarchiv* 13 (1952): 466; Frederick Law Olmsted, *A Journey to the Seaboard Slave States: In the Years 1853–1854, with Remarks on Their Economy*, New York 1904, 100–101.

69. Dennis Clark, 'Babes in Bondage: Indentured Irish Children in Philadelphia in the Nineteenth Century', *Pennsylvania Magazine of History and Biography* 101 (October 1977): 475–86; Rorabaugh, *Craft Apprentice*, 133, 140 and 167–70; Clark, *Irish in Philadelphia*, 120; *AG*, 1:58 and 94.

70. Stansell, *City of Women*, 178; S.B. Flexner and H. Wentworth, eds, *Dictionary of American Slang*, New York 1975, 577; *OED2*, 12:75.

71. Ulrich Bonnell Phillips, *American Negro Slavery*, New York, 1918, 302–3; Ernst, *Immigrant Life*, 67; Hasia Diner, *Erin's Daughters in America: Irish Immigrant Women in the Nineteenth Century*, Baltimore 1983, 91–93.

72. Man, 'Irish in New York', esp. 88–89; Man, 'Labor Competition and the New York City Draft Riots of 1863', *Journal of Negro History* 36 (October 1951): 376–405; V. Jacque

Voegeli, *Free But Not Equal: The Midwest and the Negro During the Civil War*, Chicago 1967, 5; Laurie, *Working People*, 65–66 and 157; Steven J. Ross, *Workers on the Edge: Work, Leisure and Politics in Industrializing Cincinnati, 1788–1890*, New York 1985, 195; Philip S. Foner and Ronald L. Lewis, eds, *The Black Worker: A Documentary History from Colonial Times to the Present*, Philadelphia 1978, 1:274–77; Philip S. Foner, *Organized Labor and the Black Worker*, New York 1976, 11.

73. *The Metropolitan Record*, 14 December 1861: as cited in Miller, 'Green over Black', 69; Litwack's valuable *North of Slavery: The Negro in the Free States, 1790–1860*, 161–66, too singlemindedly connects job competition and Irish racism.

74. Laurie, *Working People*, 124.

75. Brackman, 'Ebb and Flow', 235–38; Leonard P. Curry, *The Free Black in Urban America, 1800–1850*, Chicago 1981, 3–8, 14–36, 80, 259–61 and 293 n34. See also n63 above.

76. Peter Way, 'Shovel and Shamrock: Irish Workers and Labor Violence in the Digging of the Chesapeake and Ohio Canal,' *Labor History* 30 (Fall 1989): 498, 504–5; O'Hanlon, *Irish Emigrant's Guide*, 82–84; Miller, *Emigrants and Exiles*, 322; Miller, 'Green over Black', 52; Ernst, *Immigrant Life*, 105.

77. Robert Ernst, 'The Economic Status of New York City, 1850–1863', *Negro History Bulletin* 12 (March 1949): 140, quoting the New York *Herald*; Handlin, *Boston's Immigrants*, 62.

78. Stansell, *City of Women*, 156–57; Philip S. Foner, ed., *The Life and Writings of Frederick Douglass*, New York 1950, 2:249–50; Litwack, *North of Slavery*, 165–66; Commons et al., *Documentary History*, 7:60–61; Ernst, *Immigrant Life*, 131–33; Charles H. Wesley, *Negro Labor in the United States, 1850–1925*, New York 1927, 31–32; Rubin, 'Black Nativism', 199.

79. Miller, 'Green over Black', 18, 35; Bernstein, *Draft Riots*, 28, 119–20, 191–92 and 318, n88; Foner and Lewis, *Black Worker*, 1:164.

80. Berlin and Gutman, 'Natives and Immigrants', esp. 1191; Hirsch, *Roots*, 47; Rorabaugh, *Craft Apprentice*, 133 and 140; Wilentz, *Chants Democratic*, 118–19; Lane, *Solidarity or Survival?*, 28.

81. Lane, *Solidarity or Survival?*, 24–30; Ernst, *Immigrant Life*, 103 and 261 n53; Rorabaugh, *Craft Apprentice*, 133, 140 and 167–71; Robert W. Fogel, *Without Consent or Contract: The Rise and Fall of American Slavery*, New York 1989, 354–69; on the mills, see Norman Ware, *The Industrial Worker, 1840–1860*, Boston 1924, 80–88, but also for more nuance, Thomas Dublin, 'Women, Work and the Family: Female Operatives in the Lowell Mills, 1830–1860', *Feminist Studies* 3 (Fall 1975): 34–37; Jonathan Prude, *The Coming of Industrial Order: Town and Factory Life in Rural Massachusetts, 1810–1860*, Cambridge, Mass. 1983, 190 and 215; H.M. Gitelman, 'The Waltham System and the Coming of the Irish', *Labor History* 8 (Fall 1967): 227–53.

82. See Handlin, *Boston's Immigrants*, 84; Gitelman, 'Coming', passim; David Montgomery, 'The Shuttle and the Cross: Weavers and Artisans in the Kensington Riots of 1844', *Journal of Social History* 5 (1972): 411–46.

83. Miller, *Emigrants and Exiles*, 202 and 212, and Frank Walsh, 'Who Spoke for Boston's Irish? The Boston *Pilot* in the Nineteenth Century', *Journal of Ethnic Studies* 10 (Fall 1982): 27.

84. Gibson, *New York Irish*, 86–87; Edward Everett Hale, *Letters on Irish Immigration*, Boston 1852, 8; *Voice of Industry*, 7 May 1847; Thomas Ainge Devyr, *The Odd Book of the Nineteenth Century; or, 'Chivalry' in Modern Days*, Greenpoint, N.Y. 1882, 103; *Irish American*, 21 January 1860; Murphy, *Attitudes of American Catholics*, 40–41; and Chapter 5 above.

85. Douglass, as reprinted in Herbert Aptheker, ed., *A Documentary History of the Negro People in the United States*, New York 1951, 1:312; Miller, 'Green over Black', 81–83. However, see also Devyr, *Odd Book*, 164 and 168.

86. Wittke, *Irish*, 125; Rubin, 'Black Nativism', 199; *Freeman's Journal* (New York), 4 November 1843.

87. Very suggestive in this connection are Paul A.. Gilje's comments on antebellum racism as, in part, a focus for a more general hatred and contempt for unskilled workers. The Irish obviously had an interest in keeping that focus on Blacks. See Gilje, *The Road to*

Mobocracy: Popular Disorder in New York City, 1763–1834, Chapel Hill, N.C. 1987, 165; Voegeli, *Free But Not Equal*, 66 and 106. For Douglass, see P. Foner, ed., *Life and Writings*, 2:249–50.

88. Bernstein, *Draft Riots*, esp. 28–31 and 61 and Herbert Asbury, *The Gangs of New York: An Informal History of the Underworld*, New York 1928, 148–49.

89. Frantz Fanon, *Black Skins, White Masks*, New York 1967, 159 and 165.

90. Ibid., 159–66.

91. On the German-Americans' occupational structure and antislavery, see Ralf Wagner, 'Turner Societies and the Socialist Tradition' in Harmut Keil, ed., *German Workers' Culture in the United States, 1850 to 1920*, Washington, D.C. 1988, 226–28; Bruce Carlan Levine, '"In the Spirit of 1848": German-Americans and the Fight over Slavery's Expansion' (Ph.D. dissertation, University of Rochester, 1980); Fairies, 'Occupational Patterns', in Keil, ed., *German Workers' Culture*, 37–51; Carl Wittke, *Against the Current: The Life of Karl Heinzen*, Chicago 1945; James M. Berquist, 'The Mid–Nineteenth Century Slavery Crisis and the German-Americans', in Randall M. Miller, ed., *States of Progress: Germans and Blacks in America Over 300 Years*, Philadelphia 1989, 55–71.

92. Levine, 'Spirit of 1848', 60 and 62; Alexander Saxton, *The Indispensable Enemy: Labor and the Anti-Chinese Movement in California*, Berkeley, Calif. 1971, 28–29; Mack Walker, *Germany and the Emigration, 1816–1885*, Cambridge, Mass. 1964; Stanley Nadel, 'Kleindeutschland: New York City's Germans, 1845–1880' (Ph.D. dissertation, Columbia University, 1981).

93. Clark, *Irish in Philadelphia*, 26–27; Miller, *Emigrants and Exiles*, 251, and 'Green over Black', 48.

94. Quoted in Herbert Gutman, *Work, Culture and Society in Industrializing America*, New York 1976, 21; see also p. 63; Bernstein, *Draft Riots*, 30; Ernst, *Immigrant Life*, 71.

95. Gutman, *Work, Culture and Society*, 43–44 and 63–64; Wayne G. Broehl, Jr., *The Molly Maguires*, Cambridge, Mass. 1974.

96. Laurie, *Working People*, 147 and notes 1 and 2 above. On efficiency and reform, see Michael Katz, *The Irony of Early School Reform: Educational Innovation in Mid–Nineteenth Century Massachusetts*, Cambridge, Mass. 1968, and David J. Rothman, *The Discovery of the Asylum: Social Order and Disorder in the New Republic*, Boston 1971.

97. Laurie, *Working People*, 159; Bernstein, *Draft Riots*, 78–124 and notes 63–66 above. On Irish work rhythms, see Miller, *Emigrants and Exiles*, 270 and 274.

98. Clark, 'Babes in Bondage', 482; Prude, *Coming*, 117–18 and 215.

99. Wilentz, *Chants Democratic*, 267; Gutman, *Work, Culture and Society*, 21; Commons et al., *Documentary History*, 2:183; P. Foner, *Life and Writings*, 2:249–50; Shugg, *Class Struggle*, 93–119.

100. W.J. Rorabaugh, *The Alcoholic Republic: An American Tradition*, New York 1979, 10; James Barrett, 'Why Paddy Drank: The Social Significance of Whiskey in Prefamine Ireland', *Journal of Popular Culture* 11 (1977): 17–28.

101. Miller, *Emigrants and Exiles*, 241, 247, 249–50, 290 and 306; Maguire, *Father Mathew*, 470ff.

102. Eric Foner, *Free Soil, Free Labor, Free Men: The Ideology of the Republican Party Before the Civil War*, Oxford 1970, 230–39.

103. Charles Loring Brace, *The Dangerous Classes of New York, and Twenty Years Work among Them*, New York 1872, 41. See also Louis Don Scisco, *Political Nativism in New York State*, New York 1901, 18, and John D'Emilio and Estelle B. Freedman, *Intimate Matters: A History of Sexuality in America*, New York 1988, 87.

104. Stansell, *City of Women*, 83 and 178; Miller, 'Green over Black', 72; Hirsch, *Roots*, 57; Brace, *Dangerous Classes*, 41–42; D'Emilio and Freedman, *Intimate Matters*, 136; Diner, *Erin's Daughters*, 58; Elizabeth Blackmar, *Manhattan for Rent, 1785–1850*, Ithaca, N.Y. 1989, 121.

105. *Evening Day Book* (New York), 11 May 1858, as cited in Miller, 'Green over Black', 72–73; William V. Shannon, *The American Irish*, New York 1963, 20–23; D'Emilio and Freedman, *Intimate Matters*, 82.

106. Asbury, *Gangs*, 56–60.

107. George P. Rawick, *From Sundown to Sunup: The Making of the Black Community*, Westport, Conn. 1972, 132–33.

108. 'Irish Mornings and African Days on the Old Minstrel Stage', *Callahan's Irish Quarterly* 2 (Spring 1982): 49–53. The sexual puns possible in 'Carry Me Back to Old Virginny' also deserve note.

109. Miller, 'Green over Black', 42; Walsh, 'Boston Pilot', 27; O'Hanlon, *Irish Emigrant's Guide*, 199–202.

110. See Chapter 5, n60, and C. Vann Woodward, *The Strange Career of Jim Crow*, New York 1966, 15.

111. Bernstein, *Draft Riots*, 32–34 and passim.

112. Forrest G. Wood, *Black Scare: The Racist Response to Emancipation and Reconstruction*, Berkeley, Calif. 1970, 2; L. Seaman, *What Miscegenation Is and What We Are to Expect, Now That Mr Lincoln Is Re-elected*, New York 1864?, 8.

113. *Metropolitan Record* (New York), 14 December 1861. See also Sidney Kaplan, 'The Miscegenation Issue in the Election of 1864', *Journal of Negro History* 34 (July 1949): 318.

114. Man, 'Irish in New York', 100; Kaplan, 'Miscegenation Issue', 321–22 and n49 above.

115. Wood, *Black Scare*, 59–60 and 73; Kaplan, 'Miscegenation Issue', 275 and 316; Alexander Saxton, 'Blackface Minstrelsy and Jacksonian Ideology', *American Quarterly* 27 (March 1975): 22–23. On the idea that emancipation would utterly reverse roles and even enslave whites, see Baker, *Affairs of Party*, 251–53; Seaman, *What Miscegenation Is*, 4–5; Potter, *Golden Door*, 377; Miller, 'Green over Black', 46, 64 and 99; Wood, *Black Scare*, 10.

116. Quoted in Kaplan, 'Miscegenation Issue', 316.

117. Quoted in Miller, 'Green over Black', 68 and 73; see also Hernon, *Celts, Catholics and Copperheads*, 65; *Democratic Campaign Document No. 11*, New York 1864, 2–3; Kaplan, 'Miscegenation Issue', 320.

118. See Kaplan, 'Miscegenation Issue', 325 and, for the quote, 309.

119. [Croly and Wakeman], *Miscegenation*, ii; Wood, *Black Scare*, 54–58; Kaplan, 'Miscegenation Issue', 278 n6.

120. Kaplan, 'Miscegenation Issue', 278 n6; [Croly and Wakeman], *Miscegenation*, 18.

121. [Croly and Wakeman], *Miscegenation*, 29–31; Kaplan, 'Miscegenation Issue', 281.

122. Quoted in Kaplan, 'Miscegenation Issue', 308.

PART IV

The Limits of Emancipation and the Fate of Working Class Whiteness

'But out of the death of slavery
a new life at once arose.'

Karl Marx (1867)

'The resulting emotional and intellectual
rebound of the nation made it nearly incon-
ceivable in 1876 that ten years earlier most men
had believed in human equality.'

W.E.B. Du Bois (1935)

8

Epilogue: A New Life and Old Habits

In 1877, when the United States erupted in the Great Railroad Uprising, workers in St. Louis mounted a general strike. The socialist-led workers' council, which ruled the city for the better part of a week, at first seemed intent on making biracialism a centerpiece of strike strategy. At an early strike meeting, whites in the crowd screamed 'We will!' when a Black speaker asked whether whites would support demands made by Black workers. The Executive Committee running the strike and the first delegation negotiating with the mayor were both integrated. There was certainly ample reason for questioning racial divisions. The troops who menaced and finally broke the strike might have been protecting Black civil rights in the South had Reconstruction not ended with the compromise settlement of the election of 1876. The same troops might earlier and later have fought in anti-Indian wars. The *Labor Standard* bragged, 'White and black workmen stood together in ... struggle. Labor recognizes neither color, creed nor nationality.'[1]

But press reports from St. Louis also tell the story of an Irish-American worker blaming 'naygurs' for the strike, and of an increasing desire among white strike leaders to distance themselves from Black participation and to redefine the struggle as one of 'white labor'. One of the plans of the strike committee, never realized because the strike was abruptly broken, was apparently to appoint five hundred 'special policemen' to 'clean out the nigger mob'. The reminiscences of Executive Committee leader Albert Currlin indicate that the leadership backed off from public mobilizations of workers because it did not want to be identified with a 'gang of niggers'. This perception is especially significant in that the best evidence

167

suggests that the 'gangs' of roving pickets spreading the strike were not mostly Black, but were instead integrated crowds of largely unskilled workers.[2] In San Francisco, another center of the 1877 uprising, socialists initiated a movement for the eight-hour working day and nationalization of railroads but anti-Chinese clubs seized the initiative. Historically enjoying what Alexander Saxton has called 'strong working class support', the clubs transformed the strike into an anti-Chinese pogrom with astonishing speed during the 'July Days of 1877'.[3]

The tragedy of such examples might blind us to the changes they reflect. The very idea that Black–white labor unity was desirable and important, although fragile in the St. Louis case, was an essentially post–Civil War innovation. In the 1835 Philadelphia general strike, for example, it was considered remarkable that Black workers were allowed in prostrike crowds.[4] In the St. Louis general strike, Black participation and even leadership was initially encouraged. In the antebellum years, virtually no labor activists pointed to Black-white trade union unity as an issue of any importance. Recorded attempts at such unity from 1800 till the Civil War probably number less than a dozen. Ill-fated, these attempts found their temporary justification on narrow utilitarian grounds.[5]

During the period of the Civil War and Reconstruction, newspapers like the Boston *Daily Evening Voice*, the New Orleans *Tribune* and, at times, the St. Louis *Daily Press* and the Chicago *Workingmen's Advocate* emphasized that splits between white and Black workers only served capital.[6] The rationale for unity remained pragmatic, with white labor leaders asking 'Shall we make [Black workers] our friends, or shall capital be allowed to turn them as an engine against us?' But there was also a stunning 'moral impetus', as Marx put it, injected into the working class movement by the Civil War and emancipation. Antislavery luminaries were not just welcomed onto labor platforms but courted by workers' organizations.[7] Most startlingly, the abolitionist-turned-labor-reformer Wendell Phillips became one of the most sought-after speakers before massive Irish-American audiences. Eight years after the 1863 draft and anti-Black riot in New York City, African-American workers in that city's eight-hour parade heard loud cheers from white crowds watching the procession.[8]

All these changes coexisted with their opposites. William Sylvis, the National Labor Union's greatest leader, both sought to unite the 'working people of our nation, white and black', and bitterly complained of whites with daughters 'who entertain young negro gentlemen in their parlors.' The National Labor Union, which opened its 1869 convention to Black delegates, both spoke of 'know[ing] neither color nor sex, on the question of rights of labor' and neglected to push for either integrated locals or

Black civil rights.[9] Although talk of the necessity for Black–white unity increased rapidly, the rise in integrated strikes and integrated unions was far more modest. Race riots and hate strikes versus Black workers were far more common than biracial labor struggles during the Civil War, and even during Reconstruction the quickening of biracial organization only slowly took it to places other than waterfronts, mainly in the South. As Eric Foner has recently observed, 'The Northern labor movement failed to identify its aspirations and interests with those of the former slaves.'[10] Nonetheless, its occasional forays in this direction set it dramatically apart from the antebellum labor movement.

Different too were the very size, militance and capacity of the post–Civil War white labor movement. The St. Louis and San Francisco episodes were part of the first national strike of consequence in the United States, and the vacillations of the National Labor Union should not obscure the fact that a labor organization that was at least arguably national had suddenly taken shape. Workers who had accepted, or had not yet even achieved, a ten-hour working day, flocked almost overnight into Eight-Hour Leagues at the war's end. City central labor unions, especially in New York City and Chicago, gained unprecedented strength.[11] The much-quoted passage from Marx's *Capital* connecting Black emancipation and the rise of white labor identifies at least a coincidence and perhaps a relationship of cause and effect:

> In the United States of North America, every independent movement of the workers was paralysed so long as slavery disfigured a part of the Republic. Labour cannot emancipate itself in the white skin where in the black it is branded. But out of the death of slavery a new life at once arose. The first fruit of the Civil War was the eight hours' agitation, that ran with the seven-leagued boots of the locomotive from the Atlantic to the Pacific. [12]

But why? Why should Black freedom and that of the white working class have been connected at all? Why, as George Rawick put it, should 'the pressure of Blacks for equality' have 'intensified' class conflict generally?[13] Before the Civil War, figures like the German-American radicals Joseph Weydemeyer and Karl Heinzen and the labor abolitionist John A. Collins stood isolated for their suggestion that abolition was a necessary concern for those who would imagine freedom for white workers.[14] Far more common until well into the Civil War were labor and popular political leaders who predicted that Black emancipation necessarily meant the reduction of whites to slavery.[15] If Reconstruction proved Marx far closer to the mark than the proslavery Democrats, the *link* between Black freedom and white labor mobilization still needs explanation.

THE WAGES OF WHITENESS

The meager record of biracial organization does not allow us to fall back
on the generalization that Black–white unity automatically placed labor in
a better tactical position from which to attack capital. This epilogue suggests a much broader solution, arguing that the Civil War and emancipation removed the ability of white workers to derive satisfaction from
defining themselves as 'not slaves' and called into question self-definitions
that centered on being 'not Black'. The weight of whiteness by no means
completely lifted, but both the 'new life' for white workers growing out of
the Civil War and the ways in which whiteness was reasserted and continued to burden workers of all colors deserve attention.

A White Man's War

The election of 1860, no less than that of 1856, saw Democrats and
Republicans vie for votes as defenders of 'free white labor'.[16] No political
challenge to the concept of whiteness was possible, any more than was a
frontal attack on slavery. But in seeking to draw the line on the *expansion*
of slavery and thus save the West for free white labor, Lincoln and the
Republicans paradoxically opened the possibility of partially deracializ-
ing US politics. Michael Holt has observed that the Republican success
was to 'shift the focus of the sectional conflict from black slavery to
republicanism', and that Republicans attracted votes from those wanting
'to save the Republic from a Southern conspiracy and to protect themselves from enslavement, not to end black slavery.'[17] Such appeals to
whiteness also paradoxically called whiteness into question. The indictment of the South was cultural as well as political, identifying the region
as antidemocratic, reactionary, wasteful, sexually dissolute, lazy and inefficient.[18] To the considerable extent that Northern workers accepted this
critique of the South, they could make all Southerners, white and Black
– rather than all Blacks, North and South – the negative reference point
against which they projected fears and longings. In addition, Lincoln,
while ingeniously defending Republican positions against Democratic
charges that any attack on the expansion of slavery implied a support for
'political amalgamation', also suggested that there were limits beyond
which the defense of white rights could not go. While denying Stephen
A. Douglas's taunts that he wished to see Blacks vote or to promote interracial marriage, Lincoln insisted on a white republicanism that recognized that Blacks were entitled to a chance to enjoy the fruits of their
own labor and to a very limited and temporary citizenship prior to their
settlement via colonization.[19]

170

Before the Civil War, cracks in the facade of working class whiteness remained hairline ones. By no means did anti-Southern critiques of a slaveholders' conspiracy or the idea that Blacks enjoyed a natural right to control their own labor win the complete assent of workers, even in the North. The vote of the Northern working class in the 1860 presidential election divided among Lincoln, Douglas and other candidates with the Republicans making few inroads among Irish-American workers. The closest thing to 'independent movements' of the white working class commenting directly on slavery on the eve of the war were large workers' peace mobilizations, which did not imagine that emancipation and white labor's freedom were connected in the slightest degree but instead typically declared themselves 'weary of the question of slavery ... a matter which does not concern us.'[20]

So long as the Civil War itself remained what Frederick Douglass brilliantly called a war 'in the interests of slavery on both sides',[21] the tendency of white workers to construct identities around their whiteness remained intact, and probably increased. With the South fighting to preserve slavery in an independent Confederacy and with the North declaring its willingness to preserve slavery within its existing limits, none of the grandeur of emancipation was on display. But the threat of emancipation, and the reality that the war was about slavery, seldom escaped the attention of the Northern Democratic press, of minstrel performers or of suffering workers and farmers in the army. Northern white workers – skilled and unskilled, immigrant and native-born – rallied to the defense of the Republic, with organized labor punning on the words *union* and *Union*. But in measuring their own sacrifices such workers nurtured a sense of grievance based on the notion that they were being exploited as whites and that favor was being, or was about to be, lavished on Blacks.[22]

The issue of job competition between the races became vastly more immediate during the early war years. Democrats now predicted that masses of exslaves would flood into the North, either as a result of wartime escapes or of a possible Republican decision for emancipation. The idea of a Republican 'abolition-capitalist' conspiracy to unleash 'hordes of freedmen' to compete for white jobs in the North was fleshed out more completely than it ever had been before, especially since some radical Republican newspapers and politicians did almost immediately support emancipation as a war measure.[23] The movement of 'contraband' exslaves into Illinois in 1862 drew widespread criticism as a betrayal of 'white labor', with Illinois soldiers voting in 1862 for a Negro exclusion article to be inserted in the state constitution.[24] Race riots anticipating emancipation expressed white workers' fears of job competition even in cities

171

where it was highly unlikely that an exodus of freedpeople would quickly swell the population. Serious pre-emancipation hate strikes against Black employment and physical attacks on Black workers by whites thus occurred not only in Brooklyn, New York City and Cincinnati, but also in such cities as Chicago, Detroit, Boston and even St. Paul.[25]

However, even in this period it would be a mistake to focus exclusively on job competition and to ignore the wider uses of declaring oneself a white worker. Competition was, as Williston H. Lofton long ago showed, probably not sharpening, since the army's manpower needs, the death toll and the drying up of European immigration during the war more than made up for the small number of exslaves moving North.[26] Even if we allow that white workers had reason for long-term fears of competition with nearly four million freedpeople, it must be added that such fears seldom focused only on jobs. They were instead consistently alloyed with other fears ranging from political equality to sexual amalgamation and even to the peculiar terror that white women would begin to 'friz' their hair, 'à la d'Afrique'.[27]

The hardships generated by the bloodiest war in US history – and one that apparently took a greater toll on poorer and immigrant Yankee soldiers than on the wealthy – contributed to the anxieties concerning whites being victimized. As Michigan corporal Marion Munson reported, the rank-and-file of the Union Army did not want 'to go through the rough life of a soldier and perhaps get shot, for a d – d nigger.'[28] Leaving wives and lovers behind to fight in dire circumstances may well have helped to trigger the 'enflamed sexual anxiety' that, as Philip Shaw Paludan has observed, was manipulated by the proliferating number of Democratic broadsides showing Blacks 'as beasts embracing young white women [who] were usually presented as acquiescing in the alleged horror, suggesting the depth of the anxiety being probed.' Press accounts accentuating the supposedly savage sexuality of African-Americans likewise appeared at levels unprecedented in both number and pitch.[29]

Under these circumstances, the early war failed to produce decisive changes making whiteness less important as a source of Northern working class identity. Anti-Southernism did of course vastly increase, and some Protestant denominations representing the religious affiliation of a section of the working class did declare for immediate abolition, though the Catholic Church still vigorously opposed emancipation.[30] But these changes did not directly lead to any fundamental challenge to the logic of *herrenvolk* republicanism, which identified blackness with dependency and servility and therefore with a threat to white freedom. Even the heroic actions of slaves fleeing from bondage were often cast as cowardly, confused or lazy. Minstrel songs recycled 'plantation darky' images and portrayed slaves who, as Alexander Saxton has put it, 'lamented the inexplicable "white folks" war.' Movement toward freedom could easily be seen as movement away from danger: 'Niggers dey can pick de cotton – dey'll do it very freely/But when dey smell de bullets, how dey'll run for Horace Greeley.' Fleeing to Union Army camps, according to some of the same newspapers that paradoxically also regarded contrabands as formidable competitors for 'white' jobs, reflected the desire of Blacks to avoid working.[31]

Emancipation from Whiteness

Nevertheless, the literal movement of slaves toward freedom set in motion a process that created unprecedented possibilities for Northern workers to see Black freedom as increasing the well-being of whites. The unsentimental words of the popular song 'Sambo's Right to Be Kilt' best capture the most direct such connection. The song's author, Charles Graham Halpine, had served as P.T. Barnum's private secretary before the war. As a staff officer in 1862 he prepared the order mustering one of the first troops of Black soldiers into the Union Army. Aware of intense rank-and-file opposition to serving in a biracial, if segregated, army, Halpine adopted the pseudonym Private Miles O'Reilly to show how calculations regarding saving the lives of whites could lead to the conclusion that contrabands should serve as soldiers:

> Some tell me 'tis a burnin' shame
> To make the naygers fight,
> And that the trade of bein' kilt
> Belongs but to the white.
> But as for me, upon my soul!
> So lib'ral are we here,
> I'll let Sambo be shot instead of myself
> On ev'ry day of the year.[32]

Halpine's verses ran far ahead of the opinion of rank-and-file Union troops and Northern popular opinion, which only slowly came to accept that contrabands could shorten the war. White soldiers were often among the most vociferous opponents of emancipation, but they gradually came to accept Black participation in the military, first in doing work around the camps and latter as combat troops. Once this happened, the common enemies of death and Rebel troops produced a very partial and quite

173

grudging respect for Black soldiers, which could undermine firm racial distinctions even as it spoke in the language of Black and white. As Halpine wrote:

> The men who object to Sambo
> Should take his place and fight;
> And it's better to have a nayger's hue
> Than a liver that's wake and white.
> Though Sambo's black as the ace of spades,
> His fingers a trigger can pull,
> And his eye runs straight on the barrel sight,
> From under the thatch of wool.

The emancipation of slaves created broader possibilities for Black soldiering and broader challenges to the idea that whiteness alone implied freedom and dignity for workers.[33] But broader changes were also afoot.

Shortly before his death in 1866, the American Marxist Civil War officer and Republican politician Joseph Weydemeyer wrote in the St. Louis *Westliche Post:*

> With the eight-hour movement ... the labor question, i.e. the modern labor question – the question of hired labor, which is better known under the euphemistic name of 'free labor' – steps before the social forum, strips off the secondary character which heretofore adhered to it on this continent, raises itself to a social question.[34]

Weydemeyer's brilliant description of the heady changes that transformed American labor between 1863 and 1866 skips a vital step. What brought the question of hired labor to center stage, what quickened the sense of expectation and possibility for the entire working class, indeed what made the eight-hour movement itself possible, was the spectacular emancipation of slaves between 1863 and 1865. Abandoning the effort to fight a war to preserve slavery against a slaveholding power, Lincoln in effect acknowledged with the Emancipation Proclamation that the failure of the Union to defeat the South quickly and the momentous efforts of slaves to free themselves necessitated turning the Civil War into a revolution. His order, and later its expansion into the Thirteenth Amendment, provided for the greatest uncompensated revolutionary seizure of property (that is, slaves) in history prior to the Soviet revolution.

Among many other things, the fact of emancipation sharply called into question the tendency to equate Blackness and servility. To some small extent Northern popular culture acknowledged that Blacks were not only becoming free but freeing themselves. Even minstrel performances occasionally caught the drama of emancipation:

> We own de hoe, we own de plow,
> We own de hands dat hold;
> We sell de pig, we sell de cow,
> But neber chile be sold.

Other songs strangely asked white audiences to take the blackfaced performer as Black and to identify with him against (Southern) whites:

> We're gwine down to take de Souf,
> And ride 'em on a rail,
> De white folks try to win de day,
> But de nigger nebber fail;
> Dey'll think John Brown am coming down
> To make annudder raid;
> So tumble in, ye cullered folks,
> And join de Black Brigade.

Meanwhile the white composer Henry C. Work's immensely popular 'Kingdom Coming' and 'Babylon Is Fallen' gloried in the South's transformation. The latter, which one historian has argued was never equalled in popularity by any anti-Black war song, sympathized with Black joy at the turning of tables in Dixie: 'We will be de Massa,/He will be de servant.'[35]

Decades of white supremacist habits necessarily burdened all efforts to rethink working class race relations and compromised progress at every turn. The 1863 New York City draft/race riots and the vicious race baiting of the 1864 presidential campaign in some ways took working class racism to new depths.[36] But if Northern white workers developed new attitudes toward people of color only slowly and contradictorily, emancipation made for much more consistent and dramatic changes in how such workers conceived of *themselves*. No longer could whiteness be an unambiguous source of self-satisfaction. No longer could a counterpoint with slaves define whites as 'free labor'. No longer could the supposedly servile, lazy, natural and sensual African-American serve as so clear a counterpoint to white labor and as so convenient a repository for values that white workers longed for and despised.

The popular working class consciousness that emerged during the latter stages of the Civil War, especially in the North, saw the liberation of Black slaves as a *model*, and not just as a threat. Like freedpeople, white

175

workers came to see the Civil War as a 'jubilee' and, in the words of Detroit labor leader Richard Trevellick, to hope that 'we are about to be emancipated.'[37] Workers sang 'John Brown's Body' as a labor anthem and reacted to unfavorable judicial opinions as 'Dred Scott decisions' against labor.[38]

In part, these were clearly rhetorical flourishes and natural allusions. But they also represented a new millennial hope, often rooted in long-held religious beliefs but borne of witnessing the greatest transformation in United States history – the movement of millions of Blacks from slavery to full constitutional rights in less than a decade. Ira Steward, the leading theorist of the eight-hour movement and a labor leader who appropriately enough was said to have fought alongside John Brown in Kansas, thus praised the shorter workday as 'an indispensable *first step*', in labor's eventual quest 'to wholly emancipate' itself. Not insignificantly, the demand for the eight-hour day promised the same kinds of control over one's own time and opportunities for educational growth and fulfillment within families as emancipation did for slaves. Far from preaching *herrenvolk* republicanism, Steward would, as Kenneth Fones-Wolf shows, 'continually refer to abolitionist speeches on equality to drive home ideas as he criticized "wage slavery".' Steward was an extremely egalitarian example and a leader who made uncommon efforts, from a congenial Boston base, to fashion specifically abolitionist ideas into a defense of labor reform. But he was also the most influential American labor thinker of his age, a period in which the vigorous assertion that labor's freedom followed from Black liberation at least challenged the view that emancipation for African-Americans meant degradation for whites.[39]

The Legacies of White Workerism

There is a great temptation to end a story so frequently tragic on the inspiring note of emancipation, labor upsurge and what Forrest Wood calls the 'dormancy' of popular campaigns for white supremacy. We should of course be inspired by the remarkable changes that unfolded after 1863, and we should particularly note the way in which Black self-activity prepared the way for an advance by all of labor. Moreover, the aftermath of emancipation illustrates an optimistic side to the argument that working class whiteness reflects, even in a form like the minstrel show, hatreds that were profoundly mixed with a longing for values attributed to Blacks. Taking shape as it does behind dams of repression, whiteness can be swept away dramatically when the dams begin to break, as I have argued elsewhere they today may be breaking.[40]

Black emancipation, battlefield heroism and citizenship thus ensured that white workers could never again see African-Americans or themselves in just the same way. However, more than enough of the habit of whiteness and of the conditions producing it survived to ensure that white workers would be at best uncertain allies of Black freedom and would stop short of developing fully new concepts of liberation for themselves as well. White workers continued to observe war and emancipation through a lens of race, and were often loathe to credit Black military activity and Black flight from slavery as contributing to the war effort for fear this meant minimizing the 'white' role.[41] After the war, it was perhaps briefly possible that a Radical Republican party could have united Blacks with large numbers of white Northern workers around a platform of equal rights and an eight-hour working day. But such a possibility collapsed from both ends. The Radicals, as David Montgomery has superbly demonstrated, did not move to a decisive embrace of the eight-hour day and other labor reforms. Such measures violated their desire to equate free labor with an absence of government intervention (particularly prolabor intervention) in the relations between labor and capital.[42] But popular racism in the industrializing North also helped to doom Radical–labor cooperation. Postwar opposition to Black suffrage in states like New York was overwhelming.[43] Moreover, with a few exceptions like the venerable William Heighton and those around the Boston *Daily Evening Voice*, labor radicals did not agitate for confiscation of rebel land and its division into plots for freedpeople. Viewing exslaves as likely to be dependent, those who abstained from agitating for land reforms benefitting Blacks ultimately helped create the conditions for such dependency.[44]

A small incident from St. Louis in 1865 captures many of the larger tragedies. When printers there stopped work against three major newspapers, they began to publish cooperatively a paper of their own, the St. Louis *Daily Press*. Almost immediately they took note of Black replacement workers:

> Yesterday ... a negro was engaged and set to work alongside of a white man. ... As an apology for the white man, we may state that the negro keeps his person clean and works not hard enough to cause perspiration, so that no offensive smell is emitted.[45]

The curiously hedged language ran through the *Daily Press*'s editorials. The paper could attempt to be completely egalitarian, maintaining that 'the policy of elevating the black man ... as a matter of moral and political economy may be unquestionable', and then adding 'but how can the

177

same party [the Republicans] abase the working man?' Within two weeks, the emphasis would be different, and the Radical Republicans would be cast as 'running over with a sentimental sympathy for ... an inferior race ... [but] allowing white women to starve.' Finding exslaves 'ignorant, docile and easily to be led by designing men', it solved the 'nigger question' by balancing the position that 'the darkey may be improved until if not the equal of the white, he may at least claim equal privileges' with the comforting assertion that 'for the present we have done enough for the negro.'[46] Since 'the present' was the end of the summer of 1865, such a position implied opposition not only to land reform but to the very Freedmen's Bureau aid that might have supported efforts at Black education and progress. Like many other white Americans, *Daily Press* writers were able to allow that Blacks had natural rights but still to conclude that white supremacy was right or necessary. This position, endorsed by Republicans who for a time supported colonization of freed Blacks, came also to be embraced by Democrats, including labor Democrats like those then running the *Daily Press*. No longer did the dismissal of all Black claims to natural rights elicit only Democratic ridicule, but the change sometimes made little practical difference. The Boston *Pilot* in 1862, for example, held 'The negro is indeed unfortunate, and the creature has the common rights of humanity living in his breast; but, in the country of the whites where the labor of the whites has done everything, and his labor nothing, what right has the negro ... to equality or to admission.'[47]

The St. Louis case raises several other problems that would continue to divide white from Black workers. The bitter slurs against Blacks, who took jobs during the printers' strike, and later mild praise for Blacks refusing to act as strikebreakers during the gas workers' strike in St. Louis, illustrate the craft union position that became entrenched nationwide during Reconstruction: it was ridiculous for African-Americans to expect to work alongside whites in skilled jobs and criminal for them to take the jobs of whites during strikes. Just as craft unions reinforced white supremacy, so did white supremacy reinforce the formation of what Du Bois called 'craft and race unions' by helping to connect unskilled labor generally with degradation and to make integrated work unthinkable in many trades. This was true both in the postbellum North and in the postbellum South, though the different dynamics of race and labor in the latter region necessitate treating the postbellum South in a separate, forthcoming study.[48]

Nor was it accidental that the issue of 'black rats' working with 'white men' breaking strikes was raised in tandem with attacks on the use of 'female printers' to emasculate the trade.[49] The 'manly skilled worker', so central to white labor organizing after the Civil War, was, as Montgomery comments, expected to 'live up to a code of "manly" behavior usually cast in ethnic and racial terms.' A labor poem describing the unity celebration following the late nineteenth-century signing of a union scale by iron puddlers makes its ethnic exclusions from manliness clear, but the final line also suggests, in the American context, the desirability of racial exclusion:

> There were no men invited such as Slavs and 'Tally Annes',
> Hungarians and Chinamen with pigtail cues and fans.
> No, every man who got the 'pass' a union man should be;
> No blacksheep were admitted to the Puddlers' Jubilee.[50]

The use of racial language and racist precedents to oppose advancement of darker ethnic groups – the equation of blackness with the ethnicity of new immigrant groups – ran through the postbellum labor movement. The most dramatic example was of course in California, where the Chinese working population was large and where since even before statehood the definition of 'whiteness' had been an important issue involving the status not only of Blacks and Asians but of the indigenous Indian and mixed Mexican, Indian and Spanish populations. The labor and anti-Chinese movements overlapped so thoroughly as to be scarcely distinguishable in California, where the exclusion issue provided the basis for labor unity at key points.[51] Outside California the anti-Chinese movement won tremendous working class response in areas such as Chicago and Massachusetts, where threats of 'swarming' were at worst slight or episodic. The Irish, whose own status as whites had only recently been won, were among the first to ask, 'What business has the likes of him over here?'[52] Some Blacks even attempted to join the anti-Chinese movement and to change its emphasis from a defense of whiteness to a defense of Americanism.[53] But in general the Chinese and African-Americans were lumped together, with the former group being cast as nonwhites, as 'slaves' and even as Black.[54] Moreover, although the Chinese were most insistently charged with being 'nonconsuming' and undermining American standards of living, the defensive 'manliness' and perhaps the longings that characterized anti-Black attitudes among white workers also coursed through anti-Chinese propaganda, with the 'Celestials' being charged with the wholesale seduction of white women, the spread of opium addiction, and introduction of oral sex and incest into the United States.[55]

Since the Chinese had so manifestly made major contributions, especially through their mining and railroad-building, the attack by labor

[handwritten margin note: parallel to earlier strategies of Irish]

179

militants on them raised what Alexander Saxton has called 'a theoretical and moral dilemma' that undermined the grandeur of rhetoric extolling the rights and dignity of labor. As Du Bois points out, analogous dilemmas stemmed from anti-Black racism. Nor could racial exclusionism easily be tried on as a tactic to unite white workers, and then discarded in favor of class goals. 'Tactics', according to Saxton, 'have a way of becoming habits.'[56] The tactic of questioning the suitability of newcomers on racial grounds extended to the labor movement's reception of (and opposition to) the Southern and Eastern European immigrants who arrived in great numbers in the late nineteenth and early twentieth centuries and were by no means received as unambiguously white.[57] The sad drama of immigrants embracing whiteness while facing the threat of being victimized as nonwhite would have many sequels after the Irish experience.

The final legacy suggested by the St. Louis printers' strike is the most subtle, pervasive and important. The brief, sneering reference to the Black laborer as not working hard typified the manner in which whites could still use Blacks as a counterpoint to come to terms with their own acceptance of steady and even regimented labor. White workers held Blacks in contempt as both lazy and, incongruously enough, as too accepting of overly taxing 'nigger work'. It was seldom considered that there might have been something of tremendous value in what Eugene D. Genovese has called the 'Black work ethic', which was much like the work ethic that most plebeian whites had recently abandoned and the one that many immigrating whites still held. Few of them appreciated how much African-Americans, who had by far the most experience of any Americans with regimenting systems of mass labor and of successful resistance to them, had to teach white labor. As Du Bois wrote in a fascinating and romantic passage in *The Gift of Black Folk*, African-Americans carried a distinctive attitude toward labor:

> The black slave brought into common labor certain new spiritual values not yet fully realized. As a tropical product with a sensuous receptivity to the beauty of the world, he was not as easily reduced to be the mechanical draft horse which the northern European laborer became. ... [H]e brought to modern manual labor a renewed valuation of life.[58]

But this was a gift spurned by white labor.

In the middle of Reconstruction, the story of the Black steel-driving railroad or tunnel worker John Henry came to be immortalized in folklore. The song 'John Henry', recalling his freewheeling life and his epic confrontation with a newly invented steam drill almost personifies the Black work ethic. It uses, as Pete Seeger comments, a 'basically

European verse form, but the melody and rhythm are more African than European.' Some early folklorists' informants even described John Henry as white. But, as Guy Johnson's classic study observes, 'Whatever the origins of first beliefs and ballads about John Henry, Negro folk have been almost solely responsible for the preservation and diffusion of the legend.'[59] He could not have been raceless or both white and Black. As 'John Henry' was composed, white workers were still tragically set on keeping even John Henry out of the House of Labor.

Notes

1. David R. Roediger, '"Not Only the Ruling Classes to Overcome, But Also the So-Called Mob": Class, Skill and Community in the St. Louis General Strike of 1877', *Journal of Social History* 19 (Winter 1985): 213–39; St. Louis *Dispatch*, 23 July 1877; *Labor Standard*, 26 August 1877.

2. St. Louis *Globe Democrat*, 26–28 July 1877; David Thayer Burbank, *Reign of the Rabble*, New York 1966, 151; St. Louis *Times*, 4 August 1877; Roediger, '"So-Called Mob"', 225.

3. Alexander Saxton, *The Indispensable Enemy: Labor and the Anti–Chinese Movement in California*, Berkeley, Calif. 1971, 113–16.

4. Susan Davis, *Parades and Power: Street Theatre in Nineteenth Century Philadelphia*, Philadelphia 1986, 135–36.

5. Leon F. Litwack, *North of Slavery: The Negro in the Free States*, Chicago 1961, esp. 165; Philip S. Foner and Ronald L. Lewis, eds, *The Black Worker: A Documentary History from Colonial Times to the Present*, Philadelphia 1978, 1:190–96; Philip S. Foner, *Organized Labor and the Black Worker, 1619–1973*, New York 1976, 4–11.

6. P. Foner and Lewis, *Black Worker*, 1:390–406 and 2:274–75; David R. Roediger, 'Racism, Reconstruction and the Labor Press: The Rise and Fall of the St. Louis *Daily Press*, 1864–1866', *Science and Society* 42 (Summer 1978): 173–75.

7. John R. Commons et al., *A Documentary History of American Industrial Society*, Cleveland 1910, 9:157–60; Saul K. Padover, ed., *Karl Marx: On America and the Civil War*, New York 1972, 274–75 and 244; David Montgomery, *Beyond Equality: Labor and the Radical Republicans, 1862–72*, New York 1967, 123–24; Boston *Daily Evening Voice*, 12 October 1865.

8. David R. Roediger, 'What Was the Labor Movement? Organization and the St. Louis General Strike of 1877', *Mid-America*, 67 (January 1985): 47; Gilbert Osofsky, 'Abolitionists, Irish Immigrant and the Dilemmas of Romantic Nationalism', *American Historical Review* 80 (October 1975): 893; Iver Bernstein, *The New York City Draft Riots: Their Significance for American Society and Politics in the Age of the Civil War*, New York 1990, 233–34 and passim; P. Foner and Lewis, *Black Worker*, 2:279.

9. P. Foner, *Organized Labor*, 23 and 26; James C. Sylvis, ed., *The Life, Speeches and Essays of William H. Sylvis*, Philadelphia 1872, 339–46.

10. Eric Foner, *Reconstruction: America's Unfinished Revolution, 1863–1877*, New York 1988, 480; P. Foner and Lewis, *Black Worker*, 1:269–85, 352, 358–59, 392 and 398; 2:279, 282–86; P. Foner, *Organized Labor*, 22.

11. See David R. Roediger and Philip S. Foner, *Our Own Time: A History of American Labor and the Working Day*, London 1989, 81–122.

12. Marx, *Capital: A Critique of Political Economy*, New York 1967, 1:301.

13. George P. Rawick, *From Sundown to Sunup: The Making of the Black Community*, Westport, Conn. 1972, 159.

14. Karl Obermann, *Joseph Weydemeyer: Pioneer of American Socialism*, New York 1947,

103 and, more fully, in *Joseph Weydemeyer: Ein Lebensbild, 1818–1866*, Berlin 1968, 342–44; Carl Wittke, *Against the Current: The Life of Karl Heinzen*, Chicago 1945, 172–76; Herbert Shapiro, 'Labor and Antislavery: Reflections on the Literature', *Nature, Society and Thought* 2 (1989): 482.

15. See Chapter 4 above and Forrest G. Wood, *Black Scare: The Racist Response to Emancipation and Reconstruction*, Berkeley, Calif. 1970, 22 and 35; L. Seaman, *What Miscegenation Is andWhat We Are to Expect, Now That Mr Lincoln Is Re-elected*, New York 1864?, 5–6; V. Jacque Voegeli, *Free But Not Equal: The Midwest and the Negro during the Civil War*, Chicago 1967, 54–55.

16. Eric Foner, *Free Soil, Free Labor, Free Men: The Ideology of the Republican Party Before the Civil War*, New York 1970, 262–69; Voegeli, *Free But Not Equal*, 3–4.

17. Michael Holt, *The Political Crisis of the 1850s*, New York 1978, 216–17.

18. See Ronald Walters, 'The Erotic South: Civilization and Sexuality in American Abolitionism', *American Quarterly* 25 (May 1973): 177–201.

19. E. Foner, *Free Soil*, 267–300. The point is brilliantly explored by Foner and Olivia Mahoney in their permanent 'House Divided' exhibit at the Chicago Historical Society.

20. P. Foner, *Organized Labor*, 12, including the quotation from Boston in 1860; Bernstein, *Draft Riots*, 99–101.

21. W.E.B. Du Bois, *Black Reconstruction in America, 1860–1880*, New York 1971 (1935), 61, quotes Douglass and reflects Douglass's insight.

22. David Montgomery, *The American Civil War and the Meanings of Freedom*, Oxford 1987, 18; Montgomery, *Beyond Equality*, 93–101; *Finchers' Trades Review*, 1 October 1864; St. Louis *Daily Press*, 5 November 1865; Roediger and P. Foner, *Our Own Time*, 83; Jean H. Baker, *Affairs of Party: The Political Culture of Northern Democrats in the Mid-Nineteenth Century*, Ithaca, N.Y. 1983, 250–53.

23. P. Foner, *Organized Labor*, 14; Voegeli, *Free But Not Equal*, 5–6 and 82.

24. Voegeli, *Free But Not Equal*, 17 and 92 n 26.

25. Williston Lofton, 'Northern Labor and the Negro during the Civil War', *Journal of Negro History* 34 (July 1949): 259–62; Voegeli, *Free But Not Equal*, 35 and 89; David A. Gerber, *Black Ohio and the Color Line, 1860–1915*, Urbana, Ill. 1976, 28; P. Foner and Lewis, *Black Worker*, 1:276–85; Joseph M. Hernon, Jr., *Celts, Catholics and Copperheads: Ireland Views the American Civil War*, Columbus, Ohio 1968, 19.

26. Lofton, 'Northern Labor', 252–56.

27. Wood, *Black Scare*, details the various fears. On hair, see L. Seaman, *Miscegenation*, 5. See also Baker, *Affairs of Party*, 251.

28. Randall C. Jamerson, *The Private Civil War: Popular Thought during the Sectional Conflict*, Baton Rouge, La. 1988, 93–103 with the quote from p. 103; on class and casualties, see Maris A. Vinovskis, 'Have Social Historians Lost the Civil War? Some Preliminary Democraphic Speculations', *Journal of American History* 76 (June 1989): 34.

29. Philip Shaw Paludan, *'A People's Contest': The Union and Civil War, 1861–1865*, New York 1988, 95; Kerby A. Miller, 'Green over Black: The Origins of Irish–American Racism' (Unpublished paper, 1969), 73; Wood, *Black Scare*, 25–29 and 64–65.

30. Voegeli, *Free But Not Equal*, 59 and 138–39; John C. Murphy, *An Analysis of the Attitudes of American Catholics toward the Immigrant and the Negro, 1825–1925*, Washington, D.C. 1940, 50–51 and 71–79.

31. Alexander Saxton, 'Blackface Minstrelsy and Jacksonian Ideology', *American Quarterly* 27 (March 1975): 21–22; John W. Blassingame, *Black New Orleans, 1860–1880*, Chicago 1976), 27; Voegeli, *Free But Not Equal*, 7–8.

32. Irwin Silber, ed., *Songs of the Civil War*, New York 1960, 308–9 and 328–30.

33. Jimerson, *Private Civil War*, 92–111; Gerald F. Linderman, *Embattled Courage: The Experience of Combat in the American Civil War*, 4:247–48; Leon F. Litwack, *Been in the Storm So Long: The Aftermath of Slavery*, New York 1979, 71–72; James I. Robertson, Jr., *Soldiers Blue and Gray*, Columbia, S.C. 1988, 30–35; Bell Irvin Wiley, *The Life of Billy Yank: The Common Soldier in the Civil War*, Indianapolis, Ind. 1952, 40–43; and, for the quote, Silber, *Songs of the Civil War*, 330.

34. As translated and reprinted in St. Louis *Daily Press*, 8 August 1866.

35. *Buckley's Melodist*, Boston 1864, 23–24 and 109; Silber, *Songs of the Civil War*, 306–7; Du Bois, *Black Reconstruction*, 55–127, the classic account of emancipation, is peppered with insights on changing white popular attitudes toward abolition.

36. On the riots, see especially Bernstein, *New York Draft Riots*, and on the 1864 elections, see Wood, *Black Scare*, 53–79 and Sidney Kaplan, 'The Miscegenation Issue in the Election of 1864', *Journal of Negro History* 34 (July 1949): 274–343.

37. Trevellick as quoted in Albert Blum and Dan Georgakas, 24; Philip S. Foner, ed., 'Songs of the Eight-Hour Movement', *Labor History* 13 (1972): 574–80; George McNeill, 'The Labor Movement of 1878 in Chicago' (Unpublished MS, State Historical Society of Wisconsin in Madison, 1878).

38. See the Foner and McNeill references in n37 above and David R. Roediger, 'Ira Steward and the Antislavery Origins of American Eight–Hour Theory', *Labor History* 27 (Summer 1986):423.

39. Roediger, 'Steward', 411 and passim; Steward, *Poverty*, Boston 1873, preface; Commons et al., *Documentatary History*, 9:288–89; Kenneth Fones-Wolf, 'Boston Eight Hour Men, New York Marxists and the Emergence of the International Labor Union', *Historical Journal of Massachusetts* 9 (1981): 48.

40. David R. Roediger, 'Notes on Working Class Racism: A Tribute to George Rawick', in David R. Roediger and Don Fitz, eds, *Within the Shell of the Old: Essays on Workers' Self–Organization*, Chicago 1990, 11–16; Rawick, *Sundown*, 158; Wood, *Black Scare*, 79.

41. *Democratic Campaign Document No. 11; or, Miscegenation Indorsed by the Republican Party*, New York 1864, 2–3; Randall M. Miller and Jon W. Zophy, 'Unwelcome Allies: Billy Yank and the Black Soldier', *Phylon* 34 (1978): 238–40 and n33 above.

42. Montgomery, *Beyond Equality*, esp. 230–386.

43. Leslie H. Fishel, Jr., 'Northern Prejudice and Negro Suffrage, 1865–1870', *Journal of Negro History* 34 (1954): 14–15, 21–26; Montgomery, *Beyond Equality*, 186–87; Michael Allen Gordon, 'Studies in Irish and Irish-American Thought and Behavior in Gilded Age New York City' (Ph.D. dissertation, University of Rochester, 1977), 19; Phyllis F. Field, *The Politics of Race in New York: The Struggle for Black Suffrage in the Civil War Era*, Ithaca, N.Y. 1982, 117–23.

44. See *The Equality of All Men before the Law, Claimed and Defended in Speeches by Hon. William D. Kelley, Wendell Phillips and Frederick Douglass and Letters from Elizur Wright and Wm. Heighton*, Boston 1865, 42–43; Philip S. Foner, 'A Labor Voice for Black Equality: The Boston Daily Evening Voice, 1864–1867', *Science and Society* 38 (1974): 304–25.

45. St. Louis *Daily Press*, 17, 18, 24, and 28 December 1864.

46. St. Louis *Daily Press*, 14 March, 26 May, 6 and 17 August and 11 October 1865.

47. St. Louis *Daily Press*, 2 August 1865; P. Foner and Lewis, *Black Worker*, 1:270–71; compare David Warren Bowen, *Andrew Johnson and the Negro*, Knoxville, Tenn. 1989, 118.

48. Du Bois, *Black Reconstruction*, 596; Saxton, *Indispensable Enemy*, 268–73. On race and strikebreaking and Black exclusion from postbellum unions, see Sterling D. Spero and Abram L. Harris, *The Black Worker*, New York 1969, 18–35; P. Foner, *Organized Labor*, 27–29 and 82–107.

49. Roediger, 'Racism, Reconstruction and the Labor Press', 164 and 168.

50. David Montgomery, *The Fall of the House of Labor: The Workplace, the State and American Labor Activism, 1865–1925*, Cambridge, Mass. 1987, 25, includes the poem by 'puddler poet' Michael McGovern. The use of *jubilee* is worthy of note, hearkening back to emancipation as it does. John R. Commons, *Races and Immigrants in America*, New York 1913, 48–49 nicely reproduces the craft labor movement's views on the lack of 'manliness' among African-Americans. On *blacksheep* and its usage in the US and earlier in England, see Mary Ellen Freifeld, 'The Emergence of the American Working Classes' (Ph.D. dissertation, New York University, 1980), 523.

51. Saxton, *Indispensable Enemy*, 19–20 and passim; Eugene W. Berwanger, *The Frontier against Slavery: Western Anti–Negro Prejudice and the Slavery Extension Controversy*, Urbana, Ill. 1967, 60–75.

52. Robert D. Parmet, *Labor and Immigration in Industrial America*, Boston 1981, 29 and 28–30 passim; Stuart Creighton Miller, *The Unwelcome Immigrant: The American Image of the Chinese, 1785–1882*, Berkeley, Calif. 1969, 176–201; Wood, *Black Scare*, 98, for the Irish quote and 100–101.

53. Arnold Shankman, *Ambivalent Friends: Afro-Americans View the Immigrant*, Westport, Conn. 1982, 8.

54. Gunther Barth, *Bitter Strength: A History of the Chinese in America, 1850–1870*, Cambridge, Mass. 1964, 133–34; Miller, *Unwelcome Immigrant*, 178, 180 and 198; Saxton, *Indispensable Enemy*, 260; Parmet, *Labor and Immigration*, 30.

55. Wood, *Black Scare*, 99–101; Parmet, *Labor and Immigration*, 29–30; Shankman, *Ambivalent Friends*, 19; Miller, *Unwelcome Immigrants*, 180–83; Bernstein, *Draft Riots*, 227; J. Sakai, *The Mythology of the White Proletariat*, Chicago 1983, 35–37.

56. Saxton, *Indispensable Enemy*, 265–67; Du Bois, *The World and Africa: An Inquiry into the Part Which Africa Has Played in World History*, New York 1965, 18–21.

57. Saxton, *Indispensable Enemy*, 275–78; Gwendolyn Mink, *Old Labor and New Immigrants in American Political Development: Union, Party and State, 1875–1920*, Ithaca, N.Y. 1986; Herbert Hill, 'Race, Ethnicity and Organized Labor', *New Politics* (Winter 1987): 37–42.

58. Eugene D. Genovese, *Roll, Jordan, Roll: The World the Slaves Made*, New York 1974, 285–324; Du Bois, *The Gift of Black Folk*, Millwood, N.Y. 1975 (1924), 53–54; see also Edward L. Pierce, 'The Freedmen at Port Royal', *Atlantic Monthly* 12 (September 1863): 301; and P. Foner and Lewis, *Black Worker*, 2:295; R. Keith Aufhauser, 'Slavery and Scientific Management', *Journal of Economic History* 33 (December 1973): 811–24. Thanks to Sterling Stuckey for the Pierce reference.

59. Pete Seeger, 'Appleseeds', *Sing-Out!* 34 (Winter 1989): 53–54; Guy B. Johnson, *John Henry: Tracking Down a Negro Legend*, Chapel Hill, N.C. 1929, vii, 3, 20–32, 146 and passim; Brett Williams, *John Henry: A Bio-Bibliography*, Westport, Conn. 1983, vii and 3–76.

Index

NOTE: Terms whose derivation and usage are discussed in the book are shown in italics.

Burn, James D. 136

Cairo, Illinois 3–5
Calhoun, John C. 74, 76, 84
callithumpian bands 106
Campbell, John 75
Carby, Hazel 6
cartmen 26–27, 57 *see also* freemen
Caucasian 143, 154
Census Bureau 133
Chartism 11, 66–67, 75
Chicago 169, 172
Chicago *Workingmen's Advocate* 168
child labor: compared to slavery 69–70
chimney sweeps 107
Christmas 105–6
Christy Minstrels 115
Cincinnati 134, 147, 172
Civil War: minstrelsy in 124; and white
    labor 167–71, 172–77
    see also emancipation
class formation: and whiteness 95–96;
    and minstrelsy 97
coffin handbill 65, 73
Collins, John A. 82, 135, 169
Commerford, John 75–76, 80
Commons, John R. 54, 183 n50
Communist Party (USA) 9
Confidence-Man, The (Melville) 86, 99,
    119
Congo Square (New Orleans) 102
Constitution, US 34
coon 97–99
Cooper, James Fenimore 48, 54–55, 102
cordwainers, 53
Cox, Oliver Cromwell 7–8, 9, 11
craft unions 178–79
Crockett, Davy 98, 111 n12
Croly, David G. 155–56
crowds: and race-mixing 100–103; and
    mobbings 105–8 *see also* riots
Cunliffe, Marcus 27, 72
Currlin, Albert 167
Cushing, Caleb 142

Dalby, David 107
Dana, Richard Henry 68
dancing 100–103
Davis, David Brion 20, 31, 35, 87
Davis, Susan G. 105
Dawley, Alan 81
Declaration of Independence 31, 142
Democratic party 59, 172; ties of labor
    activists to 72; uses *White Slavery*
    metaphor 73; supported by Campbell
    75; and antiaristocratic racism 76;

and Evans 79–80; appeals for white,
    Irish votes 140; racism of 141–43;
    race-baiting by, in Civil War 171
de Tocqueville, Alexis 58–59, 104
DeVere, M. Schele 54
Dickinson, Anna 154–55
Diner, Hasia 147
disfranchisement 56; in New York 56; in
    Connecticut 56; in Pennsylvania
    58–59
Dixon, George Washington 98
domestic service 145–46 *see also* help
Dorr, Thomas 58
Douglas, Stephen A. 142–43, 170–71
Douglass, Frederick 82, 134, 137, 149,
    150, 171
Douglass, H. Ford 44
Dover, New Hampshire 69
Du Bois, W.E.B. 6, 11–13, 14, 75, 117,
    166, 178, 179–80
Duke, David 8
Dudden, Faye 145–46
Dutch 26, 27, 54

Edwards, Richard 10
Eight-hour Leagues 169
Eight-hour Movement 169, 174, 176
Ellison, Ralph 6
emancipation
of slaves linked to whites' freedom
    169–70, 173–74; and free white labor
    175–76
Emancipation Proclamation 174
Evans, George Henry 71, 73, 82, 110,
    116; abolitionism of, 77–78; on
    whites as 'slaves' 77–80 *see also wages
    slavery, white slavery*

'Factory Girl, The' 70
factory system 69–70
Fanon, Frantz 14, 150–51
Fields, Barbara 7
Fillmore, Millard 142
Finch, John 77, 135
Fisk, Theophilus 74
Fitzhugh, George 74
Flint, James 35–36, 49, 50, 54
Fogel, Robert 81, 148
Foner, Eric 73, 76, 81, 159 n53, 169
Foner, Philip S. 10
France 66
Fredrickson, George 10
Franklin, Benjamin 25, 29, 34, 77
free Blacks 22, 49, 52, 56–60, 72; sup-
    ported by Evans 80; temperance halls
    and churches mobbed 108; Irish

186

THE HAYMARKET SERIES

Already Published

Forthcoming

GENDER AND CLASS *by Joanna Brenner*

ENCOUNTERS WITH THE SPHINX: Journeys of a Radical in Changing Times
by Alexander Cockburn

PEOPLE'S THEATER: Orson Welles and the Mercury Theater
by Michael Denning

THE POLITICS OF SOLIDARITY: Central America and the US Left *by Van Gosse*

JAMAICA, 1945–1984 *by Winston James*

BLACK AMERICAN POLITICS: From the Washington Marches to Jesse Jackson
(Second Edition) *by Manning Marable*

THE OTHER SIDE: Los Angeles from Both Sides of the Border *by Ruben Martinez*

THE SOCIALIST REVIEW READER